Essential Latin Grammar

Bennett's Grammar Revised

Essential Latin Grammar

Bennett's Grammar Revised

Anne Mahoney

Focus Publishing
R. Pullins Company
PO Box 369
Newburyport, MA 01950
www.pullins.com

paperback
ISBN 10: 1-58510-244-x
ISBN 978-1-58510-244-0

hardcover
ISBN 10: 1-58510-274-1
ISBN 978-1-58510-274-7

Printed in the United States of America
10   9   8   7   6   5   4   3   2   1

0307TS

Preface to the Focus Edition

Bennett's *New Latin Grammar* has been a standard introductory grammar for many years. For this edition, I have updated the sections on the Indo-European language family and on Latin meter, and added a brief bibliography; I have also re-organized the index of sources to make it easier to find references to a particular text. Bennett's grammar is not as detailed as those of Allen and Greenough, Gildersleeve, Hale and Buck, or (for syntax) Woodcock, making it suitable for intermediate-level students.

Charles E. Bennett (1858-1921) spent most of his career as professor of Latin at Cornell University. In addition to the *New Latin Grammar*, he produced several commentaries on Latin authors, articles on Latin grammar, and textbooks.

He was a member of the Committee on Academic Freedom and Academic Tenure of the American Association of University Professors in 1915, and one of the original signatories of the AAUP's Declaration of Principles which helped shape the modern system of tenure in American universities.

The *New Latin Grammar* is one of a series of Latin grammars written by American scholars in the later 19th and early 20th centuries, incorporating the latest knowledge about Indo-European linguistics and the latest ways of thinking about syntax. Nearly one hundred years later, the main outlines of Bennett's approach are still sound; for this reason, the present edition has been only lightly revised.

Boston, September 2006

Preface

The present work is a revision of that published in 1908. No radical alterations have been introduced, although a number of minor changes will be noted. I have added an Introduction on the origin and development of the Latin language, which it is hoped will prove interesting and instructive to the more ambitious pupil. At the end of the book will be found an Index to the Sources of the Illustrative Examples cited in the Syntax.

C.E.B.
Ithaca, New York,
May 4, 1918

Preface to the Second Edition

The present book is a revision of my *Latin Grammar* originally published in 1895. Wherever greater accuracy or precision of statement seemed possible, I have endeavored to secure this. The rules for syllable division have been changed and made to conform to the prevailing practice of the Romans themselves. In the Perfect Subjunctive Active, the endings -*īs*, -*īmus*, -*ītis* are now marked long. The theory of vowel length before the suffixes -**gnus**, -**gna**, -**gnum**, and also before **j**, has been discarded. In the Syntax I have recognized a special category of Ablative of Association, and have abandoned the original doctrine as to the force of tenses in the Prohibitive.

Apart from the foregoing, only minor and unessential modifications have been introduced. In its main lines the work remains unchanged.

Ithaca, New York,
October 16, 1907.

From the Preface to the First Edition

The object of this book is to present *the essential facts* of Latin grammar in a direct and simple manner, and within the smallest compass consistent with scholarly standards. While intended primarily for the secondary school, it has not neglected the needs of the college student, and aims to furnish such grammatical information as is ordinarily required in undergraduate courses.

The experience of foreign educators in recent years has tended to restrict the size of school-grammars of Latin, and has demanded an incorporation of the main principles of the language in compact manuals of 250 pages. Within the past decade, several grammars of this scope have appeared abroad which have amply met the most exacting demands.

The publication in this country of a grammar of similar plan and scope seems fully justified at the present time, as all recent editions of classic texts summarize in introductions the special idioms of grammar and style peculiar to individual authors. This makes it feasible to dispense with the enumeration of many *minutiae* of usage which would otherwise demand consideration in a student's grammar.

In the chapter on Prosody, I have designedly omitted all special treatment of the lyric metres of Horace and Catullus, as well as of the measures of the comic poets. Our standard editions of these authors all give such thorough consideration to versification that repetition in a separate place seems superfluous.

Ithaca, New York,
December 15, 1894.

Contents

Introduction:
The Latin Language

1. The Indo-European Family of Languages.—Latin belongs to one group of a large family of languages, known as *Indo-European*.[1] This Indo-European family of languages embraces the following groups:

Asiatic Members of the Indo-European Family

a. Anatolian, spoken in Asia Minor, modern Turkey. Hittite dates from the latter half of the second millennium B.C and may be as early as 2000 B.C. Luvian, which dates to the fourteenth century B.C. or earlier, may be the language spoken by the Trojans. Languages of this group were written in either cuneiform[2] or hieroglyphics (not the same, however, as Egyptian hieroglyphics).

b. Indic, spoken in ancient India. Of this there were several stages, the oldest of which is Vedic Sanskrit, the language of the Vedic Hymns. These Hymns are the oldest significant literary productions known to us among all the branches of the Indo-European family. A conservative estimate places them as far back as 1500 B.C. Some scholars have even set them more than a thousand years earlier than this, *i.e.* anterior to 2500 B.C. Classical Sanskrit is the language of the great epics of India as well as a large variety of other literature. Languages of this family have always continued to be spoken in India; the group is represented today by Hindi, Urdu, Bengali, and many other languages descended from the ancient Sanskrit, and spoken by millions of people.

c. Iranian, spoken in ancient Persia, and closely related to Sanskrit. There were two main branches of the Iranian group: the Old Persian and the Avestan. Old Persian was the official language of the court, and appears in a number of cuneiform inscriptions, the earliest of which date from the time of Darius I (sixth century B.C.). The other branch of the Iranian family, Avestan, sometimes called Zend, is the language of the Avesta or sacred books of the Parsees, the followers of Zoroaster,

---

1　In the past the family was sometimes also called *Aryan* or *Indo-Germanic*.

2　Cuneiform means "wedge-shaped." The name applies to the form of the strokes the characters are made from, produced by the end of a reed pushed into wet clay.

founder of the religion of the fire-worshippers. Portions of these sacred books may have been composed as early as 1000 B.C.

Modern Persian, also called Farsi, is a living representative of the old Iranian speech. It has naturally been much modified by time, particularly through the introduction of many words from the Arabic.

d. *Armenian*, spoken in Armenia, the district near the Black Sea and Caucasus Mountains. This is closely related to Iranian, and was formerly classified under that group. It is now recognized as entitled to independent rank. The earliest literary productions of the Armenian language date from the fourth and fifth centuries of the Christian era. To this period belong the translation of the Scriptures and the old Armenian Chronicle. Armenian is still a living language, though spoken in widely separated districts, owing to the scattered locations in which the Armenians are found today.

e. *Tokharian*. This language, discovered in the early twentieth century and quickly recognized as Indo-European, was spoken in the districts east of the Caspian Sea (modern Turkestan). While in some respects closely related to the three Asiatic branches of the Indo-European family already considered, in others it shows close relationship to the European members of the family. The literature of the Tokharian, so far as it has been brought to light, consists mainly of translations from the Sanskrit sacred writings, and dates from the sixth to eighth centuries of our era.

European Members of the Indo-European Family

f. *Greek*. The Greeks had apparently long been settled in Greece and Asia Minor as far back as 1500 B.C. Probably they arrived in these districts much earlier. The earliest literary productions are the *Iliad* and the *Odyssey*, traditionally attributed to Homer, which very likely go back to the ninth century B.C. From the sixth century B.C. on, Greek literature is continuous. Modern Greek, when we consider its distance in time from antiquity, is remarkably similar to the classical Greek of the fourth and fifth centuries B.C.

g. *Italic*. The Italic Group embraces Umbrian, spoken in the northern part of the Italian peninsula (in ancient Umbria); Latin, spoken in the central part (in Latium); Oscan, spoken in the southern part (in Samnium, Campania, Lucania, etc.). Besides these, there were a number of minor dialects, such as Marsian, Volscian, etc. Of all these (barring Latin), there are no remains except a few scanty inscriptions. Latin literature begins shortly after 250 B.C. in the works of Livius Andronicus, Naevius, and Plautus, although a few brief inscriptions are found belonging to a much earlier period. Note that Italic and Greek are sister branches of the family: Latin is not in any sense descended from

Greek. Modern descendents of Latin, called the Romance languages after the Romans, include Italian, French, Spanish, Portuguese, Catalan, and others.

h. Celtic. In the earliest historical times of which we have any record, the Celts occupied extensive portions of northern Italy, as well as certain areas in central Europe; but after the second century B.C., they are found only in Gaul and the British Isles. Gallic, the language of ancient Gaul, is a Celtic language. Living languages in this group include Irish, Welsh, Scots Gaelic, and Breton, which is spoken in Brittany in France.

i. Germanic. The Germanic or Teutonic group is very extensive. Its earliest representative is Gothic, preserved for us in the translation of the scriptures by the Gothic Bishop Ulfilas (about A.D. 375). Other languages belonging to this group are Old Norse, once spoken in Scandinavia, and from which are descended modern Icelandic, Norwegian, Swedish, Danish; German; Dutch; and Old English, also called Anglo-Saxon, from which modern English is descended. Old English was spoken in England up until the Norman Conquest of the eleventh century. It is the language of *Beowulf.* It had a case system for nouns, much as Latin does, and more different verb forms than the modern language.

j. Balto-Slavic. The languages of this group belong to eastern Europe. The Baltic division of the group embraces Lithuanian and Latvian, spoken today by the people living on the eastern shores of the Baltic Sea. The earliest literary productions of these languages date from the sixteenth century. The Slavic division comprises a large number of languages, the most important of which are Russian, Ukranian, Bulgarian, Serbian (Croatian, Bosnian), Bohemian, and Polish. All of these were late in developing a literature, the earliest to do so being Old Church Slavic, in which we find a translation of the Bible dating from the ninth century.

k. Albanian, spoken in Albania and parts of Greece, Italy, and Sicily. This is most nearly related to the Balto-Slavic group, and is characterized by the very large proportion of words borrowed from Latin, Turkish, Greek, and Slavic. Its literature does not begin till the seventeenth century.

Home of the Indo-European Family

2. Despite the many outward differences of the various languages of the foregoing groups, a careful examination of their structure and vocabulary demonstrates their intimate relationship and proves overwhelmingly their descent from a common parent. We must believe, therefore, that at one time there existed a society or group of people speaking a language from which all the above enumerated languages are descended. The precise location of the home of this ancient society cannot be determined. For a long time it was assumed that it was in central Asia north of the Himalaya Mountains, but this view has long been rejected as untenable. It arose from the exaggerated importance attached for a long while to Sanskrit. The great antiquity of the earliest literary remains of Sanskrit (the Vedic Hymns) suggested that the inhabitants of India were geographically close to the original seat of the Indo-European Family. Hence the home was sought in the elevated plateau to the north. Today it is thought that central or southeastern Europe is much more likely to have been the cradle of the Indo-European parent-speech, though anything like a logical demonstration of so difficult a problem can hardly be expected.

As to the size and extent of the original group whence the Indo-European languages have sprung, we can only speculate. It probably was not large, and very likely formed a compact social and linguistic unit for centuries, possibly for thousands of years.

The time at which Indo-European unity ceased and the various individual languages began their separate existence is likewise shrouded in obscurity, though it is highly unlikely that the common language broke up before 3400 B.C. The speakers of the common Indo-European parent language may have lived around 5000 B.C. or possibly earlier.

Latin Language and Literature

3. **Stages in the Development of the Latin Language.**—The earliest remains of the Latin language are found in certain very archaic inscriptions. The oldest of these belong to the sixth and seventh centuries B.C. Roman literature does not begin till several centuries later, shortly after the middle of the third century B.C. We may recognize the following clearly marked periods of the language and literature:

a. The Preliterary Period, from the earliest times down to 240 B.C., when Livius Andronicus brought out his first play. For this period our knowledge of Latin depends almost exclusively upon the scanty inscriptions that have survived from this remote time. Few of these are of any length.

b. The Archaic Period, from Livius Andronicus (240 B.C.) to Cicero (81 B.C.). Even in this age the language had already become highly developed as a medium of expression. In the hands of certain gifted writers it had even become a vehicle of power and beauty. In its simplicity, however, it naturally marks a contrast with the more finished diction of later days. To this period belong:

Livius Andronicus, about 275-204 B.C. (Translation of Homer's
  Odyssey; Tragedies).

Plautus, about 250-184 B.C. (Comedies).

Naevius, about 270-199 B.C. (*Punic War*, an epic poem; Comedies).

Ennius, 239-169 B.C. (*Annals*, an epic; Tragedies).

Terence, about 190-159 B.C. (Comedies).

Lucilius, 180-103 B.C. (Satires).

Pacuvius, 220-about 130 B.C. (Tragedies).

Accius, 170-about 85 B.C. (Tragedies).

c. The Golden Age, from Cicero (81 B.C.) to the death of Augustus (14 A.D.). In this period the language, especially in the hands of Cicero, reaches a high degree of stylistic perfection. Its vocabulary, however, has not yet attained its greatest fullness and range. Traces of the diction of the Archaic Period are often noticed, especially in the poets, who naturally sought their effects by reverting to the speech of olden times. Literature reached its culmination in this epoch, especially in the great poets of the Augustan Age. The following writers belong here:

Lucretius, about 95-55 B.C. (Poem on Epicurean Philosophy).

Catullus, 87-about 54 B.C. (Poet).

Cicero, 106-43 B.C. (Orations; Rhetorical Works; Philosophical Works; Letters).

Caesar, 102-44 B.C. (*Commentaries* on Gallic and Civil Wars),

Sallust, 86-36 B.C. (Historian).

Nepos, about 100-about 30 B.C. (Historian).

Virgil, 70-19 B.C. (*Aeneid*; *Georgics*; *Bucolics*).

Horace, 65-8 B.C. (Odes; Satires, Epistles).

Tibullus, about 54-19 B.C. (Poet).

Propertius, about 50-about 15 B.C. (Poet).

Ovid, 43 B.C.-17 A.D. (*Metamorphoses* and other poems).

Livy. 59 B.C.-17 A.D. (Historian).

d. The Silver Latin period, from the death of Augustus (14 A.D.) to the death of Marcus Aurelius (180 A.D.), This period is marked by a certain reaction against the excessive precision of the previous age. It had become the practice to pay too much attention to standardized forms of expression, and to leave too little play to the individual writer. In the healthy reaction against this formalism, greater freedom of expression now manifests itself. We note also the introduction of idioms from the colloquial language, along with many poetical words and usages. The following authors deserve mention:

Phaedrus, flourished about 40 A.D. (Fables in Verse)

Velleius Paterculus, flourished about 30 A.D. (Historian).

Lucan, 39-65 A.D. (Poem on the Civil War).

Seneca, about 1-65 A.D. (Tragedies; Philosophical Works).

Pliny the Elder, 23-79 A.D. (*Natural History*).

Pliny the Younger, 62-about 115 A.D. (Letters).

Martial, about 45-about 104 A.D. (Epigrams).

Quintilian, about 35-about 100 A.D. (Treatise on Oratory and Education).

Tacitus, about 55-about 118 A.D. (Historian).

Juvenal, about 55-about 135 A.D. (Satirist).

Suetonius, about 73-about 118 A.D. (*Lives of the Twelve Caesars*).

Minucius Felix, flourished about 160 A.D. (First Christian Apologist).

Apuleius, 125-about 200 A.D. (*Metamorphoses*, or *Golden Ass*).

e. The Archaizing Period. This period is characterized by a conscious imitation of the Archaic Period of the second and first centuries B.C.; it overlaps the preceding period, and is of importance from a linguistic rather than from a literary point of view. Of writers who manifest the archaizing tendency most conspicuously may be mentioned Fronto, from whose hand we have a collection of letters addressed to the Emperors Antoninus Pius and Marcus Aurelius; also Aulus Gellius, author of the *Attic Nights*. Both of these writers flourished in the second half of the second century A.D.

f. The Period of the Decline, from 180 to the close of literary activity in the sixth century A.D. This period is characterized by rapid and radical alterations in the language. The features of the conversational idiom of the lower strata of society invade the literature, while in the remote provinces, such as Gaul, Spain, Africa, the language suffers from the incorporation of local peculiarities. Representative writers of this period are:

Tertullian, about 160-about 240 A.D. (Christian Writer).

Cyprian, about 200-258 A.D. (Christian Writer).

Lactantius, flourished about 300 A.D. (Defense of Christianity).

Ausonius, about 310-about 395 A.D. (Poet).

Jerome, 340-420 A.D. (Translator of the Scriptures).

Ambrose, about 340-397 (Christian Father).

Augustine, 354-430 (Christian Father—*City of God*).

Prudentius, flourished 400 A.D. (Christian Poet).

Claudian, flourished 400 A.D. (Poet).

Boëthius, about 480-524 A.D. (*Consolation of Philosophy*).

4. Subsequent History of the Latin Language.—After the sixth century A.D. Latin divides into two entirely different streams. One of these is the literary language maintained in courts, in the Church, and among scholars. This was no longer the language of people in general, and as time went on, became more and more artificial. The other stream is the colloquial idiom of the common people, which developed ultimately in the provinces into the modern so-called Romance idioms. These include Italian, Spanish, Portuguese, French, Catalan (spoken in Catalunia, in southern Spain), Provençal (spoken in Provence, *i.e.* southeastern France), Rhaeto-Romance (spoken in the Canton of the Grisons in Switzerland), and Roumanian, spoken in modern Roumania and adjacent districts. All these Romance languages bear the same relation to the Latin as the different groups of the Indo-European family of languages bear to the parent speech.

Further Reading

5. The following books provide more detail on various aspects of the Latin language, its history, and its literature.

Michael von Albrecht. *A History of Roman Literature: From Livius Andronicus to Boethius*, revised English edition. Leiden: 1997.

W. S. Allen. *Vox Latina: The Pronunciation of Classical Latin*, second edition. Cambridge: 1978.

Philip Baldi. *An Introduction to the Indo-European Languages*. Carbondale: 1983.

Benjamin W. Fortson, IV. *Indo-European Language and Culture: An Introduction*. Malden: 2004.

James W. Halporn, Martin Ostwald, and Thomas G. Rosenmeyer. *The Meters of Greek and Latin Verse*. Norman: 1980; reprinted Indianapolis: 1994.

E. J. Kenney, ed. *The Cambridge History of Classical Literature: Part 2, Latin*. Cambridge: 1982.

L. R. Palmer. *The Latin Language*. London: 1954; reprinted Norman: 1988.

Part I:
Sounds, Accent, Quantity

The Alphabet

1 The Latin Alphabet is the same as the English, except that the Latin has no **w**.

1. **K** occurs only in *Kalendae* and a few other words; **y** and **z** were introduced from the Greek about 50 B.C., and occur only in foreign words—chiefly Greek.

2. With the Romans, who regularly employed only capitals, **I** served both as vowel and consonant; so also **V**. For us, however, it is more convenient to distinguish the vowel and consonant sounds, and to write **i** and **u** for the former, **j** and **v** for the latter. Yet some scholars prefer to employ **i** and **u** in the function of consonants as well as vowels.

Classification of Sounds

2 1. The Vowels are **a, e, i, o, u, y**. The other letters are Consonants. The Diphthongs are **ae, oe, ei, au, eu, ui**.

2. Consonants are further subdivided into Mutes, Liquids, Nasals, and Spirants.

3. The Mutes (also called Stops) are **p, t, c, k, q; b, d, g; ph, th, ch**. Of these,—

a) **p, t, c, k, q** are voiceless,[3] i.e. sounded without voice or vibration of the vocal cords.

b) **b, d, g** are voiced,[4] i.e. sounded with vibration of the vocal cords.

c) **ph, th, ch** are aspirates. These are confined almost exclusively to words derived from the Greek, and were equivalent to **p + h, t + h, c + h**, *i.e.* to the corresponding voiceless mutes with a following breath, as in Eng. *loop-hole, hot-house, block-house*.

---

3   For "voiceless," the terms "surd," "hard," or "tenuis" are sometimes used.

4   For "voiced," the terms "sonant," "soft," or "media" are sometimes used.

4. The Mutes admit of classification also by point of articulation, that is, by what part of the vocal apparatus closes to stop the flow of sound:

Labials	**p, b, ph**
Dentals (or Linguals)	**t, d, th**
Gutturals (or Palatals)	**c, k, q, g, ch**

5. The Liquids are **l, r**. These sounds were voiced.

6. The Nasals are **m, n**. These were voiced. Besides its ordinary sound, **n**, when followed by a guttural mute also had another sound,—that of **ng** in *sing*,—the so-called **n** *adulterīnum*; as,—

   anceps, *double*, pronounced **angceps**.

7. The Spirants (sometimes called Fricatives) are **f, s, h**. These were voiceless.

8. The Semivowels are **j** and **v**. These were voiced.

9. Double Consonants are **x** and **z**. Of these, **x** was equivalent to **cs**, while the equivalence of **z** is uncertain. See § 3, 3.

10. The following table will indicate the relations of the consonant sounds:—

	VOICELESS,	VOICED,	ASPIRATES.	
Stops (Mutes), {	**p,**	**b,**	**ph,**	(Labials).
	t,	**d,**	**th,**	(Dentals).
	c, k, q,	**g,**	**ch,**	(Gutturals).
Liquids,		**l, r,**		
Nasals,		**m, n,**		
Fricatives (Spirants), {	**f,**			(Labial).
	s,			(Dental).
	h,			(Guttural).
Semivowels,		**j, v.**		

a) The Double Consonants, **x** and **z**, being compound sounds, do not admit of classification in the above table.

Sounds of the Letters

3 The following pronunciation (often called Roman) is substantially that employed by the Romans at the height of their civilization; *i.e.*, roughly, from 50 B.C. to 50 A.D.

1. **Vowels**

   ā as in *father*   ă as in the first syllable *ahá*
   ē as in *they*   ě as in *met*
   ī as in *machine*   ĭ as in *pin*
   ō as in *note*   ŏ as in *obey, melody*
   ū as in *rude*   ŭ as in *put*
   ȳ like French *u*, German *ü*   y similarly

2. **Diphthongs**

   ae like *ai* in *aisle*   eu with its two elements, ě
   oe like *oi* in *oil*   and ŭ, pronounced in
   ei as in *rein*   rapid succession
   au like *ow* in *how*   ui occurs almost exclusively
                                         in *cui* and *huic*. These
                                         words may be pronounced
                                         as though written *kwee*
                                         and *wheek*.

3. **Consonants**

   b, d, f, h, k, l, m, n, p, qu are pronounced as in English,
   except that **bs, bt** are pronounced *ps, pt*.

   c is always pronounced as *k*.

   t is always a plain *t*, never with the sound of *sh* as in Eng.
   oration.

   g always as in *get*; when **ngu** precedes a vowel, **gu** has the
   sound of *gw*, as in **anguis, languidus**.

   j has the sound of *y* as in *yet*.

   r was probably slightly trilled with the tip of the tongue.

   s always voiceless as in *sin*; in **suādeō, suāvis, suēscō**, and
   in compounds and derivatives of these words, **su** has the
   sound of *sw*.

   v like *w*.

   x always like *ks*; never like Eng. *gz* or *z*.

   z uncertain in sound; possibly like Eng. *zd*, possibly like *z*.
   The latter sound is recommended.

   The aspirates **ph, ch, th** were pronounced very nearly like
   our stressed Eng. *p, c, t*—so nearly so, that, for practical
   purposes, the latter sounds suffice.

   Doubled letters, like **ll, mm, tt**, *etc.*, should be so pronounced
   that both members of the combination are distinctly
   articulated.

Syllables

4 There are as many syllables in a Latin word as there are separate vowels and diphthongs. In the division of words into syllables,—

    1. A single consonant is joined to the following vowel; as, **vo-lat, ge-rit, pe-rit, a-dest**.

    2. Doubled consonants, like **tt**, **ss**, *etc.*, are always separated; as, **vit-ta, mis-sus**.

    3. Other combinations of two or more consonants are regularly separated, and the first consonant of the combination is joined with the preceding vowel; as, **ma-gis-trī, dig-nus, mōn-strum, sis-te-re**.

    4. An exception to Rule 3 occurs when the two consonants consist of a mute followed by **l** or **r** (**pl, cl, tl; pr, cr, tr,** *etc.*). In such cases both consonants are regularly joined to the following vowel; as, **a-grī, vo-lu-cris, pa-tris, mā-tris**. Yet if the **l** or **r** introduces the second part of a compound, the two consonants are separated; as, **ab-rumpō, ad-lātus**.

    5. The double consonant **x** is joined to the preceding vowel; as, **ax-is, tēx-ī**.

Quantity

5 **Quantity of Vowels**

A vowel is *long* or *short* according to the length of time required for its pronunciation. No absolute rule can be given for determining the quantity of Latin vowels. This knowledge must be gained, in large measure, by experience; but the following principles are of aid:—

    1. **A vowel is long,**[5]—

        a) before **nf** or **ns**; as, **īnfāns, īnferior, cōnsūmō, cēnseō, īnsum**.

        b) when the result of contraction; as, **nīlum** for **nihilum**.

    2. **A vowel is short—**

        a) before **nt, nd**; as, **amant, amandus**. A few exceptions occur in compounds whose first member has a long vowel; as, **nōndum** (**nōn dum**).

---

5   In this book, long vowels are indicated by a horizontal line above them, called a "macron"; as, ā, ī, ō, *etc.* Vowels not thus marked are short. Occasionally a curve (called "breve") is set above short vowels; as, ĕ, ŭ.

b) before another vowel, or **h**; as, **meus, trahō**. Some exceptions occur, chiefly in proper names derived from the Greek; as, **Aenēās**.

Quantity of Syllables

Syllables are distinguished as *long* or *short* according to the length of time required for their pronunciation.

1. **A syllable is long,**[6]—
   a) if it contains a long vowel; as, **māter, rēgnum, dīus**.
   b) if it contains a diphthong; as, **causae, foedus**.
   c) if it contains a short vowel followed by **x, z**, or any two consonants (except a mute with **l** or **r**); as, **axis, gaza, restō**. Note that the *vowel* in this case is short even though the *syllable* is long.

2. **A syllable is short**, if it contains a short vowel followed by a vowel or by a single consonant; as, **mea, amat**.

3. Sometimes a syllable varies in quantity, namely when its vowel is short and is followed by a mute with **l** or **r**, *i.e.* by **pl, cl, tl; pr, cr, tr**, *etc.*; as, **ăgrī, volucris**.[7] Such syllables are called common. In prose they were regularly short, but in verse they might be treated as long at the option of the poet.

NOTE.—These distinctions of *long* and *short* are not arbitrary and artificial, but are purely natural. Thus, a syllable containing a short vowel followed by two consonants, as **ng**, is long, because such a syllable requires *more time* for its pronunciation; while a syllable containing a short vowel followed by one consonant is short, because it takes *less time* to pronounce it. In case of the common syllables, the mute and the liquid blend so easily as to produce a combination which takes no more time than a single consonant. Yet treating the two elements as separate (as **ag-rī**) allowed the poets to use such syllables as long.

---

6   To avoid confusion, the quantity of *syllables* is not indicated by any sign.
7   But if the l or r introduces the second part of a compound, the preceding syllable is always long; as, abrumpō.

Accent

1. Words of two syllables are accented upon the first; as, **tégit, mō´rem.**

2. Words of more than two syllables are accented upon the penult (next to the last) if that is a long syllable, otherwise upon the antepenult (second from the last); as, **amā´vī, amántis, míserum.**

3. When the enclitics **-que, -ne, -ve, -ce, -met, -dum** are appended to words, if the syllable preceding the enclitic is long (either originally or as a result of adding the enclitic) it is accented; as, **miserō´que, hominísque.** But if the syllable still remains short after the enclitic has been added, it is not accented unless the word originally took the accent on the antepenult. Thus, **pórtaque;** but **míseráque.**

4. Sometimes the final **-e** of **-ne** and **-ce** disappears, but without affecting the accent; as, **tantō´n, istī´c, illū´c.**

5. In **utră´que,** *each,* and **plēră´que,** *most,* **-que** is not properly an enclitic; yet these words accent the penult, owing to the influence of their other cases, —**utérque, utrúmque, plērúmque.**

Vowel Changes

1. **In Compounds,**

   a) **ě** before a single consonant becomes **ĭ**; as, —

   colligō   for **con-legō.**

   b) **ă** before a single consonant becomes **ĭ**: as, —

   adigō   for **ad-agō.**

   c) **ă** before two consonants becomes **ē**; as, —

   expers   for **ex-pars.**

   d) **ae** becomes **ī**; as, —

   conquīrō for **con-quaerō.**

   e) **au** becomes **ū**, sometimes **ō**; as, —

   conclūdō for **con-claudō**;
   explōdō   for **ex-plaudō.**

2. **Contraction.** Concurrent vowels were frequently contracted into one long vowel. The first of the two vowels regularly prevailed; as, —

trēs	for tre-es;	cōpia	for co-opia;
mālō	for ma(v)elō;	cōgō	for co-agō;
amāstī	for amā(v)istī;	cōmō	for co-emō;
dēbeō	for dē(h)abeō;	jūnior	for ju(v)enior.
nīl	for nihil;		

3. **Parasitic Vowels.** In the environment of liquids and nasals a parasitic vowel sometimes develops; as, —

> **vinculum** for earlier **vinclum.**

So **perīculum, saeculum.**

4. **Syncope.** Sometimes a vowel drops out by syncope; as, —

> **ārdor** for **āridor** (compare *āridus*);
>
> **valdē** for **validē** (compare *validus*).

Consonant Changes[8]

8

1. **Rhotacism.** An original **s** between vowels became **r**; as, —

> **arbōs,** Gen. **arboris** (for **arbosis**);
> **genus,** Gen. **generis** (for **genesis**);
> **dirimō** (for **dis-emō**).

2. **dt, tt, ts** each give **s** or **ss**; as,—

> **pēnsum** for **pend-tum;**
> **versum** for **vert-tum;**
> **mīles** for **mīlet-s;**
> **sessus** for **sedtus;**
> **passus** for **pattus.**

3. Final consonants were often omitted; as, —

> **cor** for **cord;**
> **lac** for **lact.**

4. **Assimilation of Consonants.** Consonants are often assimilated to a following sound. Thus: **accurrō (adc-); aggerō (adg-); asserō (ads-); allātus (adl-); apportō (adp-); attulī (adt-); arrīdeō (adr-); afferō (adf-); occurrō (obc-); suppōnō (subp-); offerō (obf-); corruō (comr-); collātus (coml-);** *etc.*

5. **Partial Assimilation.** Sometimes the assimilation is only partial. Thus:—

a) **b** before **s** or **t** becomes **p**; as,—

> **scrīpsī (scrīb-sī), scrīptum (scrīb-tum).**

b) **g** before **s** or **t** becomes **c**; as,—

---

8   Only the simplest and most obvious of these are here treated.

āctus (āg-tus).

c) **m** before a dental or guttural becomes **n**; as,—

eundem (eum-dem); prīnceps (prīm-ceps).

Peculiarities of Spelling

 Many words have variable orthography (spelling).

1. Sometimes the different forms belong to different periods of the language. Thus, **quom, voltus, volnus, volt,** *etc.*, were the prevailing forms almost down to the Augustan age; after that, **cum, vultus, vulnus, vult,** *etc.* So **optumus, maxumus, lubet, lubīdō,** *etc.* down to about the same era; later, **optimus, maximus, libet, libīdō,** *etc.*

2. In some words the orthography varies at one and the same period of the language. Examples are **exspectō, expectō; exsistō, existō; epistula, epistola; adulēscēns, adolēscēns; paulus, paullus; cottīdiē, cotīdiē;** and, particularly, prepositional compounds, which often made a concession to the etymology in the spelling; as,—

ad-gerō or **aggerō;**	**ad-serō** or **asserō;**
ad-liciō or **alliciō;**	**in-lātus** or **illātus;**
ad-rogāns or **arrogāns;**	**sub-moveō** or **summoveō;**

and many others.

3. Compounds of **jaciō** were usually written **ēiciō, dēiciō, adiciō, obiciō,** *etc.*, but were probably pronounced as though written **adjiciō, objiciō,** *etc.*

4. Adjectives and nouns in **-quus, -quum; -vus, -vum; -uus, -uum** preserved the earlier forms in **-quos, -quom; -vos, -vom; -uos, -uom,** down through the Ciceronian age; as, **antīquos, antīquom; saevos; perpetuos; equos; servos.** Similarly verbs in the 3d plural present indicative exhibit the terminations **-quont, -quontur; -vont, -vontur; -uont, -uontur,** for the same period; as, **relinquont, loquontur; vīvont, metuont.**

The older spelling, while generally followed in editions of Plautus and Terence, has not yet been adopted in our prose texts.

Part II:
Inflections

10 The Parts of Speech in Latin are the same as in English, that is, Nouns, Adjectives, Pronouns, Verbs, Adverbs, Prepositions, Conjunctions, and Interjections; but Latin has no article.

11 Of these eight parts of speech the first four are capable of Inflection, *i.e.* of undergoing change of form to express modifications of meaning. In case of Nouns, Adjectives, and Pronouns, this process is called Declension; in case of verbs, Conjugation.

DECLENSION

Nouns

12 A Noun is the name of a *person, place, thing,* or *quality*; as, **Caesar,** *Caesar*; **Rōma,** *Rome*; **penna,** *feather*; **virtūs,** *courage*.

  1. Nouns are either Proper or Common. Proper nouns are permanent names of persons or places; as, **Caesar, Rōma.** Other nouns are Common: as, **penna, virtūs.**

  2. Nouns are also distinguished as Concrete or Abstract.

    a) Concrete nouns are those which designate individual objects; as, **mōns,** *mountain*; **pēs,** *foot*; **diēs,** *day*; **mēns,** *mind*.

    Under concrete nouns are included, also, collective nouns; as, **legiō,** *legion*; **comitātus,** *retinue*.

    b) Abstract nouns designate qualities; as, **cōnstantia,** *steadfastness*; **paupertās,** *poverty*.

Gender of nouns

13 There are three Genders,—Masculine, Feminine, and Neuter. Gender in Latin is either natural or grammatical.

Natural Gender

14 The gender of nouns is natural when it is based upon sex. Natural gender is confined entirely to names of persons; and these are—

1. Masculine, if they denote males; as,—

     nauta, *sailor*; **agricola**, *farmer*.

2. Feminine, if they denote females; as,—

   ' **māter**, *mother*; **rēgīna**, *queen*.

Grammatical Gender

15 Grammatical gender is determined not by sex, but by the general signification of the word, or the ending of its Nominative Singular. By grammatical gender, nouns denoting things or qualities are often Masculine or Feminine, simply by virtue of their signification or the ending of the Nominative Singular. The following are the general principles for determining grammatical gender:—

Gender determined by Signification

1. Names of *Rivers*, *Winds*, and *Months* are Masculine; as,—

     Sēquana, *Seine*; **Eurus**, *east wind*; **Aprīlis**, *April*.

2. Names of *Trees*, and such names of *Towns* and *Islands* as end in **-us**, are Feminine; as,—

     quercus, *oak*; **Corinthus**, *Corinth*; **Rhodus**, *Rhodes*.

   Other names of towns and islands follow the gender of their endings (see *B*, below); as,—

     Delphī, n.; **Leuctra**, n.; **Tībur**, n.; **Carthāgō**, f.

3. Indeclinable nouns, also infinitives and phrases, are Neuter; as,—

     nihil, *nothing*; **nefās**, *wrong*; **amāre**, *to love*.

NOTE.—Exceptions to the above principles sometimes occur; as, **Allia** (the river), f.

Gender determined by Ending of Nominative Singular

The gender of other nouns is determined by the ending of the Nominative Singular.[9]

---

9   The great majority of all Latin nouns come under this category. The principles for determining their gender are given under the separate declensions.

NOTE 1.—*Common Gender.* Certain nouns are sometimes Masculine, sometimes Feminine. Thus, **sacerdōs** may mean either *priest* or *priestess*, and is Masculine or Feminine accordingly. So also **cīvis**, *citizen*; **parēns**, *parent*; etc. The gender of such nouns is said to be *common.*

NOTE 2.—Names of animals usually have grammatical gender, according to the ending of the Nominative Singular, but the one form may designate either the male or female; as, **ānser**, m., *goose* or *gander.* So **vulpēs**, f., *fox*; **aquīla**, f., *eagle.*

Number

16 The Latin has two Numbers,—the Singular and Plural. The Singular denotes one object, the Plural, more than one.

Cases

17 There are six Cases in Latin:—

Nominative	Case of Subject
Genitive	Objective with *of*, or Possessive
Dative	Objective with *to* or *for*
Accusative	Case of Direct Object
Vocative	Case of Address
Ablative	Objective with *by, from, in, with*

1. **Locative.** Vestiges of another case, the **Locative** (denoting place where), occur in names of towns and in a few other words.

2. **Oblique Cases.** The Genitive, Dative, Accusative, and Ablative are called **Oblique Cases.**

3. **Stem and Case-Endings.** The different cases are formed by appending certain **case-endings** to a fundamental part called the **Stem.**[10] Thus, portam (Accusative Singular) is formed by adding the case-ending -m to the stem porta-. But in most cases the final vowel of the stem has coalesced so closely with the actual case-ending that the latter has become more or less obscured. The apparent case-ending thus resulting is called a termination.

---

10   The Stem is often derived from a more primitive form called the Root. Thus, the stem porta- goes back to the root per-, por-. Roots are usually monosyllabic. The addition made to a root to form a stem is called a Suffix. Thus in porta- the suffix is -ta.

The Five Declensions

18 There are five Declensions in Latin, distinguished from each other by the final letter of the Stem, and also by the Termination of the Genitive Singular, as follows:—

DECLENSION	FINAL LETTER OF STEM	GEN. TERMINATION
First	ā	-ae
Second	ŏ	-ī
Third	ĭ / Some consonant	-īs
Fourth	ŭ	-ūs
Fifth	ē	-ēī / -ĕī

Cases alike in Form

19 1. The Vocative is regularly like the Nominative, except in the singular of nouns in **-us** of the Second Declension.

2. The Dative and Ablative Plural are always alike.

3. In Neuters the Accusative and Nominative are always alike, and in the Plural end in -ă.

4. In the Third, Fourth, and Fifth Declensions, the Accusative Plural is regularly like the Nominative.

First Declension

ā-Stems

20 Pure Latin nouns of the First Declension regularly end, in the Nominative Singular, in -ă, weakened from -ā, and are of the Feminine Gender. They are declined as follows:—

Porta, *gate*; stem, **portā-**		
SINGULAR		
CASES	MEANINGS	TERMINATIONS
Nom. porta	*a gate* (as subject)	-ă
Gen. portae	*of a gate*	-ae
Dat. portae	*to* or *for a gate*	-ae
Acc. portam	*a gate* (as object)	-am
Voc. porta	*O gate!*	-ă
Abl. portā	*with, by, from, in a gate*	-ā
PLURAL		
Nom. portae	*gates* (as subject)	-ae
Gen. portārum	*of gates*	-ārum
Dat. portīs	*to* or *for gates*	-īs
Acc. portās	*gates* (as object)	-ās
Voc. portae	*O gates!*	-ae
Abl. portīs	*with, by, from, in gates*	-īs

1. Latin has no article, and **porta** may mean either *a gate* or *the gate*; and in the Plural, *gates* or *the gates*.

Peculiarities of Nouns of the First Declension

21

1. **Exceptions in Gender**. Nouns denoting males are Masculine; as, **nauta**, *sailor*; **agricola**, *farmer*; also, **Hadria**, *Adriatic Sea*.

2. Rare Case-Endings,—

   a) An old form of the Genitive Singular in -**ās** is preserved in the combination **pater familiās**, *father of a family*; also in **māter familiās, fīlius familiās, fīlia familiās**. But the regular form of the Genitive in -**ae** is also admissible in these expressions; as, **pater familiae**.

   b) In poetry a Genitive in -**āī** also occurs; as, **aulāī**. Note that **āī** is two syllables, not a diphthong.

   c) The Locative Singular ends in -**ae**; as, **Rōmae**, *at Rome*.

   d) A Genitive Plural in -**um** instead of -**ārum** sometimes occurs; as, **Dardanidum** instead of **Dardanidārum**. This termination -**um** is not a contraction of -**ārum**, but represents an entirely different case-ending.

   e) Instead of the regular ending -**īs**, we usually find -**ābus** in the Dative and Ablative Plural of **dea**, *goddess*, and **fīlia**, *daughter*, especially when it is important to distinguish these nouns from the corresponding forms of **deus**, *god*, and **fīlius**, *son*. A few other words sometimes have the same peculiarity; as, **lībertābus** (from **līberta**, *freedwoman*), **equābus** (*mares*), to avoid confusion with **lībertīs** (from **lībertus**, *freedman*) and **equīs** (from **equus**, *horse*).

Greek Nouns

22

These end in -**ē** (Feminine); -**ās** and -**ēs** (Masculine). In the Plural they are declined like regular Latin nouns of the First Declension. In the Singular they are declined as follows:—

	Archiās, *Archias*	**Epitomē**, *epitome*	**Comētēs**, *comet*
Nom.	Archiās	epitomē	comētēs
Gen.	Archiae	epitomēs	comētae
Dat.	Archiae	epitomae	comētae
Acc.	Archiam (or -ān)	epitomēn	comētēn
Voc.	Archiā	epitomē	comētē (or -ă)
Abl.	Archiā	epitomē	comētē (or -ā)

1. But most Greek nouns in -**ē** become regular Latin nouns in -**a**, and are declined like **porta**; as, **grammatica**, *grammar*; **mūsica**, *music*; **rhētorica**, *rhetoric*.

2. Some other peculiarities occur, especially in poetry.

Second Declension

ŏ-Stems

23 Pure Latin nouns of the Second Declension end in **-us, -er, -ir**, Masculine; **-um**, Neuter. Originally **-us** in the Nominative of the Masculine was **-os**; and **-um** of the Neuters **-om**. So also in the Accusative.

Nouns in **-us** and **-um** are declined as follows:—

	Hortus, *garden*; stem, **hortŏ-**	TERMINATION	**Bellum**, *war*; stem, **bellŏ-**	TERMINATION
		SINGULAR		
Nom.	hortus	-us	bellum	-um
Gen.	hortī	-ī	bellī	-ī
Dat.	hortō	-ō	bellō	-ō
Acc.	hortum	-um	bellum	-um
Voc.	horte	-e	bellum	-um
Abl.	hortō	-ō	bellō	-ō
		PLURAL		
Nom.	hortī	-ī	bella	-a
Gen.	hortōrum	-ōrum	bellōrum	-ōrum
Dat.	hortīs	-īs	bellīs	-īs
Acc.	hortōs	-ōs	bella	-a
Voc.	hortī	-ī	bella	-a
Abl.	hortīs	-īs	bellīs	-īs

Nouns in **-er** and **-ir** are declined as follows:—

	Puer, *boy*; stem, **puerŏ-**	**Ager**, *field*; stem, **agrŏ-**	**Vir**, *man*; stem, **virŏ-**	TERMINATION
		SINGULAR		
Nom.	puer	ager	vir	Wanting
Gen.	puerī	agrī	virī	-ī
Dat.	puerō	agrō	virō	-ō
Acc.	puerum	agrum	virum	-um
Voc.	puer	ager	vir	Wanting
Abl.	puerō	agrō	virō	-ō
		PLURAL		
Nom.	puerī	agrī	virī	-ī
Gen.	puerōrum	agrōrum	virōrum	-ōrum
Dat.	puerīs	agrīs	virīs	-īs
Acc.	puerōs	agrōs	virōs	-ōs
Voc.	puerī	agrī	virī	-ī
Abl.	puerīs	agrīs	virīs	-īs

1. Note that in words of the type of **puer** and **vir** the final vowel of the stem has disappeared in the Nominative and Vocative Singular.

In the Nominative and Vocative Singular of **ager**, the stem is further modified by the development of **e** before **r**.

2. The following nouns in -**er** are declined like **puer**: **adulter**, *adulterer*; **gener**, *son-in-law*; **Līber**, *Bacchus*; **socer**, *father-in-law*; **vesper**, *evening*; and compounds in -**fer** and -**ger**, as **signifer**, **armiger**.

Nouns in -*vus*, -*vum*, -*quus*

24 Nouns ending in the Nominative Singular in -**vus**, -**vum**, -**quus**, exhibited two types of inflection in the classical Latin,—an earlier and a later,—as follows:—

Earlier Inflection (including Caesar and Cicero).		
Servos, m., *slave.*	**Aevom**, n., *age.*	**Equos**, m., *horse.*
Singular		
Nom. servos	aevom	equos
Gen. servī	aevī	equī
Dat. servō	aevō	equō
Acc. servom	aevom	equom
Voc. serve	aevom	eque
Abl. servō	aevō	equō

Later inflection (after Cicero).		
Singular		
Nom. servus	aevum	equus
Gen. servī	aevī	equī
Dat. servō	aevō	equō
Act. servum	aevum	equum
Voc. serve	aevum	eque
Abl. servō	aevō	equō

1. The Plural of these nouns is regular, and always uniform.

Peculiarities of Inflection in the Second Declension

25 1. Proper names in -**ius** regularly form the Genitive Singular in -**ī** (instead of -**iī**), and the Vocative Singular in -**ī** (for -**ie**); as **Vergílī**, *of Virgil*, or *O Virgil* (instead of **Vergiliī**, **Vergilie**). In such words the accent stands upon the penult, even though that be short. Nouns in -**ajus**, -**ejus** form the Gen. in -**aī**, -**eī**, as **Pompejus**, **Pompeī**.

2. Nouns in -**ius** and -**ium**, until after the beginning of the reign of Augustus (31 B.C.), regularly formed the Genitive Singular in -**i** (instead of -**iī**); as,—

Nom.	**ingenium**	**fīlius**
Gen.	**ingénī**	**fīlī**

These Genitives accent the penult, even when it is short.

3. **Fīlius** forms the Vocative Singular in **-ī** (for **-ie**): **fīlī**, *O son!*

4. **Deus**, *god*, lacks the Vocative Singular. The Plural is inflected as follows:—

Nom.	**dī**	(**deī**)
Gen.	**deōrum**	(**deum**)
Dat.	**dīs**	(**deīs**)
Acc.	**deōs**	
Voc.	**dī**	(**deī**)
Abl.	**dīs**	(**deīs**)

5. The Locative Singular ends in **-ī**; as, **Corinthī**, *at Corinth.*

6. The Genitive Plural has **-um**, instead of **-ōrum**,—

    a) in words denoting money and measure; as, **talentum**, *of talents*; **modium**, *of pecks*; **sēstertium**, *of sesterces.*

    b) in **duumvir, triumvir, decemvir**; as, **duumvirum**.

    c) sometimes in other words; as, **līberum**, *of the children*; **socium**, *of the allies.*

Exceptions to Gender in the Second Declension

26

1. The following nouns in **-us** are Feminine by exception:—

    a) Names of **towns, islands, trees**—according to the general rule laid down in § 15, 2; also some names of countries; as Aegyptus, Egypt.

    b) Five special words,—

        alvus, *belly*
        carbasus, *flax*
        colus, *distaff*
        humus, *ground*
        vannus, *winnowing-fan*

    c) A few Greek Feminines; as,—

        atomus, *atom*
        diphthongus, *diphthong*

2. The following nouns in **-us** are Neuter:—

        pelagus, *sea*
        vīrus, *poison*
        vulgus, *crowd*

Greek Nouns of the Second Declension

27

These end in **-os**, **-ōs**, Masculine or Feminine; and **-on**, Neuter. They are mainly proper names, and are declined as follows:—

	Barbitos, m. and f., *lyre.*	Androgeōs, m., *Androgeos.*	Īlion, n., *Troy.*
Nom.	barbitos	Androgeōs	Īlion
Gen.	barbitī	Androgeō, -ī	Īliī
Dat.	barbitō	Androgeō	Īliō
Acc.	barbiton	Androgeō, -ōn	Īlion
Voc.	barbite	Androgeōs	Īlion
Abl.	barbitō	Androgeō	Īliō

1. Nouns in **-os** sometimes form the Accusative Singular in **-um** instead of **-on**; as, **Dēlum,** *Delos.*

2. The Plural of Greek nouns, when it occurs, is usually regular.

3. For other rare forms of Greek nouns the lexicon may be consulted.

Third Declension

28 Nouns of the Third Declension end in **-a, -e, -ī, -ō, -y, -c, -l, -n, -r, -s, -t, -x.** The Third Declension includes several distinct classes of Stems,—

- I.   Pure Consonant-Stems
- II. ĭ-Stems
- III. Consonant-Stems which have partially adapted themselves to the inflection of ĭ-Stems.
- IV. A very few stems ending in a long vowel or a diphthong.
- V.   Irregular Nouns

Consonant-Stems

29 1. In these the stem appears in its unaltered form in all the oblique cases, so that the actual case-endings may be clearly recognized.

2. Consonant-Stems fall into several natural subdivisions, according as the stem ends in a **Mute, Liquid, Nasal,** or **Spirant**.

Mute-Stems

30 Mute-Stems may end,—

1. In a Labial (**p**); as, **prīncep-s.**

2. In a Guttural (**g** or **c**); as, **rēmex (rēmeg-s); dux (duc-s).**

3. In a Dental (**d** or **t**); as, **lapis (lapid-s); mīles (mīlet-s).**

STEMS IN A LABIAL MUTE (P)

31 Prīnceps, m., *chief.*

	SINGULAR	TERMINATION
Nom.	prīnceps	-s
Gen.	prīncipis	-is
Dat.	prīncipī	-ī
Acc.	prīncipem	-em
Voc.	prīnceps	-s
Abl.	prīncipe	-e
	PLURAL	
Nom.	prīncipēs	-ēs
Gen.	prīncipum	-um
Dat.	prīncipibus	-ibus
Acc.	prīncipēs	-ēs
Voc.	prīncipēs	-ēs
Abl.	prīncipibus	-ibus

STEMS IN A GUTTURAL MUTE (G, C)

32 In these the termination -s of the Nominative Singular unites with the guttural, thus producing -x.

	Rēmex, m., *rower.*		Dux, c., *leader.*	
	SINGULAR	PLURAL	SINGULAR	PLURAL
Nom.	rēmex	rēmigēs	dux	ducēs
Gen.	rēmigis	rēmigum	ducis	ducum
Dat.	rēmigī	rēmigibus	ducī	ducibus
Acc.	rēmigem	rēmigēs	ducem	ducēs
Voc.	rēmex	rēmigēs	dux	ducēs
Abl.	rēmige	rēmigibus	duce	ducibus

STEMS IN A DENTAL MUTE (D, T)

33 In these the final d or t of the stem disappears in the Nominative Singular before the ending -s.

	Lapis, m., *stone.*		Mīles, m., *soldier.*	
	SINGULAR	PLURAL	SINGULAR	PLURAL
Nom.	lapis	lapidēs	mīles	mīlitēs
Gen.	lapidis	lapidum	mīlitis	mīlitum
Dat.	lapidī	lapidibus	mīlitī	mīlitibus
Acc.	lapidem	lapidēs	mīlitem	mīlitēs
Voc.	lapis	lapidēs	mīles	mīlitēs
Abl.	lapide	lapidibus	mīlite	mīlitibus

LIQUID STEMS

34

These end in **-l** or **-r**.

	Vigil, m., watchman.	**Victor**, m., conqueror.	**Aequor**, n., sea.
SINGULAR			
Nom.	vigil	victor	aequor
Gen.	vigilis	victōris	aequoris
Dat.	vigilī	victōrī	aequorī
Acc.	vigilem	victōrem	aequor
Voc.	vigil	victor	aequor
Abl.	vigile	victōre	aequore
PLURAL			
Nom.	vigilēs	victōrēs	aequora
Gen.	vigilum	victōrum	aequorum
Dat.	vigilibus	victōribus	aequoribus
Acc.	vigilēs	victōrēs	aequora
Voc.	vigilēs	victōrēs	aequora
Abl.	vigilibus	victōribus	aequoribus

1. Masculine and Feminine stems ending in a liquid form the Nominative and Vocative Singular without termination.

2. The termination is also lacking in the Nominative, Accusative and Vocative Singular of all **neuters** of the Third Declension.

NASAL STEMS

35

These end in **-n**,[11] which often disappears in the Nom. Sing.

	Leō, m., *lion.*		**Nōmen**, n., *name*	
	SINGULAR	PLURAL	SINGULAR	PLURAL
Nom.	leō	leōnēs	nōmen	nōmina
Gen.	leōnis	leōnum	nōminis	nōminum
Dat.	leōnī	leōnibus	nōminī	nōminibus
Acc.	leōnem	leōnēs	nōmen	nōmina
Voc.	leō	leōnēs	nōmen	nōmina
Abl.	leōne	leōnibus	nōmine	nōminibus

---

11   There is only one stem ending in **-m:—hiems, hiemīs,** winter.

s-Stems

36

	Mōs, m. *custom*	Genus, n., *race*	Honor, m., *honor*
	SINGULAR		
Nom.	mōs	genus	honor
Gen.	mōris	generis	honōris
Dat.	mōrī	generī	honōrī
Acc.	mōrem	genus	honōrem
Voc.	mōs	genus	honor
Abl.	mōre	genere	honōre
	PLURAL		
Nom.	mōrēs	genera	honōrēs
Gen.	mōrum	generum	honōrum
Dat.	mōribus	generibus	honōribus
Acc.	mōrēs	genera	honōrēs
Voc.	mōrēs	genera	honōrēs
Abl.	mōribus	generibus	honōribus

1. Note that the final **s** of the stem becomes **r** (between vowels) in the oblique cases. In many words (**honor, color,** and the like) the **r** of the oblique cases has, by analogy, crept into the Nominative, displacing the earlier **s,** though the forms **honōs, colōs,** *etc.,* also occur, particularly in early Latin and in poetry.

ĭ-Stems

MASCULINE AND FEMININE ĭ-STEMS

37 These regularly end in **-is** in the Nominative Singular, and always have **-ium** in the Genitive Plural. Originally the Accusative Singular ended in **-im,** the Ablative Singular in **-ī,** and the Accusative Plural in **-īs;** but these endings have been largely displaced by **-em, -e,** and **-ēs,** the endings of Consonant-Stems.

38

	Tussis, f., *cough*; stem, **tussi-**	Īgnis, m., *fire*; stem, **īgni-**	Hostis, c., *enemy*; stem, **hosti-**	
	SINGULAR			TERMINATION
Nom.	tussis	īgnis	hostis	-is
Gen.	tussis	īgnis	hostis	-is
Dat.	tussī	īgnī	hostī	-ī
Acc.	tussim	īgnem	hostem	-im, -em
Voc.	tussis	īgnis	hostis	-is
Abl.	tussī	īgnī or e	hoste	-ī, -e
	PLURAL			
Nom.	tussēs	īgnēs	hostēs	-ēs
Gen.	tussium	īgnium	hostium	-ium
Dat.	tussibus	īgnibus	hostibus	-ibus
Acc.	tussīs or -ēs	īgnīs or -ēs	hostīs or -ēs	-īs, -ēs
Voc.	tussēs	īgnēs	hostēs	-ēs
Abl.	tussibus	īgnibus	hostibus	-ibus

1. To the same class belong—

apis, *bee*	**crātis**, *hurdle*	†***secūris**, *axe*
auris, *ear*	***febris**, *fever*	**sēmentis**, *sowing*
avis, *bird*	**orbis**, *circle*	†***sitis**, *thirst*
axis, *axle*	**ovis**, *sheep*	**torris**, *brand*
***būris**, *plough-beam*	**pelvis**, *basin*	†***turris**, *tower*
clāvis, *key*	**puppis**, *stern*	**trudis**, *pole*
collis, *hill*	**restis**, *rope*	**vectis**, *lever*
	and many others.	

Words marked with a star regularly have Acc. **-im**; those marked with a † regularly have Abl. **-ī**. Of the others, many at times show **-im** and **-ī**. Town and river names in **-is** regularly have **-im, -ī**.

2. Not all nouns in **-is** are ĭ-Stems. Some are genuine consonant-stems, and have the regular consonant terminations throughout, notably, **canis**, *dog*; **juvenis**, *youth*.[12]

3. Some genuine ĭ-Stems have become disguised in the Nominative Singular; as, **pars**, *part*, for **par(ti)s**; **anas**, *duck*, for **ana(ti)s**; so also **mors**, *death*; **dōs**, *dowry*; **nox**, *night*; **sors**, *lot*; **mēns**, *mind*; **ars**, *art*; **gēns**, *tribe*; and some others.

---

12 **Mēnsis,** month, originally a consonant stem (**mēns-**), has in the Genitive Plural both **mēnsium** and **mēnsum**. The Accusative Plural is **mēnsēs**.

NEUTER Ĭ-STEMS

39 These end in the Nominative Singular in **-e**, **-al**, and **-ar**. They always have **-ī** in the Ablative Singular, **-ia** in the Nominative, Accusative, and Vocative Plural, and **-ium** in the Genitive Plural, thus holding more steadfastly to the **i**-character than do Masculine and Feminine ĭ-Stems.

	Sedile, *seat*; stem, **sedīli-**	**Animal**, *animal*; stem, **animāli-**	**Calcar**, *spur*; stem, **calcāri-**	
	SINGULAR			TERMINATION
Nom.	sedīle	animal	calcar	-e or wanting
Gen.	sedīlis	animālis	calcāris	-is
Dat.	sedīlī	animālī	calcārī	-ī
Acc.	sedīle	animal	calcar	-e or wanting
Voc.	sedīle	animal	calcar	-e or wanting
Abl.	sedīlī	animālī	calcārī	-ī
	PLURAL			
Nom.	sedīlia	animālia	calcāria	-ia
Gen.	sedīlium	animālium	calcārium	-ium
Dat.	sedīlibus	animālibus	calcāribus	-ibus
Acc.	sedīlia	animālia	calcāria	-ia
Voc.	sedīlia	animālia	calcāria	-ia
Abl.	sedīlibus	animālibus	calcāribus	-ibus

1. In most words of this class the final **-i** of the stem is lost in the Nominative Singular; in others it appears as **-e**.
2. Proper names in **-e** form the Ablative Singular in **-e**; as, **Sōracte**, *Mt. Soracte*; so also sometimes **mare**, *sea*.

Consonant-Stems that have partially adapted themselves to the Inflection of ĭ-Stems

40 Many Consonant-Stems have so far adapted themselves to the inflection of ĭ-stems as to take **-ium** in the Genitive Plural, and **-īs** in the Accusative Plural. Their true character as Consonant-Stems, however, is shown by the fact that they never take **-im** in the Accusative Singular, or **-ī** in the Ablative Singular. The following words are examples of this class:—

	Caedēs, f., *slaughter*; stem, **caed-**	**Arx**, f., *citadel*; stem, **arc-**	**Linter**, f., *small boat*; stem, **lintr-**
	SINGULAR		
Nom.	caedēs	arx	linter
Gen.	caedis	arcis	lintris
Dat.	caedī	arcī	lintrī
Acc.	caedem	arcem	lintrem
Voc.	caedēs	arx	linter
Abl.	caede	arce	lintre

		Plural	
Nom.	caedēs	arcēs	lintrēs
Gen.	caedium	arcium	lintrium
Dat.	caedibus	arcibus	lintribus
Acc.	caedēs, -īs	arcēs, -īs	lintrēs, -īs
Voc.	caedēs	arcēs	lintrēs
Abl.	caedibus	arcibus	lintribus

1. The following classes of nouns belong here:—

   a) Nouns in **-ēs**, with Genitive in **-is**; as, **nūbēs, aedēs, clādēs**, *etc.*

   b) Many monosyllables in **-s** or **-x** preceded by one or more consonants; as, **urbs, mōns, stirps, lanx.**

   c) Most nouns in **-ns** and **-rs** as, **cliēns, cohors.**

   d) **Ūter, venter; fūr, līs, mās, mūs, nix**; and the Plurals **faucēs, penātēs, Optimātēs, Samnitēs, Quirītēs.**

   e) Sometimes nouns in **-tās** with Genitive **-tātis**; as, **cīvitās, aetās. Cīvitās** *usually* has **cīvitātium.**

IV. Stems in -ī, -ū, and Diphthongs

41

	Vis, f., *force;* stem, **vī-**	**Sūs,** c., *swine;* stem, **sū-**	**Bōs,** c., *ox, cow;* stem, **bou-**	**Juppiter,** m., *Jupiter;* stem, **Jou-**
		Singular		
Nom.	vīs	sūs	bōs	Juppiter
Gen.	—	suis	bovis	Jovis
Dat.	—	suī	bovī	Jovī
Acc.	vim	suem	bovem	Jovem
Voc.	vīs	sūs	bōs	Juppiter
Abl.	vī	sue	bove	Jove
		Plural		
Nom.	vīrēs	suēs	bovēs	
Gen.	vīrium	suum	bovum, boum	
Dat.	vīribus	suibus, subus	bōbus, būbus	
Acc.	vīrēs	suēs	bovēs	
Voc.	vīrēs	suēs	bovēs	
Abl.	vīribus	suibus, subus	bōbus, būbus	

1. Notice that the oblique cases of **sūs** have **ŭ** in the root syllable.

2. **Grūs** is declined like **sūs**, except that the Dative and Ablative Plural are always **gruibus.**

3. **Juppiter** is for **Jou-pater**, and therefore contains the same stem as in **Jov-is, Jov-ī**, *etc.*

Nāvis was originally a diphthong stem ending in **au-**, but it has passed over to the ĭ-stems (§ 37). Its ablative often ends in -ī.

Irregular Nouns

42

	Senex, m., *old man.*	**Carō**, f., *flesh.*	**Os**, n., *bone.*
	SINGULAR		
Nom.	senex	carō	os
Gen.	senis	carnis	ossis
Dat.	senī	carnī	ossī
Acc.	senem	carnem	os
Voc.	senex	carō	os
Abl.	sene	carne	osse
	PLURAL		
Nom.	senēs	carnēs	ossa
Gen.	senum	carnium	ossium
Dat.	senibus	carnibus	ossibus
Acc.	senēs	carnēs	ossa
Voc.	senēs	carnēs	ossa
Abl.	senibus	carnibus	ossibus

1. **Iter, itineris,** n., *way,* is inflected regularly throughout from the stem **itiner-**.

2. **Supellex, supellectilis,** f., *furniture,* is confined to the Singular. The oblique cases are formed from the stem **supellectil-**. The ablative has both -**ī** and -**e**.

3. **Jecur,** n., *liver,* forms its oblique cases from two stems,— **jecor-** and **jecinor-**. Thus, Gen. **jecoris** or **jecinoris**.

4. **Femur,** n., *thigh,* usually forms its oblique cases from the stem **femor-**, but sometimes from the stem **femin-**. Thus, Gen. **femoris** or **feminis**.

General Principles of Gender in the Third Declension

43

1. Nouns in -**ō**, -**or**, -**ōs**, -**er**, -**ĕs** are Masculine.
2. Nouns in -**ās**, -**ēs**, -**is**, -**ys**, -**x**, -**s** (preceded by a consonant); -**dō**, -**gō** (Genitive -**inis**); -**iō** (abstract and collective), -**ūs** (Genitive -**ātis** or -**ūdis**) are Feminine.
3. Nouns ending in -**a**, -**e**, -**i**, -**y**, -**o**, -**l**, -**n**, -**t**, -**ar**, -**ur**, -**ŭs** are Neuter.

Chief Exceptions to Gender in the Third Declension

44 **Exceptions to the Rule for Masculines**

1. Nouns in -ō.
   a) Feminine: **carō**, *flesh*.
2. Nouns in -or.
   a) Feminine: **arbor**, *tree*.
   b) Neuter: **aequor**, *sea*; **cor**, *heart*; **marmor**, *marble*.
3. Nouns in -ōs.
   a) Feminine: **dōs**, *dowry*.
   b) Neuter: **ōs (ōris)**, *mouth*.
4. Nouns in -er.
   a) Feminine: linter, skiff.
   b) Neuter: **cadāver**, *corpse*; **iter**, *way*; **tūber**, *tumor*; **ūber**, *udder*. Also botanical names in -er; as, **acer**, *maple*.
5. Nouns in -ĕs.
   a) Feminine: **seges**, *crop*.

45 **Exceptions to the Rule for Feminines**

1. Nouns in -ās.
   a) Masculine: **vās**, *bondsman*.
   b) Neuter: **vās**, *vessel*.
2. Nouns in -ēs.
   a) Masculine: **ariēs**, *ram*; **pariēs**, *wall*; **pēs**, *foot*.
3. Nouns in -is.
   a) Masculine: all nouns in -nis and -guis; as, **amnis**, *river*; **īgnis**, *fire*; **pānis**, *bread*; **sanguis**, *blood*; **unguis**, *nail*.

Also—

axis, *axle*	**piscis**, *fish*
collis, *hill*	**postis**, *post*
fascis, *bundle*	**pulvis**, *dust*
lapis, *stone*	**orbis**, *circle*
mēnsis, *month*	**sentis**, *brier*

4. Nouns in -x.
   a) Masculine: **apex**, *peak*; **cōdex**, *tree-trunk*; **grex**, *flock*; **imbrex**, *tile*; **pollex**, *thumb*; **vertex**, *summit*; **calix**, *cup*.
5. Nouns in -s preceded by a consonant.
   a) Masculine: **dēns**, *tooth*; **fōns**, *fountain*; **mōns**, *mountain*; **pōns**, *bridge*.

6. Nouns in -**dō**.

   a) Masculine: **cardō**, *hinge*; **ōrdō**, *order.*

46 Exceptions to the Rule for Neuters

1. Nouns in -**l**.

   a) Masculine: **sōl**, *sun*; **sāl**, *salt.*

2. Nouns in -**n**.

   a) Masculine: **pecten**, *comb.*

3. Nouns in -**ur**.

   a) Masculine: **vultur**, *vulture.*

4. Nouns in -**ŭs**.

   a) Masculine: **lepus**, *hare.*

Greek Nouns of the Third Declension

47 The following are the chief peculiarities of these:—

1. The ending -**ă** in the Accusative Singular; as, **aetheră**, *aether*; **Salamīnă**, *Salamis.*

2. The ending -**ĕs** in the Nominative Plural; as, **Phrygĕs**, *Phrygians.*

3. The ending -**ăs** in the Accusative Plural; as, **Phrygăs**, *Phrygians.*

4. Proper names in -**ās** (Genitive -**antis**) have -**ā** in the Vocative Singular; as, **Atlās (Atlantis)**, Vocative **Atlā**, *Atlas.*

5. Neuters in -**ma** (Genitive -**matis**) have -**īs** instead of -**ibus** in the Dative and Ablative Plural; as, **poēmatīs**, *poems.*

6. **Orpheus**, and other proper names ending in -**eus**, form the Vocative Singular in -**eu** (**Orpheu**, *etc.*). But in prose the other cases usually follow the second declension; as, **Orpheī**, **Orpheō**, *etc.*

7. Proper names in -**ēs**, like **Periclēs**, form the Genitive Singular sometimes in -**is**, sometimes in -**ī**, as, **Periclis** or **Periclī**.

8. Feminine proper names in -**ō** have -**ūs** in the Genitive, but -**ō** in the other oblique cases; as,—

Nom.	Didō	*Acc.*	Didō
Gen.	Didūs	*Voc.*	Didō
Dat.	Didō	*Abl.*	Didō

9. The regular Latin endings often occur in Greek nouns.

Fourth Declension

ŭ-Stems

48 Nouns of the Fourth Declension end in **-us** Masculine, and **-ū** Neuter. They are declined as follows:—

	Frūctus, m., *fruit.*		**Cornū**, n., *horn.*	
	SINGULAR	PLURAL	SINGULAR	PLURAL
Nom.	frūctus	frūctūs	cornū	cornua
Gen.	frūctūs	frūctuum	cornūs	cornuum
Dat.	frūctuī	frūctibus	cornū	cornibus
Acc.	frūctum	frūctūs	cornū	cornua
Voc.	frūctus	frūctūs	cornū	cornua
Abl.	frūctū	frūctibus	cornū	cornibus

Peculiarities of Nouns of the Fourth Declension

49 1. Nouns in **-us**, particularly in early Latin, often form the Genitive Singular in **-ī**, following the analogy of nouns in **-us** of the Second Declension; as, **senātī**, **ōrnātī**. This is usually the case in Plautus and Terence.

2. Nouns in **-us** sometimes have **-ū** in the Dative Singular, instead of **-uī**; as, **frūctū** (for **frūctuī**).

3. The ending **-ubus**, instead of **-ibus**, occurs in the Dative and Ablative Plural of **artūs** (Plural), *limbs*; **tribus**, *tribe*; and in dis-syllables in **-cus**; as, **artubus**, **tribubus**, **arcubus**, **lacubus**. But with the exception of **tribus**, all these words admit the forms in **-ibus** as well as those in **-ubus**.

4. **Domus**, *house*, is declined according to the Fourth Declension, but has also the following forms of the Second:—

   domī (locative), *at home*
   domō, *from home*
   domum, *homewards, to one's home*
   domōs, *homewards, to their (etc.) homes*

5. The only Neuters of this declension in common use are: **cornū**, *horn*; **genū**, *knee*; and **verū**, *spit*.

Exceptions to Gender in the Fourth Declension

50 The following nouns in **-us** are Feminine: **acus**, *needle*; **domus**, *house*; **manus**, *hand*; **porticus**, *colonnade*; **tribus**, *tribe*; **Īdūs** (Plural), *Ides*; also names of trees (§ 15, 2).

Fifth Declension

ē-Stems

51 Nouns of the Fifth Declension end in **-ēs**, and are declined as follows:—

	Diēs, m., *day*		Rēs, f., *thing*	
	SINGULAR	PLURAL	SINGULAR	PLURAL
Nom.	diēs	diēs	rēs	rēs
Gen.	diēī	diērum	rĕī	rērum
Dat.	diēī	diēbus	rĕī	rēbus
Acc.	diem	diēs	rem	rēs
Voc.	diēs	diēs	rēs	rēs
Abl.	diē	diēbus	rē	rēbus

Peculiarities of Nouns of the Fifth Declension

52 1. The ending of the Genitive and Dative Singular is **-ĕī**, instead of **-ēī**, when a consonant precedes; as, **spĕī**, **rĕī**, **fidĕī**.

2. A Genitive ending **-ī** (for **-ĕī**) is found in **plēbī** (from **plēbēs** = **plēbs**) in the expressions **tribūnus plēbī**, *tribune of the people*, and **plēbī scītum**, *decree of the people*; sometimes also in other words.

3. A Genitive and Dative form in **-ē** sometimes occurs; as, **aciē**.

4. With the exception of **diēs** and **rēs**, most nouns of the Fifth Declension are not declined in the Plural. But **aciēs**, **seriēs**, **speciēs**, **spēs**, and a few others are used in the Nominative and Accusative Plural.

Gender in the Fifth Declension

53 Nouns of the Fifth Declension are regularly Feminine, except **diēs**, *day*, and **merīdiēs**, *mid-day*. But **diēs** is sometimes Feminine in the Singular, particularly when it means an *appointed day*.

Defective Nouns

54 Here belong—

1. Nouns used in the Singular only.
2. Nouns used in the Plural only.
3. Nouns used only in certain cases.
4. Indeclinable Nouns.

Nouns used in the Singular only

55 Many nouns, from the nature of their signification, are regularly used in the Singular only. Thus:—

1. **Proper names**; as, **Cicerō**, *Cicero*; **Italia**, *Italy*.

2. **Nouns denoting material**; as, **aes**, *copper*; **lac**, *milk*.

3. **Abstract nouns**; as, **ignōrantia**, *ignorance*; **bonitās**, *goodness*.

4. But the above classes of words are sometimes used in the Plural. Thus:—

   a) Proper names,—to denote different members of a family, or specimens of a type; as, **Cicerōnēs**, *the Ciceros*; **Catōnēs**, *men like Cato*.

   b) Names of materials,—to denote objects made of the material, or different kinds of the substance; as, **aera**, *bronzes* (*i.e.* bronze figures); **ligna**, *woods*.

   c) Abstract nouns,—to denote instances of the quality; as, **ignōrantiae**, *cases of ignorance*.

Nouns used in the Plural only

56 Here belong—

1. Many geographical names; as, **Thēbae**, *Thebes*; **Leuctra**, *Leuctra*; **Pompejī**, *Pompeii*.

2. Many names of festivals; as, **Megalēsia**, *the Megalesian festival*.

3. Many special words, of which the following are the most important:—

angustiae, *narrow pass*	**mānēs**, *spirits of the dead*
arma, *weapons*	**moenia**, *city walls*
dēliciae, *delight*	**minae**, *threats*
dīvitiae, *riches*	**nūptiae**, *marriage*
Īdūs, *Ides*	**posterī**, *descendants*
indūtiae, *truce*	**reliquiae**, *remainder*
īnsidiae, *ambush*	**tenebrae**, *darkness*
majōrēs, *ancestors*	**verbera**, *blows*.

Also in classical prose regularly—

cervīcēs, *neck*	**nārēs**, *nose*
fidēs, *lyre*	**vīscerā**, *viscera*

Nouns used only in Certain Cases

57

1. **Used in only One Case.** Many nouns of the Fourth Declension are found only in the Ablative Singular as, **jussū**, *by the order*; **injussū**, *without the order*; **nātū**, *by birth*.

2. **Used in Two Cases.**

   a. **Fors** (*chance*), Nom. Sing.; **forte**, Abl. Sing.

   b. **Spontis** (*free-will*), Gen. Sing.; **sponte**, Abl. Sing.

3. **Used in Three Cases.** Nēmō, *no one* (Nom.), has also the Dat. **nēminī** and the Acc. **nēminem**. The Gen. and Abl. are supplied by the corresponding cases of **nūllus, that is nūllīus** and **nūllō**.

4. **Impetus** has the Nom., Acc., and Abl. Sing., and the Nom. and Acc. Plu., so: **impetus, impetum, impetū, impetūs**.

5. a. **Precī, precem, prece**, lacks the Nom. and Gen. Sing.

   b. **Vicis, vicem, vice**, lacks the Nom. and Dat. Sing.

6. **Opis, dapis**, and **frūgis**,—all lack the Nom. Sing.

7. Many monosyllables of the Third Declension lack the Gen. Plu.: **as, cor, lūx, sōl, aes, ōs (ōris), rūs, sāl, tūs**.

Indeclinable Nouns

58

Here belong—

fās, n., *right*	**nefās**, n., *impiety*
īnstar, n., *likeness*	**nihil**, n., *nothing*
māne, n., *morning*	**secus**, n., *sex*

1. With the exception of **māne** (which may serve also as Ablative, *in the morning*), the nouns in this list are simply Neuters confined in use to the Nominative and Accusative Singular.

Heteroclites

59

These are nouns whose forms are partly of one declension, and partly of another. Thus:—

1. Several nouns have the entire Singular of one declension, while the Plural is of another; as,—

vās, vāsis (*vessel*);	Plu., **vāsa, vāsorōum, vāsīs**, *etc.*
jūgerum, jūgerī (*acre*);	Plu., **jūgera, jūgerum, jūgeribus**, *etc.*

2. Several nouns, while belonging in the main to one declension, have certain special forms belonging to another. Thus:—

a) Many nouns of the First Declension ending in -**ia** take also a Nom. and Acc. of the Fifth; as, **māteriēs, māteriem**, *material*, as well as **māteria, māteriam**.

b) **Famēs**, *hunger*, regularly of the Third Declension, has the Abl. **famē** of the Fifth.

c) **Requiēs, requiētis**, *rest*, regularly of the Third Declension, takes an Acc. of the Fifth, **requiem**, in addition to **requiētem**.

d) Besides **plēbs, plēbis**, *common people*, of the Third Declension, we find **plēbēs, plēbēī** (also **plēbī**, see § 52, 2), of the Fifth.

Heterogeneous Nouns

60 Heterogeneous nouns vary in Gender. Thus:—

1. Several nouns of the Second Declension have two forms,— one Masc. in -**us**, and one Neuter in -**um**; as, **clipeus, clipeum**, *shield*; **carrus, carrum**, *cart*.

2. Other nouns have one gender in the Singular, another in the Plural; as,—

Singular	Plural
balneum, n., *bath*	**balneae**, f., *bath-house*
epulum, n., *feast*	**epulae**, f., *feast*
frēnum, n., *bridle*	**frēnī**, m.(rarely **frēna**, n.), *bridle*
jocus, m., *jest*	**joca**, n. (also **jocī**, m.), *jests*
locus, m., *place*	**loca**, n., *places*; **locī**, m., *passages or topics in an author*
rāstrum, n., *rake*	**rāstrī**, m.; **rāstra**, n., *rakes*

a. Heterogeneous nouns may at the same time be heteroclites, as in case of the first two examples above.

Plurals with Change of Meaning

61 The following nouns have one meaning in the Singular, and another in the Plural:—

Singular	Plural
aedēs, *temple*	**aedēs**, *house*
auxilium, *help*	**auxilia**, *auxiliary troops*
carcer, *prison*	**carcerēs**, *stalls for racing-chariot*
castrum, *fort*	**castra**, *camp*
cōpia, *abundance*	**cōpiae**, *troops, resources*
fīnis, *end*	**fīnēs**, *borders, territory*
fortūna, *fortune*	**fortūnae**, *possessions, wealth*
grātia, *favor, gratitude*	**grātiae**, *thanks*
impedīmentum, *hindrance*;	**impedīmenta**, *baggage*
littera, *letter* (of the alphabet)	**litterae**, *epistle; literature*
mōs, *habit, custom*	**mōrēs**, *character*
opera, *help, service*	**operae**, *laborers*
(ops) opis, *help*	**opēs**, *resources*
pars, *part*	**partēs**, *party; rōle*
sāl, *salt*	**sălēs**, *wit*

Adjectives

62 Adjectives denote *quality*. They are declined like nouns, and fall into two classes,—

1. Adjectives of the First and Second Declensions.
2. Adjectives of the Third Declension.

Adjectives of the First and Second Declensions

63 In these the Masculine is declined like **hortus**, **puer**, or **ager**, the Feminine like **porta**, and the Neuter like **bellum**. Thus, Masculine like **hortus**:—

Bonus, *good*			
SINGULAR	MASCULINE	FEMININE	NEUTER
Nom.	bonus	bona	bonum
Gen.	bonī	bonae	bonī
Dat.	bonō	bonae	bonō
Acc.	bonum	bonam	bonum
Voc.	bone	bona	bonum
Abl.	bonō	bonā	bonō
PLURAL			
Nom.	bonī	bonae	bona
Gen.	bonōrum	bonārum	bonōrum
Dat.	bonīs	bonīs	bonīs
Acc.	bonōs	bonās	bona
Voc.	bonī	bonae	bona
Abl.	bonīs	bonīs	bonīs

1. The Gen. Sing. Masc. and Neut. of Adjectives in **-ius** ends in **-iī** (not in **-ī** as in case of Nouns; see § 25, 1; 2). So also the Voc. Sing. of such Adjectives ends in -ie, not in ī. Thus eximius forms Gen. eximiī; Voc. eximie.

2. Distributives (see § 78, 1, c) regularly form the Gen. Plu. Masc. and Neut. in -um instead of -ōrum (compare § 25, 6); as, dēnum centēnum; but always singulōrum.

64 Masculine like **puer:**—

Tener, *tender*			
SINGULAR	MASCULINE	FEMININE	NEUTER
Nom.	tener	tenera	tenerum
Gen.	tenerī	tenerae	tenerī
Dat.	tenerō	tenerae	tenerō
Acc.	tenerum	teneram	tenerum
Voc.	tener	tenera	tenerum
Abl.	tenerō	tenerā	tenerō
PLURAL			
Nom.	tenerī	tenerae	tenera
Gen.	tenerōrum	tenerārum	tenerōrum
Dat.	tenerīs	tenerīs	tenerīs
Acc.	tenerōs	tenerās	tenera
Voc.	tenerī	tenerae	tenera
Abl.	tenerīs	tenerīs	tenerīs

65

Masculine like **ager:—**

Sacer, *sacred*			
SINGULAR	MASCULINE	FEMININE	NEUTER
Nom.	sacer	sacra	sacrum
Gen.	sacrī	sacrae	sacrī
Dat.	sacrō	sacrae	sacrō
Acc.	sacrum	sacram	sacrum
Voc.	sacer	sacra	sacrum
Abl.	sacrō	sacrā	sacrō
PLURAL			
Nom.	sacrī	sacrae	sacra
Gen.	sacrōrum	sacrārum	sacrōrum
Dat.	sacrīs	sacrīs	sacrīs
Acc.	sacrōs	sacrās	sacra
Voc.	sacrī	sacrae	sacra
Abl.	sacrīs	sacrīs	sacrīs

1. Most adjectives in **-er** are declined like **sacer**. The following however, are declined like **tener: asper**, *rough*; **lacer**, *torn*; **līber**, *free*; **miser**, *wretched*; **prōsper**, *prosperous*; compounds in **-fer** and **-ger**; sometimes **dexter**, *right*.

2. **Satur**, *full*, is declined: **satur, satura, saturum**.

Nine Irregular Adjectives

66

Here belong—

alius, *another*	**alter**, *the other*
ūllus, *any*	**nūllus**, *none*
uter, *which?* (of two)	**neuter**, *neither*
sōlus, *alone*	**tōtus**, *whole*
ūnus, *one, alone*	

They are declined as follows:—

	SINGULAR					
	MASCULINE	FEMININE	NEUTER	MASCULINE	FEMININE	NEUTER
Nom.	alius	alia	aliud	alter	altera	alterum
Gen.	alterĭus	alterĭus	alterĭus[13]	alterĭus	alterĭus	alterĭus
Dat.	aliī	aliī	aliī	alterī	alterī[14]	alterī
Acc.	alium	aliam	aliud	alterum	alteram	alterum
Voc.	—	—	—	—	—	—
Abl.	aliō	aliā	aliō	alterō	alterā	alterō
Nom.	uter	utra	utrum	tōtus	tōta	tōtum
Gen.	utrīus	utrīus	utrīus	tōtīus	tōtīus	tōtīus
Dat.	utrī	utrī	utrī	tōtī	tōtī	tōtī
Acc.	utrum	utram	utrum	tōtum	tōtam	tōtum
Voc.	—	—	—	—	—	—
Abl.	utrō	utrā	utrō	tōtō	tōtā	tōtō

1. All these words lack the Vocative. The Plural is regular.
2. **Neuter** is declined like **uter**.

Adjectives of the Third Declension

67 These fall into three classes,—

1. Adjectives of three terminations in the Nominative Singular,—one for each gender.
2. Adjectives of two terminations.
3. Adjectives of one termination.
    a. With the exception of Comparatives, and a few other words mentioned below in § 70, 1, all Adjectives of the Third Declension follow the inflection of ĭ-stems; i.e. they have the Ablative Singular in -ī, the Genitive Plural in -ium, the Accusative Plural in -īs (as well as -ēs) in the Masculine and Feminine, and the Nominative and Accusative Plural in -ia in Neuters.

---

13   This is practically always used instead of **alīus** in the Genitive.
14   A Dative Singular Feminine **alterae** also occurs.

Adjectives of Three Terminations

68 These are declined as follows:—

Ācer, *sharp*		
SINGULAR		
MASCULINE	FEMININE	NEUTER
Nom. ācer	ācris	ācre
Gen. ācris	ācris	ācris
Dat. ācrī	ācrī	ācrī
Acc. ācrem	ācrem	ācre
Voc. ācer	ācris	ācre
Abl. ācrī	ācrī	ācrī
PLURAL		
Nom. ācrēs	ācrēs	ācria
Gen. ācrium	ācrium	ācrium
Dat, ācribus	ācribus	ācribus
Acc. ācrēs, -īs	ācrēs, -īs	ācria
Voc. ācrēs	ācrēs	ācria
Abl. ācribus	ācribus	ācribus

1. Like **ācer** are declined **alacer**, *lively*; **campester**, *level*; **celeber**, *famous*; **equester**, *equestrian*; **palūster**, *marshy*; **pedester**, *pedestrian*; **puter**, *rotten*; **salūber**, *wholesome*; **silvester**, *woody*; **terrester**, *terrestrial*; **volucer**, *winged*; also names of months in -**ber**, as **September**.

2. **Celer, celeris, celere**, *swift*, retains the **e** before **r**, but lacks the Genitive Plural.

3. In the Nominative Singular of Adjectives of this class the Feminine form is sometimes used for the Masculine. This is regularly true of **salūbris, silvestris**, and **terrestris**. In case of the other words in the list, the use of the Feminine for the Masculine is confined chiefly to early and late Latin, and to poetry.

Adjectives of Two Terminations

69 These are declined as follows:—

	Fortis, *strong*		**Fortior,** *stronger*	
		SINGULAR		
	M. AND F.	NEUT.	M. AND F.	NEUT.
Nom.	fortis	forte	fortior	fortius
Gen.	fortis	fortis	fortiōris	fortiōris
Dat.	fortī	fortī	fortiōrī	fortiōrī
Acc.	fortem	forte	fortiōrem	fortius
Voc.	fortis	forte	fortior	fortius
Abl.	fortī	fortī	fortiōre	fortiōre
		PLURAL		
Nom.	fortēs	fortia	fortiōrēs	fortiōra
Gen.	fortium	fortium	fortiōrum	fortiōrum
Dat.	fortibus	fortibus	fortiōribus	fortiōribus
Acc.	fortēs, -īs	fortia	fortiōrēs, -īs	fortiōra
Voc.	fortēs	fortia	fortiōrēs	fortiōra
Abl.	fortibus	fortibus	fortiōribus	fortiōribus

1. **Fortior** is the Comparative of **fortis**. All Comparatives are regularly declined in the same way. The Acc. Plu. in -īs is rare.

Adjectives of One Termination

70

	Fēlīx, *happy*		**Prūdēns,** *prudent*	
		SINGULAR		
	M. AND F.	NEUT.	M. AND F.	NEUT.
Nom.	fēlīx	fēlīx	prūdēns	prūdēns
Gen.	fēlīcis	fēlīcis	prūdentis	prūdentis
Dat.	fēlīcī	fēlīcī	prūdentī	prūdentī
Acc.	fēlīcem	fēlīx	prūdentem	prūdēns
Voc.	fēlīx	fēlīx	prūdēns	prūdēns
Abl.	fēlīcī	fēlīcī	prūdentī	prūdentī
		PLURAL		
Nom.	fēlīcēs	fēlīcia	prūdentēs	prūdentia
Gen.	fēlīcium	fēlīcium	prūdentium	prūdentium
Dat.	fēlīcibus	fēlīcibus	prūdentibus	prūdentibus
Acc.	fēlīcēs, -īs	fēlīcia	prūdentēs, -īs	prūdentia
Voc.	fēlīcēs	fēlīcia	prūdentēs	prūdentia
Abl.	fēlīcibus	fēlīcibus	prūdentibus	prūdentibus

	Vetus, *old*		**Plūs,** *more*	
		SINGULAR		
	M. AND F.	NEUT.	M. AND F.	NEUT.
Nom.	vetus	vetus	—	plūs
Gen.	veteris	veteris	—	plūris
Dat.	veterī	veterī	—	—
Acc.	veterem	vetus	—	plūs
Voc.	vetus	vetus	—	—
Abl.	vetere	vetere	—	plūre
		PLURAL		
Nom.	veterēs	vetera	plūrēs	plūra
Gen.	veterum	veterum	plūrium	plūrium
Dat.	veteribus	veteribus	plūribus	plūribus
Acc.	veterēs	vetera	plūrēs, -īs	plūra
Voc.	veterēs	vetera	—	—
Abl.	veteribus	veteribus	plūribus	plūribus

1. It will be observed that **vetus** is declined as a pure Consonant-Stem; *i.e.* Ablative Singular in -**e**, Genitive Plural in -**um**, Nominative Plural Neuter in -**a**, and Accusative Plural Masculine and Feminine in -**ēs** only. In the same way are declined **compos,** *controlling*; **dīves,** *rich*; **particeps,** *sharing*; **pauper,** *poor*; **prīnceps,** *chief*; **sōspes,** *safe*; **superstes,** *surviving*. Yet **dīves** always has Neut. Plu. **dītia.**

2. **Inops,** *needy*, and **memor,** *mindful*, have Ablative Singular **inopī, memorī,** but Genitive Plural **inopum, memorum.**

3. Participles in -**āns** and -**ēns** follow the declension of ī-stems. But they do not have -ī the Ablative, except when employed as adjectives; when used as participles or as substantives, they have -**e**; as,—

    ā sapientī virō, *by a wise man*; but
    ā sapiente, *by a philosopher*
    Tarquiniō rēgnante, *under the reign of Tarquin*

4. **Plūs,** in the Singular, is always a noun.

5. In the Ablative Singular, adjectives, when used as substantives,—

    a) usually retain the adjective declension; as,—

        aequālis, *contemporary*, Abl. **aequālī**
        cōnsulāris, *ex-consul*, Abl. **cōnsulārī**

        So names of Months; as, **Aprīlī,** *April*; **Decembrī,** *December.*

b) But adjectives used as proper names have **-e** in the Ablative Singular; as, **Celere**, Celer; **Juvenāle**, *Juvenal.*

c) Patrials in **-ās**, **-ātis** and **-īs**, **-ītis**, when designating places regularly have **-ī**; as, **in Arpīnātī**, *on the estate at Arpinum,* yet **-e**, when used of persons; as, **ab Arpīnāte**, *by an Arpinatian.*

6. A very few indeclinable adjectives occur, the chief of which are **frūgī**, *frugal;* **nēquam**, *worthless.*

7. In poetry, adjectives and participles in **-ns** sometimes form the Gen. Plu. in **-um** instead of **-ium**; as, **venientum**, *of those coming.*

Comparison of Adjectives

71

1. There are three degrees of Comparison,—the Positive, the Comparative, and the Superlative.

2. The Comparative is regularly formed by adding **-ior** (Neut. **-ius**), and the Superlative by adding **-issimus** (**-a**, **-um**), to the Stem of the Positive deprived of its final vowel; as,—

altus, *high*	alt**ior**, *higher*	alt**issimus**,
		highest, very high
fortis, *brave*	fort**ior**	fort**issimus**
fēlīx, *fortunate*	fēlīc**ior**	fēlīc**issimus**

So also Participles, when used as Adjectives; as,—

| doctus, *learned* | doct**ior** | doct**issimus** |
| egēns, *needy* | egent**ior** | egent**issimus** |

3. Adjectives in **-er** form the Superlative by appending **-rimus** to the Nominative of the Positive. The Comparative is regular. Thus:—

asper, *rough*	asper**ior**	asper**rimus**
pulcher, *beautiful*	pulchr**ior**	pulcher**rimus**
ācer, *sharp*	ācr**ior**	ācer**rimus**
celer, *swift*	celer**ior**	celer**rimus**

a. Notice mātū**rus**, mātū**rior**, mātū**rissimus** or mātū**rrimus**.

4. Five Adjectives in **-ilis** form the Superlative by adding -**limus** to the Stem of the Positive deprived of its final vowel. The Comparative is regular. Thus:—

facilis, *easy*	facil**ior**	facil**limus**
difficilis, *diffcult*	difficil**ior**	difficil**limus**
similis, *like*	simil**ior**	simil**limus**
dissimilis, *unlike*	dissimil**ior**	dissimil**limus**
humilis, *low*	humil**ior**	humil**limus**

5. Adjectives in -**dicus**, -**ficus**, and -**volus** form the Comparative and Superlative as though from forms in -**dīcēns**, -**ficēns**, -**volēns**. Thus:—

maledicus, *slanderous*	maledīcent**ior**	maledīcent**issimus**
magnificus, *magnificent*	magnificent**ior**	magnificent**issimus**
benevolus, *kindly*	benevolent**ior**	benevolent**issimus**

   a. Positives in -**dīcēns** and -**volēns** occur in early Latin; as **maledīcēns**, **benevolēns**.

6. **Dīves** has the Comparative **dīvitior** or **dītior**; Superlative **dīvitissimus** or **dītissimus**.

Irregular Comparison

72 Several Adjectives vary the Stem in Comparison, namely:—

bonus, *good*	mel**ior**	opt**imus**
malus, *bad*	pe**jor**	pess**imus**
parvus, *small*	min**or**	min**imus**
magnus, *large*	ma**jor**	max**imus**
multus, *much*	plūs	plūr**imus**
frūgī, *thrifty*	frūgāl**ior**	frūgāl**issimus**
nēquam, *worthless*	nēqu**ior**	nēqu**issimus**

Defective Comparison

73 1. Positive lacking entirely,—

(Cf. **prae**, *in front of*)	prior, *former*	prīmus, *first*
(Cf. **citrā**, *this side of*)	citerior, *on this side*	citimus, *near*
(Cf. **ultrā**, *beyond*)	ulterior, *farther*	ultimus, *farthest*
(Cf. **intrā**, *within*)	interior, *inner*	intimus, *inmost*

(Cf. **prope**, *near*)	prop**ior**, *nearer*	prox**imus**, *nearest*
(Cf. **dē**, *down*)	dēter**ior**, *inferior*	dēter**rimus**, *worst*
(Cf. archaic **potis**, *possible*)	pot**ior**, *preferable*	pot**issimus**, *chiefest*

2. Positive occurring only in special cases,—

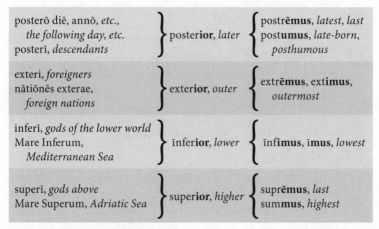

posterō diē, annō, *etc.*, *the following day, etc.* posterī, *descendants*	poster**ior**, *later*	postrēmus, *latest, last* post**umus**, *late-born, posthumous*
exteri, *foreigners* nātiōnēs exterae, *foreign nations*	exter**ior**, *outer*	extrēmus, extimus, *outermost*
inferī, *gods of the lower world* Mare Inferum, *Mediterranean Sea*	īnfer**ior**, *lower*	īnfimus, īmus, *lowest*
superī, *gods above* Mare Superum, *Adriatic Sea*	super**ior**, *higher*	suprēmus, *last* sum**mus**, *highest*

3. Comparative lacking.

vetus, *old*	——[15]	veter**rimus**
fīdus, *faithful*	——	fīdis**simus**
novus, *new*	——[16]	novis**simus**,[17] *last*
sacer, *sacred*	——	sacer**rimus**
falsus, *false*	——	fals**issimus**

Also in some other words less frequently used.

4. Superlative lacking.

alacer, *lively*	alacr**ior**	——
ingēns, *great*	ingent**ior**	——
salūtāris, *wholesome*	salūtār**ior**	——
juvenis, *young*	jūn**ior**	——[18]
senex, *old*	sen**ior**	——[19]

    a. The Superlative is lacking also in many adjectives in **-ālis, -īlis, -ĭlis, -bilis**, and in a few others.

---

15   Supplied by **vetustior**, from **vetustus**.
16   Supplied by **recentior**.
17   For *newest*, **recentissimus** is used.
18   Supplied by **minimus nātū**.
19   Supplied by **maximus nātū**.

Comparison by *Magis* and *Maximē*

74 Many adjectives do not admit terminational comparison, but form the Comparative and Superlative degrees by prefixing **magis** (*more*) and **maximē** (*most*). Here belong—

1. Many adjectives ending in -**ālis**, -**āris**, -**idus**, -**īlis**, -**icus**, **imus**, **īnus**, -**ōrus**.
2. Adjectives in -**us**, preceded by a vowel; as, **idōneus**, *adapted*; **arduus**, *steep*; **necessārius**, *necessary*.
   a. Adjectives in -**quus**, of course, do not come under this rule. The first **u** in such cases is not a vowel, but a consonant.

Adjectives not admitting Comparison

75 Here belong—

1. Many adjectives, which, from the nature of their signification, do not admit of comparison; as, **hodiernus**, *of today*; **annuus**, *annual*; **mortālis**, *mortal*.
2. Some special words; as, **mīrus**, **gnārus**, **merus**; and a few others.

Formation and Comparison of Adverbs

76 Adverbs are for the most part derived from adjectives, and depend upon them for their comparison.

1. Adverbs derived from adjectives of the First and Second Declensions form the Positive by changing -ī of the Genitive Singular to -**ē**; those derived from adjectives of the Third Declension, by changing -**is** of the Genitive Singular to -**iter**; as,—

cārus	cārē, *dearly*
pulcher	pulchrē, *beautifully*
ācer	ācr**iter**, *fiercely*
levis	lev**iter**, *lightly*

   a. But Adjectives in -**ns**, and a few others, add -**er** (instead of -**iter**), to form the Adverb; as,—

sapiēns	sapient**er**, *wisely*
sollers	sollert**er**, *skillfully*

   Note **audāx**, **audācter**, *boldly*.

2. The Comparative of all Adverbs regularly consists of the Accusative Singular Neuter of the Comparative of the Adjective; while the Superlative of the Adverb is formed by changing the -ī of the Genitive Singular of the Superlative of the Adjective to -ē. Thus—

(cārus)	cārē, *dearly*	cārius	cārissimē
(pulcher)	pulchrē, *beautifully*	pulchrius	pulcherrimē
(ācer)	ācriter, *fiercely*	ācrius	ācerrimē
(levis)	leviter, *lightly*	levius	levissimē
(sapiēns)	sapienter, *wisely*	sapientius	sapientissimē
(audāx)	audācter, *boldly*	audācius	audācissimē

Adverbs Peculiar in Comparison and Formation

77

1.

benĕ, *well*	melius	optimē
malĕ, *ill*	pejus	pessimē
magnopere, *greatly*	magis	maximē
multum, *much*	plūs	plūrimum
nōn multum, parum } *little*	minus	minimē
diū, *long*	diūtius	diūtissimē
nēquiter, *worthlessly*	nēquius	nēquissimē
saepe, *often*	saepius	saepissimē
mātūrē, *betimes*	mātūrius	{ mātūrrimē mātūrissimē
prope, *near*	propius	proximē
nūper, *recently*	—	nūperrimē
	potius, *rather*	potissimum *especially*
	prius { *previously, before* }	prīmum, *first*
secus, *otherwise*	sētius, *less*	

2. A number of adjectives of the First and Second Declensions form an Adverb in -ō, instead of -ē; as,—

crēbrō, *frequently*   **falsō**, *falsely*

continuō, *immediately*   **subitō**, *suddenly*

rārō, *rarely*, and a few others.

a. **cito**, quickly, has -ŏ.

3. A few adjectives employ the Accusative Singular Neuter as the Positive of the Adverb; as,—

multum, *much*   **paulum**, *little*   **facile**, *easily*

4. A few adjectives of the First and Second Declensions form the Positive in -**iter**; as,—

fīrmus, fīrmiter, *firmly*	**hūmānus, hūmāniter,** *humanly*
largus, largiter, *copiously*	**alius, aliter,** *otherwise*

   a. **violentus** has **violenter**.

5. Various other adverbial suffixes occur, the most important of which are -**tus** and -**tim**; as, **antīquitus**, *anciently*; **paulātim**, *gradually*.

Numerals

78 Numerals may be divided into—

I. Numeral Adjectives, comprising—

   a. *Cardinals*; as, **ūnus**, *one*; **duo**, *two*; *etc.*

   b. *Ordinals*; as, **prīmus**, *first*; **secundus**, *second*; *etc.*

   c. *Distributives*; as, **singulī**, *one by one*; **bīnī**, *two by two*; *etc.*

II. Numeral Adverbs; as, **semel**, *once*; **bis**, *twice*; *etc.*

79 Table of Numeral Adjectives and Adverbs

	CARDINALS	ORDINALS	DISTRIBUTIVES	ADVERBS
1.	ūnus, ūna, ūnum	prīmus, *first*	singulī, *one by one*	semel, *once*
2.	duo, duae, duo	secundus, *second*	bīnī, *two by two*	bis
3.	trēs, tria	tertius, *third*	ternī (trīnī)	ter
4.	quattuor	quārtus, *fourth*	quaternī	quater
5.	quīnque	quīntus, *fifth*	quīnī	quīnquiēs
6.	sex	sextus	sēnī	sexiēs
7.	septem	septimus	septēnī	septiēs
8.	octō	octāvus	octōnī	octiēs
9.	novem	nōnus	novēnī	noviēs
10.	decem	decimus	dēnī	deciēs
11.	ūndecim	ūndecimus	ūndēnī	ūndeciēs
12.	duodecim	duodecimus	duodēnī	duodeciēs
13.	tredecim	tertius decimus	ternī dēnī	terdeciēs
14.	quattuordecim	quārtus decimus	quaternī dēnī	quaterdeciēs
15.	quīndecim	quīntus decimus	quīnī dēnī	quīnquiēs deciēs
16.	sēdecim, sexdecim	sextus decimus	sēnī dēnī	sexiēs deciēs
17.	septendecim	septimus decimus	septēnī dēnī	septiēs deciēs
18.	duodēvīgintī	duodēvīcēsimus	duodēvīcēnī	octiēs deciēs
19.	ūndēvīgintī	ūndēvīcēsimus	ūndēvīcēnī	noviēs deciēs
20.	vīgintī	vīcēsimus	vīcēnī	vīciēs
21.	vīgintī ūnus, ūnus et vīgintī	vīcēsimus prīmus, ūnus et vīcēsimus	vīcēnī singulī, singulī et vīcēni	vīciēs semel
22.	vīgintī duo, duo et vīgintī	vīcēsimus secundus, alter et vīcēsimus	vīcēnī bīnī, bīnī et vīcēnī	vīciēs bis
30.	trīgintā	trīcēsimus	trīcēnī	triciēs
40.	quadrāgintā	quadrāgēsimus	quadrāgēnī	quadrāgiēs
50.	quīnquāgintā	quīnquāgēsimus	quinquāgēnī	quīnquāgiēs
60.	sexāgintā	sexāgēsimus	sexāgēnī	sexāgiēs
70.	septuāgintā	septuāgēsimus	septuāgēnī	septuāgiēs
80.	octōgintā	octōgēsimus	octōgēnī	octōgiēs
90.	nōnāgintā	nōnāgēsimus	nōnāgēnī	nōnāgiēs
100.	centum	centēsimus	centēnī	centiēs
101.	centum ūnus, centum et ūnus	centēsimus prīmus, centēsimus et prīmus	centēnī singulī, centēnī et singulī	centiēs semel
200.	ducentī, -ae, -a	ducentēsimus	ducēnī	ducentiēs
300.	trecentī	trecentēsimus	trecēnī	trecentiēs
400.	quadringentī	quadringentēsimus	quadringēnī	quadringentiēs
500.	quīngentī	quīngentēsimus	quīngēnī	quīngentiēs
600.	sescentī	sescentēsimus	sescēnī	sescentiēs
700.	septingentī	septingentēsimus	septingēnī	septingentiēs
800.	octingentī	octingentēsimus	octingēnī	octingentiēs
900.	nōngentī	nōngentēsimus	nōngēnī	nōngentiēs
1,000.	mīlle	mīllēsimus	singula mīlia	mīliēs
2,000.	duo mīlia	bis mīllēsimus	bīna mīlia	bis mīliēs
100,000.	centum mīlia	centiēs mīllēsimus	centēna mīlia	centiēs mīliēs
1,000,000.	deciēs centēna mīlia	deciēs centiēs mīllēsimus	deciēs centēna mīlia	deciēs centiēs mīliēs

NOTE   **-ēnsimus** and **-iēns** are often written in the numerals instead of **-ēsimus** and **-iēs.**

Declension of the Cardinals

80

1. The declension of **ūnus** has already been given under § 66.
2. **Duo** is declined as follows:—

Nom.	duo	duae	duo
Gen.	duōrum	duārum	duōrum
Dat.	duōbus	duābus	duōbus
Acc.	duōs, duo	duās	duo
Abl.	duōbus	duābus	duōbus

   a. So **ambō**, *both*, except that its final **o** is long.

3. **Trēs** is declined,—

Nom.	trēs	tria
Gen.	trium	trium
Dat.	tribus	tribus
Acc.	trēs (trīs)	tria
Abl.	tribus	tribus

4. The hundreds (except **centum**) are declined like the Plural of **bonus**.
5. **Mīlle** is regularly an adjective in the Singular, and indeclinable. In the Plural it is a substantive (followed by the Genitive of the objects enumerated; § 201, 1), and is declined,—

Nom.	mīlia	Acc.	mīlia
Gen.	mīlium	Voc.	mīlia
Dat.	mīlibus	Abl.	mīlibus

Thus **mīlle hominēs**, *a thousand men*; but **duo mīlia hominum**, *two thousand men*, literally *two thousands of men*.

   a. Occasionally the Singular admits the Genitive construction; as, **mīlle hominum**.

6. Other Cardinals are indeclinable. Ordinals and Distributives are declined like Adjectives of the First and Second Declensions.

Peculiarities in the Use of Numerals

81

1. The compounds from 21 to 99 may be expressed either with the larger or the smaller numeral first. In the latter case, **et** is used. Thus:—

    trīgintā sex or **sex et trīgintā**, *thirty-six*

2. The numerals under 90, ending in 8 and 9, are often expressed by subtraction; as,—

> **duodēvīgintī,** *eighteen* (but also **octōdecim**)
> **ūndēquadrāgintā,** *thirty-nine* (but also **trīgintā novem** or **novem et trīgintā**)

3. Compounds over 100 regularly have the largest number first; the others follow without **et**; as,—

> **centum vīgintī septem,** *one hundred and twenty-seven*
> **annō octingentēsimō octōgēsimō secundō,** *in the year 882*

Yet **et** may be inserted where the smaller number is either a digit or one of the tens; as,—

> **centum et septem,** *one hundred and seven*
> **centum et quadrāgintā,** *one hundred and forty*

4. The Distributives are used—

   a) To denote *so much each, so many apiece*; as,—

   > **bīna talenta eīs dedit,** *he gave them two talents each*

   b) When those nouns that are ordinarily Plural in form, but Singular in meaning, are employed in a Plural sense; as,—

   > **bīnae litterae,** *two epistles*

   But in such cases, **ūnī** (not **singulī**) is regularly employed for *one*, and **trīnī** (not **ternī**) for three; as,—

   > **ūnae litterae,** *one epistle*
   > **trīnae litterae,** *three epistles*

   c) In multiplication; as,—

   > **bis bīna sunt quattuor,** *twice two are four*

   d) Often in poetry, instead of the cardinals; as,—

   > **bīna hastīlia,** *two spears*

Pronouns

82 A Pronoun is a word that indicates something without naming it.

83 There are the following classes of pronouns:—

I. Personal	V. Intensive
II. Reflexive	VI. Relative
III. Possessive	VII. Interrogative
IV. Demonstrative	VIII. Indefinite

Personal Pronouns

84 These correspond to the English *I*, *you*, *he*, *she*, *it*, *etc.*, and are declined as follows:—

	First Person	Second Person	Third Person
Singular			
Nom.	ego, *I*	tū, *thou*	is, *he*; ea, *she*; id, *it*
Gen.	meī	tuī	(For declension see § 87.)
Dat.	mihi	tibi	
Acc.	mē	tē	
Voc.	—	tū	
Abl.	mē	tē	
Plural			
Nom.	nōs, *we*	vōs, *you*	
Gen.	nostrum, nostrī	vestrum, vestrī	
Dat.	nōbīs	vōbīs	
Acc.	nōs	vōs	
Voc.	—	vōs	
Abl.	nōbīs	vōbīs	

1. A Dative Singular **mī** occurs in poetry. The final i of *mihi* and *tibi* is sometimes long in poetry.

2. Emphatic forms in **-met** are occasionally found; as, **egomet**, *I myself*; **tibimet**, *to you yourself*; **tū** has **tūte** and **tūtemet** (written also **tūtimet**).

3. In early Latin, **mēd** and **tēd** occur as Accusative and Ablative forms.

Reflexive Pronouns

85 These refer to the subject of the sentence or clause in which they stand; like *myself, yourself,* in *'I see myself,'* etc. They are declined as follows:—

	FIRST PERSON Supplied by oblique cases of **ego**.	SECOND PERSON Supplied by oblique cases of **tū**.	THIRD PERSON
Gen.	meī, *of myself*	tuī, *of thyself*	suī
Dat.	mihi, *to myself*	tibi, *to thyself*	sibi
Acc.	mē, *myself*	tē, *thyself*	sē or sēsē
Voc.	—	—	—
Abl.	mē, *with myself,* etc.	tē, *with thyself,* etc.	sē or sēsē

1. The Reflexive of the Third Person serves for *all genders* and for *both numbers.* Thus **sui** may mean, *of himself, herself, itself,* or *of themselves*; and so with the other forms.

2. All of the Reflexive Pronouns have at times a *reciprocal* force; as,—

    inter sē pugnant, *they fight with each other.*

3. In early Latin, **sēd** occurs as Accusative and Ablative.

4. The final i of *sibi* may be long in poetry.

Possessive Pronouns

86 These are strictly adjectives of the First and Second Declensions, and are inflected as such. They are—

FIRST PERSON	SECOND PERSON
meus, -a, -um, *my*; noster, nostra, nostrum, *our*;	tuus, -a, -um, *thy*; vester, vestra, vestrum, *your*;
THIRD PERSON	
suus, -a, -um, *his, her, its, their.*	

1. **Suus** is exclusively Reflexive; as,—

    pater līberōs suōs amat, *the father loves his children.*

    Otherwise, *his, her, its* are regularly expressed by the Genitive Singular of **is**, that is, **ejus**; and *their* by the Genitive Plural, **eōrum, eārum**.

2. The Vocative Singular Masculine of **meus** is **mī**.

3. The enclitic **-pte** may be joined to the Ablative Singular of the Possessive Pronouns for the purpose of emphasis. This is particularly common in case of **suō, suā**; as, **suōpte, suāpte**.

Demonstrative Pronouns

87 These point out an object as **here** or **there**, or as **previously mentioned**. They are—

> **hīc**, *this* (where I am)
> **iste**, *that* (where you are)
> **ille**, *that* (something distinct from the speaker)
> **is**, *that* (weaker than **ille**)
> **īdem**, *the same*

Hīc, **iste**, and **ille** are accordingly the Demonstratives of the First, Second, and Third Persons respectively.

Hīc, *this*

	SINGULAR			PLURAL		
	MASCULINE	FEMININE	NEUTER	MASCULINE	FEMININE	NEUTER
Nom.	hīc	haec	hōc	hī	hae	haec
Gen.	hūjus[20]	hūjus	hūjus	hōrum	hārum	hōrum
Dat.	huic	huic	huic	hīs	hīs	hīs
Acc.	hunc	hanc	hōc	hōs	hās	haec
Abl.	hōc	hāc	hōc	hīs	hīs	hīs

Iste, *that, that of yours*

	SINGULAR			PLURAL		
	MASCULINE	FEMININE	NEUTER	MASCULINE	FEMININE	NEUTER
Nom.	iste	ista	istud[21]	istī	istae	ista
Gen.	istīus	istīus	istīus	istōrum	istārum	istōrum
Dat.	istī	istī	istī	istīs	istīs	istīs
Acc.	istum	istam	istud	istōs	istās	ista
Abl.	istō	istā	istō	istīs	istīs	istīs

Ille (archaic **olle**), *that, that one, he*, is declined like **iste**.[22]

Is, *he, this, that*

	SINGULAR			PLURAL		
	MASCULINE	FEMININE	NEUTER	MASCULINE	FEMININE	NEUTER
Nom.	is	ea	id	eī, iī (ī)	eae	ea
Gen.	ejus	ejus	ejus	eōrum	eārum	eōrum
Dat.	eī	eī	eī	eīs, iīs	eīs, iīs	eīs, iīs
Acc.	eum	eam	id	eōs	eās	ea
Abl.	eō	eā	eō	eīs, iīs	eīs, iīs	eīs, iīs

---

20   Forms of **hīc** ending in **-s** sometimes append **-ce** for emphasis; as, **hūjusce**, *this...here*; **hōsce**, **hīsce**. When **-ne** is added, **-c** and **-ce** become **-ci**; as, **huncine**, **hōscine**.

21   For **istud**, **istūc** sometimes occurs; for **ista**, **istaec**.

22   For **illud**, **illūc** sometimes occurs.

Īdem, *the same*					
SINGULAR			PLURAL		
MASCULINE	FEMININE	NEUTER	MASCULINE	FEMININE	NEUTER
Nom. īdem	eadem	idem	eīdem, iīdem	eaedem	eadem
Gen. ejusdem	ejusdem	ejusdem	eōrundem	eārundem	eōrundem
Dat. eīdem	eīdem	eīdem	eīsdem	eīsdem	eīsdem
Acc. eundem	eandem	idem	eōsdem	eāsdem	eadem
Abl. eōdem	eādem	eōdem	eīsdem	eīsdem	eīsdem

The Nom. Plu. Masc. also has **īdem**, and the Dat. Abl. Plu.
īsdem or **iīsdem**

The Intensive Pronoun

88 The Intensive Pronoun in Latin is **ipse**. It corresponds to the English *myself, etc.*, in '*I myself, he himself.*'

	SINGULAR			PLURAL		
	MASCULINE	FEMININE	NEUTER	MASCULINE	FEMININE	NEUTER
Nom.	ipse	ipsa	ipsum	ipsī	ipsae	ipsa
Gen.	ipsīus	ipsīus	ipsīus	ipsōrum	ipsārum	ipsōrum
Dat.	ipsī	ipsī	ipsī	ipsīs	ipsīs	ipsīs
Acc.	ipsum	ipsam	ipsum	ipsōs	ipsās	ipsa
Abl.	ipsō	ipsā	ipsō	ipsīs	ipsīs	ipsīs

The Relative Pronoun

89 The Relative Pronoun is **quī**, who. It is declined:—

	SINGULAR			PLURAL		
	MASCULINE	FEMININE	NEUTER	MASCULINE	FEMININE	NEUTER
Nom.	quī	quae	quod	quī	quae	quae
Gen.	cūjus	cūjus	cūjus	quōrum	quārum	quōrum
Dat.	cui	cui	cui	quibus[24]	quibus	quibus
Acc.	quem	quam	quod	quōs	quās	quae
Abl.	quō[23]	quā	quō	quibus	quibus	quibus

Interrogative Pronouns

90 The Interrogative Pronouns are **quis**, *who?* (substantive) and **quī**, *what? what kind of?* (adjective).

---

23   An ablative **quī** occurs in **quīcum**, *with whom.*
24   Sometimes **quīs.**

1. **Quis**, *who?*

	SINGULAR		PLURAL
	Masc. and Fem.	Neuter	
Nom.	quis	quid	The rare Plural follows
Gen.	cūjus	cūjus	the declension of the
Dat.	cui	cui	Relative Pronoun.
Acc.	quem	quid	
Abl.	quō	quō	

2. **Quī**, *what? what kind of?* is declined precisely like the Relative Pronoun: **quī, quae, quod**, *etc.*

   a. An old Ablative **quī** occurs, in the sense of *how? why?*

   b. **Quī** is sometimes used for **quis** in Indirect Questions.

   c. **Quis**, when limiting words denoting persons, is sometimes an adjective. But in such cases **quis homō** = *what man?* whereas **quī homō** = *what sort of man?*

   d. **Quis** and **quī** may be strengthened by adding -**nam**. Thus:—

Substantive:	**quisnam**, *who, pray?*
	quidnam, *what, pray?*
Adjective:	**quīnam, quaenam, quodnam**, *of what kind, pray?*

Indefinite Pronouns

 91 These have the general force of *some one, any one.*

SUBSTANTIVES M. AND F.	Neuter	ADJECTIVES Masc.	Fem.	Neuter
quis, *any one, anything*	quid, *any*	quī	quae, qua	quod
aliquis, *some one, something*	aliquid, *any*	aliquī	aliqua	aliquod
quisquam, *any one, anything*	quidquam, *any* (rare)	quisquam		quidquam
quispiam, *any one, anything*	quidpiam, *any*	quispiam	quaepiam	quodpiam
quisque, *each*	quidque, *each*	quisque	quaeque	quodque
quīvīs, quaevīs, quīlibet, quaelibet, *any one (anything) you wish*	quidvīs, quidlibet *any you wish*	quīvis, quilibet	quaevīs, quaelibet	quodvis, quodlibet
quīdam, quaedam *a certain person, or thing*	quiddam, *a certain*	quīdam	quaedam	quoddam

1. In the Indefinite Pronouns, only the pronominal part is declined. Thus: Genitive Singular **alicūjus, cūjuslibet**, *etc.*

2. Note that **aliquī** has **aliqua** in the Nominative Singular Feminine, also in the Nominative and Accusative Plural

Neuter. **Quī** has both **qua** and **quae** in these same cases.

3. **Quīdam** forms Accusative Singular **quendam, quandam**; Genitive Plural **quōrundam, quārundam**; the **m** being assimilated to **n** before **d**.

4. **Aliquis** may be used adjectively, and (occasionally) **aliquī** substantively.

5. In combination with **nē, sī, nisi, num**, either **quis** or **quī** may stand as a Substantive. Thus: **sī quis** or **sī quī**.

6. **Ecquis**, *any one*, though strictly an Indefinite, generally has interrogative force. It has both substantive and adjective forms,—substantive, **ecquis, ecquid**; adjective, **ecquī, ecquae** and **ecqua, ecquod**.

7. **Quisquam** is not used in the Plural.

8. There are two Indefinite Relatives,—**quīcumque** and **quisquis**, *whoever*. **Quīcumque** declines only the first part; **quisquis** declines both but has only **quisquis, quidquid, quōquō**, in common use.

Pronominal Adjectives

92 The following adjectives, also, frequently have pronominal force:—

1.

alius, *another*	**alter**, *the other*
uter, *which of two?* (interr.)	**neuter**, *neither*
whichever of two (rel.)	
ūnus, *one*	**nūllus**, *no one*
(in oblique cases)	

2. The compounds,—

uterque, utraque, utrumque, *each of two*;
utercumque, utracumque, utrumcumque, *whoever of two*;
uterlibet, utralibet, utrumlibet, *either one you please*;
utervīs, utravīs, utrumvīs, *either one you please*;
alteruter, alterutra, alterutrum, *the one or the other*.

In these, **uter** alone is declined. The rest of the word remains unchanged, except in case of **alteruter**, which may decline both parts; as,—

Nom.	**alteruter**	**altera utra**	**alterum utrum**
Gen.	**alterius utrīus**, *etc.*		

CONJUGATION

93 A Verb is a word which asserts something; as, **est**, *he is*; **amat**, *he loves*. The Inflection of Verbs is called Conjugation.

94 Verbs have Voice, Mood, Tense, Number, and Person:—

1. Two Voices,—Active and Passive.
2. Three Moods,—Indicative, Subjunctive, Imperative.
3. Six Tenses,—

Present,	Perfect,
Imperfect,	Pluperfect,
Future,	Future Perfect.

But the Subjunctive lacks the Future and Future Perfect; while the Imperative employs only the Present and Future.

4. Two Numbers,—Singular and Plural.
5. Three Persons,—First, Second, and Third.

95 These make up the so-called *Finite Verb*. Besides this, we have the following Noun and Adjective Forms:—

1. Noun Forms,—Infinitive, Gerund, and Supine.
2. Adjective Forms,—Participles (including the Gerundive).

96 The Personal Endings of the Verb are,—

		ACTIVE	PASSIVE
Sing.	1.	**-ō; -m; -ī** (Perf. Ind.)	**-r**
	2.	**-s; -stī** (Perf Ind.); **-tō** or wanting (Impv.)	**-rīs, -re; -re, -tor** (Impv.)
	3.	**-t; -tō** (Impv.)	**-tur; -tor** (Impv.)
Plu.	1.	**-mus**	**-mur**
	2.	**-tis; -stis** (Perf. Ind.); **-te, -tōte** (Impv.)	**-minī**
	3.	**-nt; -ērunt** (Perf Ind.);**-ntō** (Impv.);	**-ntur; -ntor** (Impv.).

Verb Stems

97 Conjugation consists in appending certain endings to the Stem. We distinguish three different stems in a fully inflected verb,—

Present Stem, from which are formed—

1. Present, Imperfect, and Future Indicative,

2. Present and Imperfect Subjunctive,

   } Active and Passive

3. The Imperative,

4. The Present Infinitive,

5. The Present Active Participle, the Gerund, and Gerundive.

Perfect Stem, from which are formed—

1. Perfect, Pluperfect, and Future Perfect Indicative,

2. Perfect and Pluperfect Subjunctive,   } Active

3. Perfect Infinitive,

Participial Stem, from which are formed—

1. Perfect Participle,

2. Perfect, Pluperfect, and Future Perfect Indicative,

   } Passive

3. Perfect and Pluperfect Subjunctive,

4. Perfect Infinitive,

Apparently from the same stem, though really of different origin, are the Supine, the Future Active Participle, the Future Infinitive Active and Passive.

The Four Conjugations

98 There are in Latin four regular Conjugations, distinguished from each other by the vowel of the termination of the Present Infinitive Active, as follows:—

CONJUGATION	INFINITIVE TERMINATION	DISTINGUISHING VOWEL
I.	-āre	ā
II.	-ēre	ē
III.	-ĕre	ĕ
IV.	-īre	ī

99 **Principal Parts**. The Present Indicative, Present Infinitive, Perfect Indicative, and the Perfect Participle[25] constitute the Principal Parts of a Latin verb,—so called because they contain the different stems, from which the full conjugation of the verb may be derived.

---

25   Where the Perfect Participle is not in use, the Future Active Participle, if it occurs, is given as one of the Principal Parts.

Conjugation of *Sum*

100 The irregular verb **sum** is so important for the conjugation of all other verbs that its inflection is given at the outset. It has no Perfect Participle, nor does it have any passive forms at all.

PRINCIPAL PARTS

Pres. Ind.	Pres. Inf.	Perf. Ind.	Fut. Partic.
sum	**esse**	**fuī**	**futūrus**

INDICATIVE MOOD

Present Tense

Singular	Plural
su**m**, *I am*	su**mus**, *we are*
e**s**, *thou art*	es**tis**, *you are*
es**t**, *he is*	su**nt**, *they are*

Imperfect

era**m**, *I was*	erā**mus**, *we were*
erā**s**, *thou wast*	erā**tis**, *you were*
era**t**, *he was*	era**nt**, *they were*

Future

er**ō**, *I shall be*	eri**mus**, *we shall be*
eri**s**, *thou wilt be*	eri**tis**, *you will be*
eri**t**, *he will be*	eru**nt**, *they will be*

Perfect

fu**ī**, *I have been, I was*	fu**imus**, *we have been, we were*
fu**istī**, *thou hast been, thou wast*	fu**istis**, *you have been, you were*
fu**it**, *he has been, he was*	fu**ērunt**, fu**ēre**, *they have been, they were*

Pluperfect

fu**eram**, *I had been*	fu**erāmus**, *we had been*
fu**erās**, *thou hadst been*	fu**erātis**, *you had been*
fu**erat**, *he had been*	fu**erant**, *they had been*

Future Perfect

fu**erō**, *I shall have been*	fu**erimus**, *we shall have been*
fu**eris**, *thou wilt have been*	fu**eritis**, *you will have been*
fu**erit**, *he will have been*	fu**erint**, *they will have been*

SUBJUNCTIVE[26]

PRESENT

SINGULAR	PLURAL
sim, *may I be*	**sīmus**, *let us be*
sīs, *mayst thou be*	**sītis**, *be ye, may you be*
sit, *let him be, may he be*	**sint**, *let them be*

IMPERFECT[27]

essem, I should be	**essēmus**, *we should be*
essēs, thou wouldst be	**essētis**, *you would be*
esset, he would be	**essent**, they would be

PERFECT

fuerim, *I may have been*	**fuerīmus**, *we may have been*
fuerīs, *thou mayst have been*	**fuerītis**, *you may have been*
fuerit, *he may have been*	**fuerint**, *they may have been*

PLUPERFECT

fuissem, *I should have been*	**fuissēmus**, *we should have been*
fuissēs, *thou wouldst have been*	**fuissētis**, *you would have been*
fuisset, *he would have been*	**fuissent**, *they would have been*

IMPERATIVE

Pres.	**es**, *be thou*	**este**, *be ye*
Fut.	**estō**, *thou shalt be*	**estōte**, *ye shall be*
	estō, *he shall be*	**suntō**, *they shall be*

INFINITIVE   PARTICIPLE

Pres.	**esse**, *to be*		
Perf.	**fuisse**, *to have been*		
Fut.	**futūrus** esse,[28] to be about to be	*Fut.*	**futūrus**,[29] about to be

---

26 The meanings of the different tenses of the Subjunctive are so many and so varied, particularly in subordinate clauses, that no attempt can be made to give them here. For fuller informtion the pupil is referred to the Syntax.

27 For **essem, essēs, esset**, the forms **forem, forēs, foret, forent** are sometimes used.

28 For **futūrus esse**, the form **fore** is often used.

29 Declined like **bonus, -a, -um**.

First (or ā-) Conjugation

101

Active Voice—Amō, *I love.*

PRINCIPAL PARTS

Pres. Ind.	Pres. Inf.	Perf. Ind.	Perf. Pass. Partic.
amō	amāre	amāvī	amātus

INDICATIVE MOOD	

PRESENT TENSE

SINGULAR	PLURAL
amō, *I love*	amāmus, *we love*
amās, *you love*	amātis, *you love*
amat, *he loves*	amant, *they love*

IMPERFECT

amābam, *I was loving*[30]	amābāmus, *we were loving*
amābās, *you were loving*	amābātis, *you were loving*
amābat, *he was loving*	amābant, *they were loving*

FUTURE

amābō, *I shall love*	amābimus, *we shall love*
amābis, *you will love*	amābitis, *you will love*
amābit, *he will love*	amābunt, *they will love*

PERFECT

amāvī, *I have loved, I loved*	amāvimus, *we have loved, we loved*
amāvistī, *you have loved, you loved*	amāvistis, *you have loved, you loved*
amāvit, *he has loved, he loved*	amāvērunt, -ēre, *they have loved, they loved*

PLUPERFECT

amāveram, *I had loved*	amāverāmus, *we had loved*
amāverās, *you had loved*	amāverātis, *you had loved*
amāverat, *he had loved*	amāverant, *they had loved*

FUTURE PERFECT

amāverō, *I shall have loved*	amāverimus, *we shall have loved*
amāveris, *you will have loved*	amāveritis, *you will have loved*
amāverit, *he will have loved*	amāverint, *they will have loved*

---

30   The Imperfect also means *I loved.*

SUBJUNCTIVE

PRESENT

SINGULAR	PLURAL
amem, *may I love*	amēmus, *let us love*
amēs, *may you love*	amētis, *may you love*
amet, *let him love*	ament, *let them love*

IMPERFECT

amārem, *I should love*	amārēmus, *we should love*
amārēs, *you would love*	amārētis, *you would love*
amāret, *he would love*	amārent, *they would love*

PERFECT

amāverim, *I may have loved*	amāverīmus, *we may have loved*
amāverīs, *you may have loved*	amāverītis, *you may have loved*
amāverit, *he may have loved*	amāverint, *they may have loved*

PLUPERFECT

amāvissem, *I should have loved*	amāvīssēmus, *we should have loved*
amāvissēs, *you would have loved*	amāvissētis, *you would have loved*
amāvisset, *he would have loved*	amāvissent, *they would have loved*

IMPERATIVE

Pres.	amā, *love thou*	amāte, *love ye*
Fut.	amātō, *thou shalt love*	amātōte, *ye shall love*
	amātō, *he shall love*	amantō, *they shall love*

INFINITIVE   PARTICIPLE

Pres.	amāre, *to love*	Pres.	amāns, loving (Gen. amantis; for declension see § 70, 3.)
Perf.	amāvisse, *to have loved*		
Fut.	amātūrus esse, *to be about to love*	Fut.	amātūrus, *about to love*

GERUND   SUPINE

Gen.	amandī, *of loving*		
Dat.	amandō, *for loving*		
Acc.	amandum, *loving*	Acc.	amātum, *to love*
Abl.	amandō, *by loving*	Abl.	amātū, *to love, be loved*

102

Passive Voice—Amor, *I am loved.*

PRINCIPAL PARTS

Pres. Ind.	Pres. Inf.	Perf. Ind.
amōr	amārī	amātus sum

INDICATIVE MOOD

Present Tense
I am loved.

Singular	Plural
amor	amāmur
amāris	amāminī
amātur	amantur

Imperfect
I was loved.

amābar	amābāmur
amābāris, *or* -re	amābāmini
amābātur	amābantur

Future
I shall be loved.

amābor	amābimur
amāberis, *or* -re	amābiminī
amābitur	amābuntur

Perfect
I have been loved, or *I was loved.*

amātus (-a, -um) sum[31]	amātī (-ae, -a) sumus
amātus es	amātī estis
amātus est	amātī sunt

Pluperfect
I had been loved.

amātus eram	amātī erāmus
amātus erās	amātī erātis
amātus erat	amātī erant

Future Perfect
I shall have been loved.

amātus erō	amātī erimus
amātus eris	amātī eritis
amātus erit	amātī erunt

---

31   **Fuī, fuistī**, etc., are sometimes used for **sum, es**, etc. So **fueram, fuerās**, etc., for **eram**, etc.; **fuerō**, etc., for **erō**, etc.

SUBJUNCTIVE

PRESENT
May I be loved, let him be loved.

SINGULAR	PLURAL
amer	amēmur
amēris, *or* -re	amēmini
amētur	amentur

IMPERFECT
I should be loved, he would be loved.

amārer	amārēmur
amārēris, *or* -re	amārēminī
amārētur	amārentur

PERFECT
I may have been loved.

amātus sim[32]	amātī sīmus
amātus sīs	amāti sītis
amātus sit	amāti sint

PLUPERFECT
I should have been loved, he would have been loved.

amātus essem	amātī essēmus
amātus essēs	amātī essētis
amātus esset	amāti essent

IMPERATIVE

Pres.	amāre,[33] be thou loved	amāminī, *be ye loved*	
Fut.	amātor, *thou shalt be loved,*		
	amātor, *he shall be loved*	amantor, *they shall be loved*	

INFINITIVE   PARTICIPLE

	INFINITIVE		PARTICIPLE	
Pres.	amārī, *to be loved*	*Perf.*	amātus, *loved, having*	
Perf.	amātus esse, *to have been loved*		*been loved*	
Fut.	amātum īrī, *to be about to be loved*	*Ger.*	amandus, *to be loved, deserving to be loved*	

---

32   **Fuerim**, etc., are sometimes used for **sim**; so **fuissem**, etc., for **essem**.

33   In actual usage passive imperatives occur only in deponents (§ 112).

Second (or ē-) Conjugation

103

Active voice—Moneō, *I advise.*

PRINCIPAL PARTS

Pres. Ind.	Pres. Inf.	Perf. Ind.	Perf. Pass. Partic.
moneō	monēre	monuī	monitus

INDICATIVE MOOD	
PRESENT TENSE *I advise.*	
SINGULAR	PLURAL
moneō	monēmus
monēs	monētis
monet	monent
IMPERFECT *I was advising,* or *I advised.*	
monēbam	monēbāmus
monēbās	monēbātis
monēbat	monēbant
FUTURE *I shall advise.*	
monēbō	monēbimus
monēbis	monēbitis
monēbit	monēbunt
PERFECT *I have advised,* or *I advised.*	
monuī	monuimus
monuistī	monuistis
monuit	monuērunt, *or* -ēre
PLUPERFECT *I had advised.*	
monueram	monuerāmus
monuerās	monuerātis
monuerat	monuerant
FUTURE PERFECT *I shall have advised.*	
monuerō	monuerimus
monueris	monueritis
monuerit	monuerint

SUBJUNCTIVE	
PRESENT	
May I advise, let him advise.	
SINGULAR	PLURAL
mone**am**	mone**āmus**
mone**ās**	mone**ātis**
mone**at**	mone**ant**
IMPERFECT	
I should advise, he would advise.	
mon**ērem**	mon**ērēmus**
mon**ērēs**	mon**ērētis**
mon**ēret**	mon**ērent**
PERFECT	
I may have advised.	
monu**erim**	monu**erīmus**
monu**erīs**	monu**erītis**
monu**erit**	monu**erint**
PLUPERFECT	
I should have advised, he would have advised.	
monu**issem**	monu**issēmus**
monu**issēs**	monu**issētis**
monu**isset**	monu**issent**

IMPERATIVE		
Pres.	mon**ē**, *advise thou*	mon**ēte**, *advise ye*
Fut.	mon**ētō**, *thou shall advise,*	mon**ētōte**, *ye shall advise*
	mon**ētō**, *he shall advise*	mon**entō**, *they shall advise*

INFINITIVE		PARTICIPLE	
Pres.	mon**ēre**, *to advise*	*Pres.*	mon**ēns**, *advising*
Perf.	monu**isse**, *to have advised*		(Gen. mon**entis**.)
Fut.	monit**ūrus esse**, *to be about to advise*	*Fut.*	monit**ūrus**, *about to advise*

GERUND		SUPINE	
Gen.	mon**endī**, *of advising*		
Dat.	mon**endō**, *for advising*		
Acc.	mon**endum**, *advising*	*Acc.*	monit**um**, *to advise*
Abl.	mon**endō**, *by advising*	*Abl.*	monit**ū**, *to advise, be advised*

104

Passive voice—Moneor, *I am advised.*

PRINCIPAL PARTS

PRES. IND.	PRES. INF.	PERF. IND.
moneor	monērī	monitus sum

INDICATIVE MOOD	

PRESENT TENSE
I am advised.

SINGULAR	PLURAL
moneor	monēmur
monēris	monēminī
monētur	monentur

IMPERFECT
I was advised.

monēbar	monēbāmur
monēbāris, *or* -re	monēbāminī
monēbātur	monēbantur

FUTURE
I shall be advised.

monēbor	monēbimur
monēberis, *or* -re	monēbiminī
monēbitur	monēbuntur

PERFECT
I have been advised, or *I was advised.*

monitus sum	monitī sumus
monitus es	monitī estis
monitus est	monitī sunt

PLUPERFECT
I had been advised.

monitus eram	monitī erāmus
monitus erās	monitī erātis
monitus erat	monitī erant

FUTURE PERFECT
I shall have been advised.

monitus erō	monitī erimus
monitus eris	monitī eritis
monitus erit	monitī erunt

SUBJUNCTIVE

PRESENT
May I be advised, let him be advised.

SINGULAR	PLURAL
monear	moneāmur
moneāris, *or* -re	moneāminī
moneātur	moneantur

IMPERFECT
I should be advised, he would be advised.

monērer	monērēmur
monērēris, *or* -re	monērēminī
monērētur	monērentur

PERFECT
I may have been advised.

monitus **sim**	monitī **sīmus**
monitus **sīs**	monitī **sītis**
monitus **sit**	monitī **sint**

PLUPERFECT
I should have been advised, he would have been advised.

monitus **essem**	monitī **essēmus**
monitus **essēs**	monitī **essētis**
monitus **esset**	monitī **essent**

IMPERATIVE

Pres.	monēre, *be thou advised*	monēminī, *be ye advised*
Fut.	monētor, *thou shalt be advised,*	
	monētor, *he shall be advised*	monentor, *they shall be advised*

INFINITIVE — PARTICIPLE

	INFINITIVE		PARTICIPLE
Pres.	monērī, *to be advised*	*Perf.*	monitus, *advised, having been advised*
Perf.	monitus esse, *to have been advised*		
Fut.	monitum īrī, *to be about to be advised*	*Ger.*	monendus, *to be advised, deserving to be advised*

Third (or Consonant-) Conjugation

105   Active Voice—Regō, *I rule.*

PRINCIPAL PARTS

Pres. Ind.	Pres. Inf.	Perf. Ind.	Perf. Pass. Partic.
regō	reg**ere**	rēx**ī**	rēc**tus**

INDICATIVE MOOD

PRESENT TENSE *I rule.*	
Singular	**Plural**
reg**ō**	reg**imus**
reg**is**	reg**itis**
reg**it**	reg**unt**

IMPERFECT *I was ruling,* or *I ruled.*	
regē**bam**	regē**bāmus**
regē**bās**	regē**bātis**
regē**bat**	regē**bant**

FUTURE *I shall rule.*	
reg**am**	reg**ēmus**
reg**ēs**	reg**ētis**
reg**et**	reg**ent**

PERFECT *I have ruled,* or *I ruled.*	
rēx**ī**	rēx**imus**
rēx**istī**	rēx**istis**
rēx**it**	rēx**ērunt,** *or* **-ēre**

PLUPERFECT *I had ruled.*	
rēx**eram**	rēx**erāmus**
rēx**erās**	rēx**erātis**
rēx**erat**	rēx**erant**

FUTURE PERFECT *I shall have ruled.*	
rēx**erō**	rēx**erimus**
rēx**eris**	rēx**eritis**
rēx**erit**	rēx**erint**

SUBJUNCTIVE

PRESENT
May I rule, let him rule.

SINGULAR	PLURAL
regam	regāmus
regās	regātis
regat	regant

IMPERFECT
I should rule, he would rule.

regerem	regerēmus
regerēs	regerētis
regeret	regerent

PERFECT
I may have ruled.

rēxerim	rēxerīmus
rēxerīs	rēxerītis
rēxerit	rēxerint

PLUPERFECT
I should have ruled, he would have ruled.

rēxissem	rēxissēmus
rēxissēs	rēxissētis
rēxisset	rēxissent

IMPERATIVE

Pres.	rege, *rule thou*	regite, *rule ye*
Fut.	regitō, *thou shall rule,*	regitōte, *ye shall rule*
	regitō, *he shall rule*	reguntō, *they shall rule*

INFINITIVE		PARTICIPLE	
Pres.	regere, *to rule*	*Pres.*	regēns, *ruling*
Perf.	rēxisse, *to have ruled*		(Gen. regentis.)
Fut.	rēctūrus esse, *to be about to rule*	*Fut.*	rēctūrus, *about to rule*

GERUND		SUPINE	
Gen.	regendī, *of ruling*		
Dat.	regendō, *for ruling*		
Acc.	regendum, *ruling*	*Acc.*	rēctum, *to rule*
Abl.	regendō, *by ruling*	*Abl.*	rēctū, *to rule, be ruled*

106

Passive Voice—Regor, *I am ruled.*

PRINCIPAL PARTS

Pres. Ind.	Pres. Inf.	Perf. Ind.
regor	regī	rēctus sum

INDICATIVE MOOD	

PRESENT TENSE
I am ruled.

SINGULAR	PLURAL
regor	regimur
regeris	regiminī
regitur	reguntur

IMPERFECT
I was ruled.

regēbar	regēbāmur
regēbāris, *or* -re	regēbāminī
regēbātur	regēbantur

FUTURE
I shall be ruled.

regar	regēmur
regēris, *or* -re	regēminī
regētur	regentur

PERFECT
I have been ruled, or *I was ruled.*

rēctus sum	rēctī sumus
rēctus es	rēctī estis
rēctus est	rēctī sunt

PLUPERFECT
I had been ruled.

rēctus eram	rēctī erāmus
rēctus erās	rēctī erātis
rēctus erat	rēctī erant

FUTURE PERFECT
I shall have been ruled.

rēctus erō	rēctī erimus
rēctus eris	rēctī eritis
rēctus erit	rēctī erunt

SUBJUNCTIVE

PRESENT
May I be ruled, let him be ruled.

SINGULAR	PLURAL
regar	regāmur
regāris, *or* -re	regāminī
regātur	regantur

IMPERFECT
I should be ruled, he would be ruled.

regerer	regerēmur
regerēris, *or* -re	regerēminī
regerētur	regerentur

PERFECT
I may have been ruled.

rēctus sim	rēctī sīmus
rēctus sīs	rēctī sītis
rēctus sit	rēctī sint

PLUPERFECT
I should have been ruled, he would have been ruled.

rēctus essem	rēctī essēmus
rēctus essēs	rectī essētis
rēctus esset	rectī essent

IMPERATIVE

Pres.	regere, *be thou ruled*	regiminī, *be ye ruled*
Fut.	regitor, *thou shalt be ruled,*	
	regitor, *he shall be ruled*	reguntor, *they shall be ruled*

INFINITIVE / PARTICIPLE

	INFINITIVE		PARTICIPLE
Pres.	regī, *to be ruled*	*Perf.*	rēctus, *ruled, having been ruled*
Perf.	rēctus esse, *to have been ruled*		
Fut.	rēctum īrī, *to be about to be ruled*	*Ger.*	regendus, *to be ruled, deserving to be ruled*

Fourth (or ī-) Conjugation

107

Active Voice—Audiō, *I hear.*

PRINCIPAL PARTS

Pres. Ind.	Pres. Inf.	Perf. Ind.	Perf. Pass. Partic.
audiō	audīre	audīvī	audītus

INDICATIVE MOOD	
Present Tense *I hear.*	
Singular	Plural
audiō	audīmus
audīs	audītis
audit	audiunt
Imperfect *I was hearing,* or *I heard.*	
audiēbam	audiēbāmus
audiēbās	audiēbātis
audiēbat	audiēbant
Future *I shall hear.*	
audiam	audiēmus
audiēs	audiētis
audiet	audient
Perfect *I have heard,* or *I heard.*	
audīvī	audīvimus
audīvistī	audīvistis
audīvit	audīvērunt, *or* -ēre
Pluperfect *I had heard.*	
audīveram	audīverāmus
audīverās	audīverātis
audīverat	audīverant
Future Perfect *I shall have heard.*	
audīverō	audīverimus
audīveris	audīveritis
audīverit	audīverint

SUBJUNCTIVE

PRESENT
May I hear, let him hear.

SINGULAR	PLURAL
audiam	audiāmus
audiās	audiātis
audiat	audiant

IMPERFECT
I should hear, he would hear.

audīrem	audīrēmus
audīrēs	audīrētis
audīret	audīrent

PERFECT
I may have heard.

audīverim	audīverīmus
audīverīs	audīverītis
audīverit	audīverint

PLUPERFECT
I should have heard, he would have heard.

audīvissem	audīvissēmus
audīvissēs	audīvissētis
audīvisset	audīvissent

IMPERATIVE

Pres.	audī, *hear thou*	audīte, *hear ye*
Fut.	audītō, *thou shalt hear,*	audītōte, *ye shall hear*
	audītō, *he shall hear*	audiuntō, *they shall hear*

INFINITIVE   PARTICIPLE

Pres.	audīre, *to hear*	Pres.	audiēns, *hearing*
Perf.	audīvisse, *to have heard*		(Gen. audientis.)
Fut.	audītūrus esse, *to be about to hear*	Fut.	audītūrus, *about to hear*

GERUND   SUPINE

Gen.	audiendī, *of hearing*		
Dat.	audiendō, *for hearing*		
Acc.	audiendum, *hearing*	Acc.	audītum, *to hear*
Abl.	audiendō, *by hearing*	Abl.	audītū, *to hear, be heard*

108

Passive Voice—Audior, *I am heard.*

PRINCIPAL PARTS

PRES. IND.	PRES. INF.	PERF. IND.
audior	audīrī	audītus sum

INDICATIVE MOOD

PRESENT TENSE
I am heard.

SINGULAR	PLURAL
audior	audīmur
audīris	audīminī
audītur	audiuntur

IMPERFECT
I was heard.

audiēbar	audiēbāmur
audiēbāris, *or* -re	audiēbāminī
audiēbātur	audiēbantur

FUTURE
I shall be heard.

audiar	audiēmur
audiēris, *or* -re	audiēminī
audiētur	audientur

PERFECT
I have been heard, or *I was heard.*

audītus sum	audītī sumus
audītus es	audītī estis
audītus est	audītī sunt

PLUPERFECT
I had been heard.

audītus eram	audītī erāmus
audītus erās	audītī erātis
audītus erat	audītī erant

FUTURE PERFECT
I shall have been heard.

audītus erō	audītī erimus
audītus eris	audītī eritis
audītus erit	audītī erunt

SUBJUNCTIVE

PRESENT
May I be heard, let him be heard.

SINGULAR	PLURAL
audiar	audiāmur
audiāris, *or* -re	audiāminī
audiātur	audiantur

IMPERFECT
I should be heard, he would be heard.

audīrer	audīrēmur
audīrēris, *or* -re	audīrēminī
audīrētur	audīrentur

PERFECT
I may have been heard.

audītus sim	audītī sīmus
audītus sīs	audītī sītis
audītus sit	audītī sint

PLUPERFECT
I should have been heard, he would have been heard.

audītus essem	audītī essēmus
audītus essēs	audītī essētis
audītus esset	audītī essent

IMPERATIVE

Pres.	audīre, *be thou heard*	audīminī, *be ye heard*
Fut.	audītor, *thou shalt be heard,*	
	audītor, *he shall be heard*	audiuntor, *they shall be heard*

INFINITIVE / PARTICIPLE

INFINITIVE		PARTICIPLE	
Pres.	audīrī, *to be heard*	*Perf.*	audītus, *heard, having*
Perf.	audītus esse, *to have*		*been heard*
	been heard		
Fut.	audītum īrī, *to be about*	*Ger.*	audiendus, *to be heard,*
	to be heard		*deserving to be heard*

Verbs in -iō of the Third Conjugation

109

1. Verbs in **-iō** of the Third Conjugation take the endings of the Fourth Conjugation wherever the latter endings have two successive vowels. This occurs only in the Present System.

2. Here belong—

   a) **capiō**, *to take*; **cupiō**, *to desire*; **faciō**, *to make*; **fodiō**, *to dig*; **fugiō**, *to flee*; **jaciō**, *to throw*; **pariō**, *to bear*; **quatiō**, *to shake*; **rapiō**, *to seize*; **sapiō**, *to taste*.

   b) Compounds of **laciō** and **speciō** (both ante-classical); as, **alliciō**, *entice*; **cōnspiciō**, *behold*.

   c) The deponents **gradior**, *to go*; **morior**, *to die*, **patior**, *to suffer*.

110   **Active Voice**—Capiō, *I take*.

PRINCIPAL PARTS

Pres. Ind.	Pres. Inf.	Perf. Ind.	Perf. Pass. Partic.
capiō	capere	cēpī	captus

INDICATIVE MOOD	
Present Tense	
Singular	Plural
capiō, capis, capit	capimus, capitis, capiunt
Imperfect	
capiēbam, -iēbās, -iēbat	capiēbāmus, -iēbātis, -iēbant
Future	
capiam, -iēs, -iet	capiēmus, -iētis, -ient
Perfect	
cēpī, -istī, -it	cēpimus, -istis, -ērunt or -ēre
Pluperfect	
cēperam, -erās, -erat	cēperāmus, -erātis, -erant
Future Perfect	
cēperō, -eris, -erit	cēperimus, -eritis, -erint

SUBJUNCTIVE	
PRESENT	
SINGULAR	PLURAL
capiam, -iās, -iat	capiāmus, -iātis, -iant
IMPERFECT	
caperem, -erēs, -eret	caperēmus, -erētis, -erent
PERFECT	
cēperim, -eris, -erit	cēperīmus, -erītis, -erint
PLUPERFECT	
cēpissem, -issēs, -isset	cēpissēmus, -issētis, -issent

IMPERATIVE		
Pres.	cape	capite
Fut.	capitō	capitōte
	capitō	capiuntō

INFINITIVE		PARTICIPLE	
Pres.	capere	*Pres.*	capiēns
Perf.	cēpisse		
Fut.	captūrus esse	*Fut.*	captūrus

GERUND		SUPINE	
Gen.	capiendī		
Dat.	capiendō		
Acc.	capiendum	*Acc.*	captum
Abl.	capiendō	*Abl.*	captū

111   **Passive Voice**—Capior, *I am taken.*

PRINCIPAL PARTS

Pres. Ind.	Pres. Inf.	Perf. Ind.
capior	capī	captus sum

INDICATIVE MOOD	
PRESENT TENSE	
SINGULAR	PLURAL
capior, caperis, capitur	capimur, capiminī, capiuntur
IMPERFECT	
capiēbar, -iēbāris, -iēbātur	capiēbāmur, -iēbāminī, -iēbantur
FUTURE	
capiar, -iēris, -iētur	capiēmur, -iēminī, -ientur
PERFECT	
captus sum, es, est	captī sumus, estis, sunt
PLUPERFECT	
captus eram, erās, erat	captī erāmus, erātis, erant
FUTURE PERFECT	
captus erō, eris, erit	captī erimus, eritis, erunt

SUBJUNCTIVE	
PRESENT	
SINGULAR	PLURAL
capiar, -iāris, -iātur	capiāmur, -iāminī, -iantur
IMPERFECT	
caperer, -erēris, -erētur	caperēmur, -erēminī, -erentur
PERFECT	
captus sim, sīs, sit	captī sīmus, sītis, sint
PLUPERFECT	
captus essem, essēs, esset	captī essēmus, essētis, essent

IMPERATIVE		
Pres.	capere	capiminī
Fut.	capitor	
	capitor	capiuntor

INFINITIVE		PARTICIPLE	
Pres.	capī		
Perf.	captus esse	*Perf.*	captus
Fut.	captum īrī	*Ger.*	capiendus

Deponent Verbs

112 Deponent Verbs have in the main Passive *forms* with Active or Neuter *meaning*. But—

a. They have the following Active forms: Future Infinitive, Present and Future Participles, Gerund, and Supine.

b. They have the following Passive meanings: always in the Gerundive, and sometimes in the Perfect Passive Participle; as—

sequendus, *to be followed*; **adeptus**, *attained*.

113 Paradigms of Deponent Verbs are—

I. Conj.   **mīror, mīrārī, mīrātus sum**, *admire.*
II. Conj.   **vereor, verērī, veritus sum**, *fear.*
III. Conj. **sequor, sequī, secūtus sum**, *follow.*
IV. Conj. **largior, largīrī, largītus sum**, *give.*
III. (in -ior) **patior, patī, passus sum**, *suffer.*

INDICATIVE MOOD				
	I.	II.	III.	IV.	III (in -ior)

	I.	II.	III.	IV.	III (in -ior)
Pres.	mīror	vereor	sequor	largior	patior
	mīrāris	verēris	sequeris	largiris	pateris
	mīrātur	verētur	sequitur	largītur	patitur
	mīrāmur	verēmur	sequimur	largīmur	patimur
	mīrāminī	verēminī	sequiminī	largīminī	patiminī
	mīrantur	verentur	sequuntur	largiuntur	patiuntur
Impf.	mīrābar	verēbar	sequēbar	largiēbar	patiēbar
Fut.	mīrābor	verēbor	sequar	largiar	patiar
Perf.	mīrātus sum	veritus sum	secūtus sum	largītus sum	passus sum
Plup.	mīrātus eram	veritus eram	secūtus eram	largītus eram	passus eram
F.P.	mīrātus erō	veritus erō	secūtus erō	largītus erō	passus erō

SUBJUNCTIVE

Pres.	mīrer	verear	sequar	largiar	patiar
Impf.	mīrārer	verērer	sequerer	largīrer	paterer
Perf.	mīrātus sim	veritus sim	secūtus sim	largītus sim	passus sim
Plup.	mīrātus essem	veritus essem	sectūtus essem	largītus essem	passus essem

IMPERATIVE

Pres.	mīrāre, *etc.*	verēre, *etc.*	sequere, *etc.*	largīre, *etc.*	patere, *etc.*
Fut.	mīrātor, *etc.*	verētor, *etc.*	sequitor, *etc.*	largītor, *etc.*	patitor, *etc.*

INFINITIVE

Pres.	mīrārī	verērī	sequī	largīrī	patī
Perf.	mīrātus esse	veritus esse	secūtus esse	largītus esse	passus esse
Fut.	mīrātūrus esse	veritūrus esse	secūtūrus esse	largītūrus esse	passūrus esse

PARTICIPLES

Pres.	mīrāns	verēns	sequēns	largiēns	patiēns
Fut.	mīrātūrus	veritūrus	secūtūrus	largitūrus	passūrus
Perf.	mīrātus	veritus	secūtus	largitus	passus
Ger.	mīrandus	verendus	sequendus	largiendus	patiendus

GERUND

	mīrandī	verendī	sequendī	largiendī	patiendī
	mirandō, *etc.*	verendō, *etc.*	sequendō, *etc.*	largiendō, *etc.*	patiendō, *etc.*

SUPINE

	mīrātum, -tū	veritum, -tū	secūtum, -tū	largītum, -tū	passum, -sū

Semi-Deponents

114

1. Semi-Deponents are verbs which have the Present System in the Active Voice, but the Perfect System in the Passive without change of meaning. Here belong—

> **audeō, audēre, ausus sum,** *to dare*
> **gaudeō, gaudēre, gāvīsus sum,** *to rejoice*
> **soleō,   solēre,   solitus sum,** *to be wont*
> **fīdō,   fīdere,   fīsus sum,** *to trust*

2. The following verbs have a Perfect Passive Participle with Active meaning:—

> **adolēscō,** *grow up*   **adultus,** *having grown up*
> **cēnāre,** *dine*   **cēnātus,** *having dined*
> **placēre,** *please*   **placitus,** *having pleased, agreeable*
> **prandēre,** *lunch*   **prānsus,** *having lunched*
> **pōtāre,** *drink*   **pōtus,** *having drunk*
> **jūrāre,** *swear*   **jūrātus,** *having sworn*

> a. **Jūrātus** is used in a passive sense also.

3. **Revertor** and **dēvertor** both regularly form their Perfect in the Active Voice:—

revertor	**revertī (Inf.)**	**revertī (Perf.),** *to return*
dēvertor	**dēvertī (Inf.)**	**dēvertī (Perf.),** *to turn aside*

Periphrastic Tenses

115

There are two Periphrastic Conjugations,—the Active and the Passive. The Active is formed by combining the Future Active Participle with the auxiliary **sum**, the Passive by combining the Gerundive with the same auxiliary.

ACTIVE PERIPHRASTIC CONJUGATION

INDICATIVE MOOD

Pres.	**amātūrus (-a, -um) sum,** *I am about to love.*
Inf.	**amātūrus eram,** *I was about to love.*
Fut.	**amātūrus erō,** *I shall be about to love.*
Perf.	**amātūrus fuī,** *I have been (was) about to love.*
Plup.	**amātūrus fueram,** *I had been about to love.*
Fut. P.	**amātūrus fuerō,** *I shall have been about to love.*

SUBJUNCTIVE

Pres.	**amātūrus sim,** *may I be about to love.*
Imp.	**amātūrus essem,** *I should be about to love.*
Perf.	**amātūrus fuerim,** *I may have been about to love.*
Plup.	**amātūrus fuissem,** *I should have been about to love.*

INFINITIVE

Pres.	**amātūrus esse,** *to be about to love*
Perf.	**amātūrus fuisse,** *to have been about to love*

PASSIVE PERIPHRASTIC CONJUGATION

INDICATIVE

Pres.	**amandus (-a, -um) sum,** *I am to be loved, must be loved.*
Inf.	**amandus eram,** *I was to be loved.*
Fut.	**amandus erō,** *I shall deserve to be loved.*
Perf.	**amandus fuī,** *I was to be loved.*
Plup.	**amandus fueram,** *I had deserved to be loved.*
Fut. P.	**amandus fuerō,** *I shall have deserved to be loved.*

SUBJUNCTIVE

Pres.	**amandus sim,** *may I deserve to be loved.*
Imp.	**amandus essem,** *I should deserve to be loved.*
Perf.	**amandus fuerim,** *I may have deserved to be loved.*
Plup.	**amendus fuissem,** *I should have deserved to be loved.*

INFINITIVE

Pres.	**amandus esse,** *to deserve to be loved*
Perf.	**amantus fuisse,** *to have deserved to be loved*

Peculiarities of Conjugation

116

1. Perfects in -āvī, -ēvī, and -īvī, with the forms derived from them, often drop the **ve** or **vi** before endings beginning with **r** or **s**. So also **nōvī** (from **nōscō**) and the compounds of **mōvī** (from **moveō**). Thus:—

amāvistī	amāstī	dēlēvistī	dēlēstī
amāvisse	amāsse	dēlēvisse	dēlēsse
amāvērunt	amārunt	dēlēvērunt	dēlērunt
amāverim	amārim	dēlēverim	dēlērim
amāveram	amāram	dēlēveram	dēlēram
amāverō	amārō	dēlēverō	dēlērō
nōvistī	nōstī	nōverim	nōrim
nōvisse	nōsse	nōveram	nōram
audīvistī	audīstī	audīvisse	audīsse

2. In the Gerund and Gerundive of the Third and Fourth Conjugations; the endings -**undus**, -**undī**, often occur instead of -**endus** and -**endī**, as **faciundus, faciundī**.

3. **Dīcō, dūcō, faciō**, form the Imperatives, **dīc, dūc, fac.** But compounds of **faciō** form the Imperative in -**fice**, as **cōnfice**. Compounds of **dīcō, dūcō**, accent the ultima; as, **ēdū´c, ēdī´c.**

4. Archaic and Poetic forms:—

    a. The ending -**ier** in the Present Infinitive Passive; as, **amārier, monērier, dīcier**, for **amārī, monērī, dīcī.**

    b. The ending -**ībam** for -**iēbam** in Imperfects of the Fourth Conjugation, and -**ībō** for -**iam** in Futures; as, **scībam, scībō**, for **sciēbam, sciam.**

    c. Instead of the fuller forms, in such words as **dīxistī, scrīpsistis, surrēxisse**, we sometimes find **dīxtī, scrīpstis, surrēxe**, *etc.*

    d. The endings -**im**, -**īs**, *etc.* (for -**am**, -**ās**, *etc.*) occur in a few Subjunctive forms; as, **edim** (*eat*), **duint, perduint.**

5. In the Future Active and Perfect Passive Infinitive, the auxiliary **esse** is often omitted; as, **āctūrum** for **āctūrum esse**; **ējectus** for **ējectus esse.**

Formation of the Verb Stems

Formation of the Present Stem

117 Many verbs employ the simple Verb Stem for the Present Stem;[34] as, dīcere, amāre, monēre, audīre. Others modify the Verb Stem to form the Present, as follows:—

1. By appending the vowels, **ā, ē, ī**; as,—

	PRESENT STEM	VERB STEM
juvāre	juvā-	juv-
augēre	augē-	aug-
vincīre	vincī-	vinc-

2. By adding **i**, as **capiō**, Present Stem **capi-** (Verb Stem **cap-**).

3. By the insertion of **n** (**m** before labial-mutes) before the final consonant of the Verb Stem; as, **fundō** (Stem **fud-**), **rumpō** (Stem **rup-**).

4. By appending **-n** to the Verb Stem; as,—

   cern-ō   **pell-ō** (for **pel-nō**)

5. By appending **t** to the Verb Stem; as,—

   flect-ō

6. By appending **sc** to the Verb Stem; as,—

   crēsc-ō   **scīsc-ō**

7. By Reduplication, that is, by prefixing the initial consonant of the Verb Stem with **i**; as,—

   gi-gn-ō (root **gen-**)   **si-st-ō** (root **sta-**).

Formation of the Perfect Stem

118 The Perfect Stem is formed from the Verb Stem—

1. By adding **v** (in case of Vowel Stems); as,—

   amāv-ī   **dēlēv-ī**   **audīv-ī**

2. By adding **u** (in case of some Consonant Stems); as,—

   strepu-ī   genu-ī   alu-ī

---

34 Strictly speaking, the Present Stem always ends in a Thematic Vowel (**ĕ** or **ŏ**); as, **dīc-ĕ-, dīc-ŏ-; amā-ĕ-, amā-ŏ-**. But the multitude of phonetic changes involved prevents a scientific treatment of the subject here. See Bennett's *Latin Language*.

3. By adding **s** (in case of most Consonant Stems); as,—

carp-ō	*Perfect*	carps-ī
scrīb-ō	"	scrīps-ī (for scrīb-sī)
rīd-eō	"	rīs-ī (for rīd-sī)
sent-iō	"	sēns-ī (for sent-sī)
dīc-ō	"	dīx-ī (*i.e.* dīc-sī)

  a. Note that before the ending -**sī** a Dental Mute (**t, d**) is lost; a Guttural Mute (**c, g**) unites with **s** to form **x**; while the Labial **b** is changed to **p**.

4. Without addition. Of this formation there are three types:—

  a) The Verb Stem is reduplicated by prefixing the initial consonant with the following vowel or **e**; as,—

currō	*Perfect*	cu-currī
poscō	"	po-poscī
pellō	"	pe-pulī

NOTE 1.   Compounds, with the exception of **dō, stō, sistō, discō, poscō**, omit the reduplication. Thus: **com-pulī**, but **re-poposcī**.

NOTE 2.   Verbs beginning with **sp** or **st** retain both consonants in the reduplication, but drop **s** from the stem; as, **spondeō, spo-pondī; stō, stetī**.

---

  b) The short vowel of the Verb Stem is lengthened; as, **legō, lēgī; agō, ēgī**. Note that **ă** by this process becomes **ē**.

  c) The vowel of the Verb Stem is unchanged; as, **vertō, vertī; minuō, minuī**.

Formation of the Participial Stem

119 The Perfect Passive Participle, from which the Participial Stem is derived by dropping **-us**, is formed:—

1. By adding **-tus** (sometimes to the Present Stem, sometimes to the Verb Stem); as,—

amā-re	*Participle*	amā-tus
dēlē-re	"	dēlē-tus
audī-re	"	audī-tus
leg-ere	"	lēc-tus
scrīb-ere	"	scrīp-tus
sentī-re	"	sēn-sus (for sent-tus)
caed-ere	"	cae-sus (for caed-tus)

   a. Note that **g**, before **t**, becomes **c** (see § 8, 5); **b** becomes **p**; while **dt** or **tt** becomes **ss**, which is then often simplified to **s** (§ 8, 2).

2. After the analogy of Participles like **sēnsus** and **caesus**, where **-sus** arises by phonetic change, **-sus** for **-tus** is added to other Verb Stems; as,—

lāb-ī	*Participle*	lāp-sus
fīg-ere	*Participle*	fī-xus

   a. The same consonant changes occur in appending this ending **-sus** to the stem as in the case of the Perfect ending **-si** (see § 118, 3, a).

3. A few Verbs form the Participle in **-ĭtus**; as,—

domā-re	**dom-ĭtus**
monē-re	**mon-ĭtus**

4. The Future Active Participle is usually identical in its stem with the Perfect Passive Participle; as, **amā-tus**, **amātūrus**; **moni-tus**, **monitūrus**. But—

juvā-re	*Perf. Partic.*	**jūtus**	*has Fut. Act. Partic.*	**juvātūrus**[35]
lavā-re	"	**lautus**	"	**lavātūrus**
par-ere	"	**partus**	"	**paritūrus**
ru-ere	"	**rutus**	"	**ruitūrus**
secă-re	"	**sectus**	"	**secātūrus**
fru-ĭ	"	**frūctus**	"	**fruitūrus**
mor-ī	"	**mortuus**	"	**moritūrus**
orī-rī	"	**ortus**	"	**oritūrus**

---

35 But the compounds of **juvō** sometimes have **-jūtūrus**; as, **adjūtūrus**.

List of the Most Important Verbs, with Principal Parts

First (Ā-) Conjugation

120
I. Perfect in -vī

| amō | amāre | amāvī | amātus | *love* |

All regular verbs of the First Conjugation follow this model.

| pōtō | pōtāre | pōtāvī | pōtus (§ 114, 2) | *drink* |

II. Perfect in -uī

crepō	crepāre	crepuī	crepitūrus	*rattle*
cubō	cubāre	cubuī	cubitūrus	*lie down*
domō	domāre	domuī	domitus	*tame*
fricō	fricāre	fricuī	frictus *and* fricātus	*rub*
micō	micāre	micuī	—	*glitter*
dīmicō	dīmicāre	dīmicāvī	dīmicātum (est)[36]	*fight*
ex-plicō	explicāre	explicāvī (-uī)	explicātus (-itus)	*unfold*
im-plicō	implicāre	implicāvī (-uī)	implicātus (-itus)	*entwine*
secō	secāre	secuī	sectus	*cut*
sonō	sonāre	sonuī	sonātūrus	*sound*
tonō	tonāre	tonuī	—	*thunder*
vetō	vetāre	vetuī	vetitus	*forbid*

III. Perfect in -ī with Lengthening of the Stem Vowel

| juvō | juvāre | jūvī | jūtus | *help* |
| lavō | lavāre | lāvī | lautus | *wash* |

IV. Perfect Reduplicated

| stō | stāre | stetī | stātūrus | |

V. Deponents
These are all regular, and follow *mīror, mīrārī, mīrātus sum.*

Second (Ē-) Conjugation

121
I. Perfect in -vī

dēleō	dēlēre	dēlēvī	dēlētus	*destroy*
fleō	flēre	flēvī	flētus	*weep, lament*
com-pleō[37]	complēre	complēvī	complētus	*fill up*
aboleō	abolēre	abolēvī	abolitus	*destroy*
cieō[38]	ciēre	cīvī	citus	*set in motion*

---

36   Used only impersonally.
37   So **impleō, expleō**.
38   Compounds follow

II.   Perfect in -**uī**

a. Type -**eō**, -**ēre**, -**uī**, -**itus**

arceō	arcēre	arcuī		*keep off*
coerceō	coercēre	coercuī	coercitus	*hold in check*
exerceō	exercēre	exercuī	exercitus	*practise*
caleō	calēre	caluī	calitūrus	*be warm*
careō	carēre	caruī	caritūrus	*be without*
doleō	dolēre	doluī	dolitūrus	*grieve*
habeō	habēre	habuī	habitus	*have*
dēbeō	dēbēre	dēbuī	dēbitus	*owe*
praebeō	praebēre	praebuī	praebitus	*offer*
jaceō	jacēre	jacuī	jacitūrus	*lie*
mereō	merēre	meruī	meritus	*earn, deserve*
moneō	monēre	monuī	monitus	*advise*
noceō	nocēre	nocuī	nocitum (est)	*injure*
pāreō	pārēre	pāruī	pāritūrus	*obey*
placeō	placēre	placuī	placitūrus	*please*
taceō	tacēre	tacuī	tacitūrus	*be silent*
terreō	terrēre	terruī	territus	*frighten*
valeō	valēre	valuī	valitūrus	*be strong*

NOTE 1.—The following lack the Participial Stem:

egeō	egēre	eguī	—	*want*
ēmineō	ēminēre	ēminuī	—	*stand forth*
flōreō	flōrēre	flōruī	—	*bloom*
horreō	horrēre	horruī	—	*bristle*
lateō	latēre	latuī	—	*lurk*
niteō	nitēre	nituī	—	*gleam*
oleō	olēre	oluī	—	*smell*
palleō	pallēre	palluī	—	*be pale*
pateō	patēre	patuī	—	*lie open*
rubeō	rubēre	rubuī	—	*be red*
sileō	silēre	siluī	—	*be silent*
splendeō	splendēre	splenduī	—	*gleam*
studeō	studēre	studuī	—	*study*
stupeō	stupēre	stupuī	—	*be amazed*
timeō	timēre	timuī	—	*fear*
torpeō	torpēre	torpuī	—	*be dull*
vigeō	vigēre	viguī	—	*flourish*
vireō	virēre	viruī	—	*be green*
and others.				

NOTE 2.—The following are used only in the Present System:

aveō	avēre	—	—	*wish*
frīgeō	frīgēre	—	—	*be cold*
immineō	imminēre	—	—	*overhang*
maereō	maerēre	—	—	*mourn*
polleō	pollēre	—	—	*be strong*
and others.				

b. Type -eō, -ēre, -uī, -tus (-sus)

cēnseō	cēnsēre	cēnsuī	cēnsus	*estimate*
doceō	docēre	docuī	doctus	*teach*
misceō	miscēre	miscuī	mixtus	*mix*
teneō	tenēre	tenuī	—	*hold*

So *contineō* and *sustineō*; but

retineō	retinēre	retinuī	retentus	*retain*
obtineō	obtinēre	obtinuī	obtentus	*maintain*
torreō	torrēre	torruī	tostus	*bake*

III. Perfect in -sī

augeō	augēre	auxī	auctus	*increase*
torqueō	torquēre	torsī	tortus	*twist*
indulgeō	indulgēre	indulsī	—	*indulge*
lūceō	lūcēre	lūxī	—	*be light*
lūgeō	lūgēre	lūxī	—	*mourn*
jubeō	jubēre	jussī	jussus	*order*
per-mulceō	permulcēre	permulsī	permulsus	*soothe*
rīdeō	rīdēre	rīsī	rīsum (est)	*laugh*
suādeō	suādēre	suāsī	suāsum (est)	*advise*
abs-tergeō	abstergēre	abstersī	abstersus	*wipe off*
ārdeō	ārdēre	ārsī	ārsūrus	*burn*
haereō	haerēre	haesī	haesūrus	*stick*
maneō	manēre	mānsī	mānsūrus	*stay*
algeō	algēre	alsī	—	*be cold*
fulgeō	fulgēre	fulsī	—	*gleam*
urgeō	urgēre	ursī	—	*press*

IV. Perfect in -ī with Reduplication

mordeō	mordēre	momordī	morsus	*bite*
spondeō	spondēre	spopondī	spōnsus	*promise*
tondeō	tondēre	totondī	tōnsus	*shear*
pendeō	pendēre	pependī	—	*hang*

V. Perfect in -ī with Lengthening of Stem Vowel

caveō	cavēre	cāvī	cautūrus	*take care*
faveō	favēre	fāvī	fautūrus	*favor*
foveō	fovēre	fōvī	fōtus	*cherish*
moveō	movēre	mōvī	mōtus	*move*
paveō	pavēre	pāvī	—	*fear*
sedeō	sedēre	sēdī	sessūrus	*sit*
videō	vidēre	vīdī	vīsus	*see*
voveō	vovēre	vōvī	vōtus	*vow*

VI. Perfect in -ī without Either Reduplication or Lengthening of Stem Vowel

ferveō	fervēre	(fervī, ferbuī)	—	*boil*
prandeō	prandēre	prandī	prānsus (§114, 2)	*lunch*
strīdeō	strīdēre	strīdī	—	*creak*

VII. Deponents

liceor	licērī	licitus sum	*bid*
polliceor	pollicērī	pollicitus sum	*promise*
mereor	merērī	meritus sum	*earn*
misereor	miserērī	miseritus sum	*pity*
vereor	verērī	veritus sum	*fear*
fateor	fatērī	fassus sum	*confess*
cōnfiteor	cōnfitērī	cōnfessus sum	*confess*
reor	rērī	ratus sum	*think*
medeor	medērī	—	*heal*
tueor	tuērī	—	*protect*

Third (Consonant) Conjugation

122   I. Verbs with Present Stem Ending in a Consonant

1. Perfect in -sī

a. Type -ō, -ĕre, -sī, -tus

carpō	carpere	carpsī	carptus	*pluck*
sculpō	sculpere	sculpsī	sculptus	*chisel*
rēpō	rēpere	rēpsī .	—	*creep*
serpō	serpere	serpsī	—	*crawl*
scrībō	scrībere	scrīpsī	scrīptus	*write*
nūbō	nūbere	nūpsī	nūpta (woman only)	*marry*
regō	regere	rēxī	rēctus	*govern*
tegō	tegere	tēxī	tēctus	*cover*
af-flīgō	afflīgere	afflīxī	afflīctus	*shatter*
dīcō	dīcere	dīxī	dictus	*say*
dūcō	dūcere	dūxī	ductus	*lead*
coquō	coquere	coxī	coctus	*cook*
trahō	trahere	trāxī	trāctus	*draw*
vehō	vehere	vexī	vectus	*carry*
cingō	cingere	cīnxī	cīnctus	*gird*
tingō	tingere	tīnxī	tīnctus	*dip*
jungō	jungere	jūnxī	jūnctus	*join*
fingō	fingere	fīnxī	fīctus	*would*
pingō	pingere	pīnxī	pīctus	*paint*
stringō	stringere	strīnxī	strictus	*bind*
-stinguō[39]	-stinguere	-stīnxī	-stīnctus	*blot out*
unguō	unguere	ūnxī	ūnctus	*anoint*
vīvō	vīvere	vīxī	vīctum (est)	*live*
gerō	gerere	gessī	gestus	*carry*
ūrō	ūrere	ussī	ūstus	*burn*
temnō	temnere	con-tempsī	con-temptus	*despise*

---

39   Fully conjugated only in the compounds: **exstinguō, restinguō, distinguō**.

b. Type -ō, -ĕre, -sī, -sus

fīgō	fīgere	fīxī	fīxus	*fasten*
mergō	mergere	mersī	mersus	*sink*
spargō	spargere	sparsī	sparsus	*scatter*
flectō	flectere	flexī	flexus	*bend*
nectō	nectere	nexuī (nexī)	nexus	*twine*
mittō	mittere	mīsī	missus	*send*
rādō	rādere	rāsī	rāsus	*shave*
rōdō	rōdere	rōsī	rōsus	*gnaw*
vādō	vādere	-vāsī[40]	-vāsum (est)	*march, walk*
lūdō	lūdere	lūsī	lūsum (est)	*play*
trūdō	trūdere	trūsī	trūsus	*push*
laedō	laedere	laesī	laesus	*injure, hurt*
claudō	claudere	clausī	clausus	*close*
plaudō	plaudere	plausī	plausum (est)	*clap*
explōdō	explōdere	explōsī	explōsus	*hoot off*
cēdō	cēdere	cessī	cessum (est)	*withdraw*
dīvidō	dīvidere	dīvīsī	dīvīsus	*divide*
premō	premere	pressī	pressus	*press*

2. Perfect in -ī with Reduplication

ab-dō	abdere	abdidī	abditus	*conceal*
red-dō	red-dere	reddidī	redditus	*return*

So *addō, condō, dēdō, perdō, prōdō, trādō,* etc.

cōn-sistō	cōnsistere	cōnstitī	—	*take one's stand*
resistō	resistere	restitī	—	*resist*
circumsistō	circumsistere	circumstetī	—	*surround*
cadō	cadere	cecidī	cāsūrus	*fall*
caedō	caedere	cecīdī	caesus	*kill*
pendō	pendere	pependī	pēnsus	*weigh, pay*
tendō	tendere	tetendī	tentus	*stretch*
tundō	tundere	tutudī	tūsus, tūnsus	*beat*
fallō	fallere	fefellī	(falsus, *as Adj.*)	*deceive*
pellō	pellere	pepulī	pulsus	*drive out*
currō	currere	cucurrī	cursum (est)	*run*
parcō	parcere	pepercī	parsūrus	*spare*
canō	canere	cecinī	—	*sing*
tangō	tangere	tetigī	tāctus	*touch*
pungō	pungere	pupugī	pūnctus	*prick*

NOTE.—In the following verbs the perfects were originally reduplicated, but have lost the reduplicating syllable:

per-cellō	percellere	perculī	perculsus	*strike down*
findō	findere	fidī	fissus	*split*
scindō	scindere	scidī	scissus	*tear apart*
tollō	tollere	sus-tulī	sublātus	*remove*

---

40   Only in the compounds: **ēvādō, invādō, pervādō.**

3. Perfect in -ī with Lengthening of Stem Vowel

agō	agere	ēgī	āctus	*drive, do*
peragō	peragere	perēgī	perāctus	*finish*
subigō	subigere	subēgī	subāctus	*subdue*
cōgō	cōgere	coēgī	coāctus	*force, gather*
frangō	frangere	frēgī	frāctus	*break*
perfringō	perfringere	perfrēgī	perfrāctus	*break down*
legō	legere	lēgī	lēctus	*gather, read*
perlegō	perlegere	perlēgī	perlēctus	*read through*
colligō	colligere	collēgī	collēctus	*collect*
dēligō	dēligere	dēlēgī	dēlēctus	*choose*
dīligō	dīligere	dīlēxī	dīlēctus	*love*
intellegō	intellegere	intellēxī	intellēctus	*understand*
neglegō	neglegere	neglēxī	neglēctus	*neglect*
emō	emere	ēmī	ēmptus	*buy*
coëmō	coëmere	coëmī	coëmptus	*buy up*
redimō	redimere	redēmī	redēmptus	*buy back*
dirimō	dirimere	dirēmī	dirēmptus	*destroy*
dēmō	dēmere	dēmpsī	dēmptus	*take away*
sūmō	sūmere	sūmpsī	sūmptus	*take*
prōmō	prōmere	prōmpsī	(prōmptus, as Adj.)	*take out*
vincō	vincere	vīcī	victus	*conquer*
re-linquō	relinquere	relīquī	relīctus	*leave*
rumpō	rumpere	rūpī	ruptus	*break*
edō	ēsse (§128)	ēdī	ēsus	*eat*
fundō	fundere	fūdī	fūsus	*four*

4. Perfect in -ī without either Reduplication or Lengthening of Stem Vowel

excūdō	excūdere	excūdī	excūsus	*hammer*
cōnsīdō	cōnsīdere	cōnsēdī	—	*take one's seat*
possīdō	possīdere	possēdī	possessus	*take possession*
accendō	accendere	accendī	accēnsus	*kindle*
a-scendō	ascendere	ascendī	ascēnsum (est)	*climb*
dē-fendō	dēfendere	dēfendī	dēfēnsus	*defend*
pre-hendō	prehendere	prehendī	prehēnsus	*seize*
īcō	īcere	īcī	ictus	*strike*
vellō	vellere	vellī	vulsus	*pluck*
vertō	vertere	vertī	versus	*turn*
pandō	pandere	pandī	passus	*spread*
solvō	solvere	solvī	solūtus	*loose*
vīsō	vīsere	vīsī	vīsus	*visit*
volvō	volvere	volvī	volūtus	*roll*
verrō	verrere	verrī	versus	*sweep*

5. Perfect in -uī

in-cumbō	incumbere	incubuī	incubitūrus	*lean on*
gignō	gignere	genuī	genitus	*bring forth*
molō	molere	moluī	molitus	*grind*
vomō	vomere	vomuī	vomitus	*vomit*
fremō	fremere	fremuī	—	*snort*
gemō	gemere	gemuī	—	*sigh*
metō	metere	messuī	messus	*reap*
tremō	tremere	tremuī	—	*tremble*
strepō	strepere	strepuī	—	*rattle*
alō	alete	aluī	altus (alitus)	*nourish*
colō	colere	coluī	cultus	*cultivate*
incolō	incolere	incoluī	—	*inhabit*
excolō	excolere	excoluī	excultus	*perfect*
cōnsulō	cōnsulere	cōnsuluī	cōnsultus	*consult*
cōnserō	cōnserere	cōnseruī	cōnsertus	*join*
dēserō	dēserere	dēseruī	dēsertus	*desert*
disserō	disserere	disseruī	—	*discourse*
texō	texere	texuī	textus	*weave*

6. Perfect in -vī

sinō	sinere	sīvī	situs	*allow*
desinō	dēsinere	dēsiī	dēsitus	*cease*
ponō	pōnere	posuī	positus	*place*
ob-linō	oblinere	oblēvī	oblitus	*smear*
serō	serere	sēvī	satus	*sow*
cōnserō	cōnserere	cōnsēvī	cōnsitus	*plant*
cernō	cernere	—	—	*separate*
discernō	discernere	discrēvī	discrētus	*distinguish*
dēcernō	dēcernere	dēcrēvī	dēcrētus	*decide*
spernō	spernere	sprēvī	sprētus	*scorn*
sternō	sternere	strāvī	strātus	*spread*
prō-sternō	prōsternere	prōstrāvī	prōstrātus	*overthrow*
petō	petere	petīvī (petiī)	petītus	*seek*
appetō	appetere	appetīvī	appetītus	*long for*
terō	terere	trīvī	trītus	*rub*
quaerō	quaerere	quaesīvī	quaesītus	*seek*
acquīrō	acquīrere	acquīsīvī	acquīsītus	*acquire*
arcessō	arcessere	arcessīvī	arcessītus	*summon*
capessō	capessere	capessīvī	capessītus	*seize*
lacessō	lacessere	lacessīvī	lacessītus	*provoke*

7. Used only in Present System

angō	angere	—	—	*choke*
lambō	lambere	—	—	*lick*
claudō	claudere	—	—	*be lame*
furō	furere	—	—	*rave*
vergō	vergere	—	—	*bend*

and a few others.

II. Verbs with Present Stems Ending in -u

induō	induere	induī	indūtus	*put on*
imbuō	imbuere	imbuī	imbūtus	*moisten*
luō	luere	luī	—	*wash*
polluō	polluere	polluī	pollūtus	*defile*
minuō	minuere	minuī	minūtus	*lessen*
statuō	statuere	statuī	statūtus	*set up*
cōnstituō	cōnstituere	cōnstituī	cōnstitūtus	*determine*
suō	suere	suī	sūtus	*sew*
tribuō	tribuere	tribuī	tribūtus	*allot*
ruō	ruere	ruī	ruitūrus	*fall*
dīruō	dīruere	dīruī	dīrutus	*destroy*
obruō	obruere	obruī	obrutus	*overwhelm*
acuō	acuere	acuī	—	*sharpen*
arguō	arguere	arguī	—	*accuse*
congruō	congruere	congruī	—	*agree*
metuō	metuere	metuī	—	*fear*
ab-nuō	abnuere	abnuī	—	*decline*
re-spuō	respuere	respuī	—	*reject*
struō	struere	strūxī	strūctus	*build*
fluō	fluere	flūxi	(flūxus, *as Adj.*)	*flow*

III. Verbs with Present Stem Ending in -i

capiō	cupere	cupīvī	cupītus	*wish*
sapiō	sapere	sapīvī	—	*taste*
rapiō	rapere	rapuī	raptus	*snatch*
dīripiō	dīripere	dīripuī	dīreptus	*plunder*
cōnspiciō	cōnspicere	cōnspexī	cōnspectus	*gaze at*
aspiciō	aspicere	aspexī	aspectus	*behold*
illiciō	illicere	illexī	illectus	*allure*
pelliciō	pellicere	pellexī	pellectus	*allure*
ēliciō	ēlicere	ēlicuī	ēlicitus	*elicit*
quatiō	quatere	—	quassus	*shake*
concutiō	concutere	concussī	concussus	*shake*
pariō	parere	peperī	partus	*bring forth*
capiō	capere	cēpī	captus	*take*
accipiō	accipere	accēpī	acceptus	*accept*
incipiō	incipere	incēpī	inceptus	*begin*
faciō	facere	fēcī	factus	*make*
afficiō	afficere	affēcī	affectus	*affect*
Passive, afficior, afficī, affectus sum				

So other prepositional compounds, *perficiō, perficior; interficiō, interficior; etc.* But

assuēfaciō	assuēfacere	assuēfēcī	assuēfactus	*accustom*
Passive, assuēfiō, assuēfieri, assuēfactus sum				

So also *patefaciō*, *patefīō*; *calefaciō*, *calefīō*; and all non-prepositional compounds.

jaciō	jacere	jēcī	jactus	*hurl*
abiciō	abicere	abjēcī	abjectus	*throw away*
fodiō	fodere	fōdī	fossus	*dig*
fugiō	fugere	fūgī	fugitūrus	*flee*
effugiō	effugere	effūgī	—	*escape*

IV. Verbs in **-scō**

1. Verbs in **-scō** from Simple Roots

poscō	poscere	poposcī	—	*demand*
discō	discere	didicī	—	*learn*
pāscō	pāscere	pāvī	pāstus	*feed*
pāscor	pāscī	pāstus sum		*graze*
crēscō	crēscere	crēvī	crētus	*grow*
cōnsuēscō	cōnsuēscere	cōnsuēvī	cōnsuētus	*accustom one's self*
quiēscō	quiēscere	quiēvī	quiētūrus	*be still*
adolēscō	adolēscere	adolēvi	adultus	*grow up*
obsolēscō	obsolēscerē	obsolēvī	—	*grow old*
nōscō	nōscere	nōvī	—	*become acquainted with*
ignōscō	ignōscere	ignōvī	ignōtūrus	*pardon*
agnōscō	agnōscere	agnōvī	agnitus	*recognize*
cognōscō	cognōscere	cognōvī	cognitus	*get acquainted with*

2. Verbs in **-scō** formed from other Verbs

These usually have Inchoative or Inceptive meaning (see §155, 1). When they have the Perfect, it is the same as that of the Verbs from which they are derived.

flōrēscō	flōrēscere	flōruī	*begin to bloom*	(flōreō)
scīscō	scīscere	scīvī	*enact*	(scīo)
ārēscō	ārēscere	āruī	*become dry*	(āreō)
calēscō	calēscere	caluī	*become hot*	(caleō)
cōnsenēscō	cōnsenēscere	cōnsenuī	*grow old*	(seneō)
extimēscō	extimēscere	extimuī	*fear greatly*	(timeō)
ingemīscō	ingemīscere	ingemuī	*sigh*	(gemō)
adhaerēscō	adhaerēscere	adhaesī	*stick*	(haereō)

3. Verbs in **-scō** derived from Adjectives, usually with Inchoative meaning.

obdūrēscō	obdūrēscere	obdūruī	*grow hard*	(dūrus)
ēvanēscō	ēvanēscere	ēvinuī	*disappear*	(vānus)
percrēbrēsco	percrēbrēscere	percrēbruī	*grow fresh*	(crēber)
mātūrescō	mātūrēscere	mātūruī	*grow ripe*	(mātūrus)
obmūtēscō	obmūtēscere	obmūtuī	*grow dumb*	(mūtus)

V. Deponents

fungor	fungi	fūnctus sum	*perform*
queror	querī	questus sum	*complain*
loquor	loquī	locūtus sum	*speak*
sequor	sequī	secūtus sum	*follow*
fruor	fruī	fruitūrus	*enjoy*
perfruor	perfruī	perfrūctus sum	*thoroughly enjoy*
lābor	lābi	lāpsus sum	*glide*
amplector	amplectī	amplexus sum	*embrace*
nītor	nītī	nīsus sum, nīxus sum	*strive*
gradior	gradī	gressus sum	*walk*
patior	patī	passus sum	*suffer*
perpetior	perpetī	perpessus sum	*endure*
ūtor	ūtī	ūsus sum	*use*
morior	morī	mortuus sum	*die*
adipīscor	adipīscī	adeptus sum	*acquire*
comminīscor	comminīscī	commentus sum	*invent*
reminīscor	reminīscī	—	*remember*
nancīscor	nancīscī	nanctus (nactus) sum	*acquire*
nāscor	nāscī	nātus sum	*be born*
oblīvīscor	oblīvīscī	oblītus sum	*forget*
pacīscor	pacīscī	pactus sum	*covenant*
proficīscor	proficīscī	profectus sum	*set out*
ulcīscor	ulcīscī	ultus sum	*avenge*
īrāscor	īrāscī	(īrātus, *as Adj.*)	*be angry*
vescor	vescī	—	*eat*

Fourth Conjugation

123

I. Perfect Ends in -**vī**

audiō	audīre	audīvī	audītus	*hear*

So all regular Verbs of the Fourth Conjugation

sepeliō	sepelīre	sepelīvī	sepultus	*bury*

II. Perfect Ends in -**uī**

aperiō	aperīre	aperuī	apertus	*open*
operiō	operīre	operuī	opertus	*cover*
saliō	salīre	saluī	—	*leap*

III. Perfect Ends in -**sī**

saepiō	saepīre	saepsī	saeptus	*hedge in*
sanciō	sancīre	sānxī	sānctus	*ratify*
vinciō	vincīre	vinxī	vinctus	*bind*
amiciō	amicīre	—	amictus	*envelop*
fulciō	fulcīre	fulsī	fultus	*prop up*
referciō	refercīre	refersī	refertus	*fill*
sarciō	sarcīre	sarsī	sartus	*patch*
hauriō	haurīre	hausī	haustus	*draw*
sentiō	sentīre	sēnsī	sēnsus	*feel*

IV. Perfect in -ī with Lengthening of Stem Vowel

veniō	venīre	vēnī	ventum (est)	*come*
adveniō	advenīre	advēnī	adventum (est)	*arrive*
inveniō	invenīre	invēnī	inventus	*find*

V. Perfect with Loss of Reduplication

| reperiō | reperīre | repperī | repertus | *find* |
| comperiō | comperīre | comperī | compertus | *learn* |

VI. Used Only in the Present

| feriō | ferīre | — | — | *strike* |
| ēsuriō | ēsurīre | — | — | *be hungry* |

VII. Deponents

| largior | largīrī | largītus sum | | *bestow* |
| So many others. | | | | |

experior	experīrī	expertus sum		*try*
opperior	opperīrī	oppertus sum		*await*
ōrdior	ōrdīrī	ōrsus sum		*begin*
orior	orīrī	ortus sum		*arise*

Orior usually follows the Third Conjugation in its inflection; as *oreris, orĭtur, orĭmur*; *orerer* (Imp. Subj.); *orere* (Imper.).

| mētior | mētīrī | mēnsus sum | | *measure* |
| assentior | assentīrī | assēnsus sum | | *assent* |

Irregular Verbs

124 A number of Verbs are called Irregular. The most important are **sum, dō, edō, ferō, volō, nōlō, mālō, eō, fīō**. The peculiarity of these Verbs is that they append the personal endings in many forms directly to the stem, instead of employing a connecting vowel, as **fer-s** (2d Sing. of **fer-ō**), instead of **fer-i-s**. They are but the relics of what was once in Latin a large class of Verbs.

125 The Inflection of **sum** has already been given. Its various compounds are inflected in the same way. They are—

absum	abesse	āfuī	*am absent*
Pres. Partic. absēns (absentis), *absent*			
adsum	adesse	adfuī	*am present*
dēsum	deesse	dēfuī	*am lacking*
insum	inesse	īnfuī	*am in*
intersum	interesse	interfuī	*am among*
praesum	praeesse	praefuī	*am in charge of*

Pres. Partic. praesēns (praesentis), *present*

obsum	obesse	obfuī	*hinder*
prōsum	prōdesse	prōfuī	*am of advantage*
subsum	subesse	subfuī	*am underneath*
supersum	superesse	superfuī	*am left*

NOTE—**Prōsum** is compounded of **prōd** (earlier form of **prō**) and **sum**; the **d** disappears before consonants, as **prōsumus**; but **prōdestis**.

126

Possum. In its Present System **possum** is a compound of **pot-** (for **pote**, able) and **sum**; **potuī** is from an obsolete **potēre**.

PRINCIPAL PARTS

| possum | posse | potuī | *to be able* |

INDICATIVE MOOD

	SINGULAR	PLURAL
Pres.	possum, potes, potest	possumus, potestis, possunt
Imp.	poteram	poterāmus
Fut.	poterō	poterimus
Perf.	potuī	potuimus
Plup.	potueram	potuerāmus
Fut. P.	potuerō	potuerimus

SUBJUNCTIVE

	SINGULAR	PLURAL
Pres.	possim, possīs, possit	possīmus, possītis, possint
Imp.	possem	possēmus
Perf.	potuerim	potuerīmus
Plup.	potuissem	potuissēmus

INFINITIVE		PARTICIPLE
Pres. posse	*Pres.*	potēns (*as an adjective*)
Perf. potuisse		

127   Dō, *I give.*

PRINCIPAL PARTS

dō	dăre	dedī	dătus

INDICATIVE MOOD

	Singular	Plural
Pres.	dō, dās, dat	dămus, dătis, dant
Imp.	dăbam, *etc.*	dăbāmus
Fut.	dăbō, *etc.*	dăbimus
Perf.	dedī	dedimus
Plup.	dederam	dederāmus
Fut. P.	dederō	dederimus

SUBJUNCTIVE

	Singular	Plural
Pres.	dem	dēmus
Imp.	dărem	dărēmus
Perf.	dederim	dederīmus
Plup.	dedissem	dedissēmus

IMPERATIVE

Pres.	dă	dăte
Fut.	dătō	dătōte
	dătō	dantō

INFINITIVE   PARTICIPLE

	INFINITIVE	PARTICIPLE
Pres.	dăre	dāns
Perf.	dedisse	
Fut.	dătūrus esse	dătūrus

GERUND	SUPINE
dandī, *etc.*	dătum, dătū

1. The passive is inflected regularly with the short vowel. Thus: **dărī, dătur, dărētur,** *etc.*

2. The archaic and poetic Present Subjunctive forms **duim, duint, perduit, perduint,** *etc.*, are not from the root **da-,** but from **du-,** a collateral root of similar meaning.

128   Edō, *I eat.*

PRINCIPAL PARTS

edō	esse	ēdī	ēsus

ACTIVE VOICE

INDICATIVE MOOD

Pres.	edō	edimus
	ēs	ēstis
	ēst	edunt

SUBJUNCTIVE

Imp.	ēssem	ēssēmus
	ēssēs	ēssētis
	ēsset	ēssent

IMPERATIVE

Pres.	ēs	ēste
Fut.	ēstō	ēstōte
	ēstō	eduntō

INFINITIVE

Pres.	ēsse

PASSIVE VOICE

INDICATIVE MOOD

Pres. 3d Sing.	ēstur

SUBJUNCTIVE

Imp. 3d Sing.	ēssētur

1. Observe the long vowel of the forms in **ēs-**, which alone distinguishes them from the corresponding forms of **esse**, *to be.*

2. Note **comedō, comēsse, comēdī, comēsus** or **comēstus**, *consume.*

3. The Present Subjunctive has **edim, -īs, -it,** *etc.*, less often **edam, -ās,** *etc.*

129 Ferō, *I bear.*[41]

PRINCIPAL PARTS

ferō	ferre	tulī	lātus

ACTIVE VOICE

INDICATIVE MOOD

Pres.	ferō, fers, fert	ferimus, fertis, ferunt.[41]
Imp.	ferēbam	ferēbāmus
Fut.	feram	ferēmus
	tulī	tulimus
	tuleram	tulerāmus
Fut. P.	tulerō	tulerimus

SUBJUNCTIVE

Pres.	feram	ferāmus
Imp.	ferrem	ferrēmus
Perf.	tulerim	tulerīmus
Plup.	tulissem	tulissēmus

IMPERATIVE

Pres.	fer	ferte
Fut.	fertō	fertōte
	fertō	feruntō

	INFINITIVE		PARTICIPLE
Pres.	ferre	*Pres.*	ferēns
Perf.	tulisse		
Fut.	lātūrus esse	*Fut.*	lātūrus

	GERUND		SUPINE
Gen.	ferendī		
Dat.	ferendō		
Acc.	ferendum	*Acc.*	lātum
Abl.	ferendō	*Abl.*	lātū

---

41 It will be observed that not all the forms of **ferō** lack the connecting vowel. Some of them, as **ferimus**, **ferunt**, follow the regular inflection of verbs of the Third Conjugation.

PASSIVE VOICE			
feror	**ferrī**	**lātus sum**	*to be borne*

INDICATIVE MOOD	
SINGULAR	PLURAL
Pres. feror, ferris, fertur	ferimur, feriminī, feruntur
Imp. ferēbar	ferēbāmur
Fut. ferar	ferēmur
Perf. lātus sum	lātī sumus
Plup. lātus eram	lātī erāmus
Fut. P. lātus erō	lātī erimus

SUBJUNCTIVE	
Pres. ferar	ferāmur
Imp. ferrer	ferrēmur
Perf. lātus sim	lātī sīmus
Plup. lātus essem	lātī essēmus

IMPERATIVE	
Pres. ferre	ferimimī
Fut. fertor	—
fertor	feruntor

INFINITIVE		PARTICIPLE	
Pres.	ferrī	*Pres.*	lātus
Perf.	lātus esse		
Fut.	lātum īrī	*Fut.*	ferendus

So also the Compounds—

afferō	afferre	attulī	allātus	*bring toward*
auferō	auferre	abstulī	ablātus	*take away*
cōnferō	cōnferre	contulī	collātus	*compare*
differō	differre	distulī	dīlātus	*put off*
efferō	efferre	extulī	ēlātus	*carry out*
īnferō	īnferre	intulī	illātus	*bring against*
offerō	offerre	obtulī	oblātus	*present*
referō	referre	rettulī	relātus	*bring back*

NOTE—The forms **sustulī** and **sublātus** belong to **tollō**.

130 Volō, nōlō, mālō

PRINCIPAL PARTS

volō	velle	voluī	*to wish*
nōlō	**nōlle**	**nōluī,**	*to be unwilling*
mālō	**mālle**	**māluī**	*to prefer*

INDICATIVE MOOD

Pres.	volō	nōlō	mālō
	vīs	nōn vīs	māvīs
	vult	nōn vult	māvult
	volumus	nōlumus	mālumus
	vultis	nōn vultis	māvultis
	volunt	nōlunt	mālunt
Imp.	volēbam	nōlēbam	mālēbam
Fut.	volam	nōlam	mālam
Perf.	voluī	nōluī	māluī
Plup.	volueram	nōlueram	mālueram
Fut. P.	voluerō	nōluerō	māluerō

SUBJUNCTIVE

Pres.	velim, -īs, -it, *etc.*	nōlim	mālīm
Imp.	vellem, -ēs, -et, *etc.*	nōllem	māllem
Perf.	voluerim	nōluerim	māluerim
Plup.	voluissem	nōluissem	māluissem

IMPERATIVE

Pres.	nōlī	nōlīte
Fut.	nōlītō	nōlītōte
	nōlītō	nōluntō

INFINITIVE

Pres.	velle	nōlle	mālle
Perf.	voluisse	nōluisse	māluisse

PARTICIPLE

Plup.	volēns	nōlēns	—

131   Fīō

PRINCIPAL PARTS

fīō	fīerī	**factus sum**	*to become, be made*

INDICATIVE MOOD

	SINGULAR	PLURAL
Pres.	fīō, fīs, fit	fīmus, fītis, fīunt
Inf.	fīēbam	fīēbāmus
Fut.	fīam	fīēmus
Perf.	factus sum	factī sumus
Pluf.	factus eram	factī erāmus
Fut. P.	factus erō	factī erimus

SUBJUNCTIVE

	SINGULAR	PLURAL
Pres.	fīam	fīāmus.
Imp.	fierem	fierēmus
Perf.	factus sim	factī sīmus
Plup.	factus essem	factī essēmus

IMPERATIVE

Pres.	fī	fīte

INFINITIVE   PARTICIPLE

	INFINITIVE		PARTICIPLE
Pres.	fierī		
Perf.	factus esse	*Perf.*	factus
Fut.	factum īrī	*Ger.*	faciendus

NOTE—A few isolated forms of compounds of **fīō** occur; as, **dēfit** *lacks*; **īnfit**, *begins*.

132 ^{Eō}

PRINCIPAL PARTS

eō	īre	īvī	itum (est)	*to go*

INDICATIVE MOOD

	SINGULAR	PLURAL
Pres.	eō, īs, it	īmus, ītis, eunt
Imp.	ībam	ībāmus
Fut.	ībō	ībimus
Perf.	īvī (iī)	īvimus (iimus)
Plup.	īveram (ieram)	īverāmus (ierāmus)
Fut. P.	īverō (ierō)	īverimus (ierimus)

SUBJUNCTIVE

	SINGULAR	PLURAL
Pres.	eam	eāmus
Inf.	īrem	īrēmus
Perf.	īverim (ierim)	īverīmus (ierīmus)
Pluf.	īvissem (iissem, īssem)	īvissēmus (iissēmus, īssēmus)

IMPERATIVE

Pres.	ī	īte
Fut.	ītō	ītōte
	ītō	euntō

INFINITIVE / PARTICIPLE

INFINITIVE		PARTICIPLE	
Pres.	īre	*Pres.*	iēns
Perf.	īvisse (īsse)		(*Gen.* euntis.)
Fut.	itūrus esse	*Fut.*	itūrus.
			Gerundive, eundum

GERUND / SUPINE

GERUND	SUPINE
eundī, *etc.*	itum, itū

1. Transitive compounds of **eō** admit the full Passive inflection; as **adeor, adīris, adītur,** *etc.*

Defective Verbs

Defective Verbs lack certain forms. The following are the most important:—

133   Used Mainly in the Perfect System

	Coepī *I have begun*	**Meminī** *I remember*	**Ōdī** *I hate*
	INDICATIVE MOOD		
Perf.	coepī	meminī	ōdī
Plup.	coeperam	memineram	ōderam
Fut. P.	coeperō	meminerō	ōderō
	SUBJUNCTIVE		
Perf.	coeperim	meminerim	ōderim
Pluf.	coepissem	meminissem	ōdissem
	IMPERATIVE		
	Sing. mementō; *Plur.* mementōte		
	INFINITIVE		
Perf.	coepisse	meminisse	ōdisse
Fut.	coeptūrus esse		ōsūrus esse
	PARTICIPLE		
Perf.	coeptus, *begun*		ōsus
Fut.	coeptūrus		ōsūrus

1. When **coepī** governs a Passive Infinitive it usually takes the form **coeptus est**; as, **amārī coeptus est**, *he began to be loved.*

2. Note that **meminī** and **ōdī**, though Perfect in form, are Present in sense. Similarly the Pluperfect and Future Perfect have the force of the Imperfect and Future; as, **memineram**, *I remembered*; **ōderō**, *I shall hate.*

134   Inquam, *I say* (inserted between words of a direct quotation)

INDICATIVE MOOD		
	SINGULAR	PLURAL
Pres.	inquam	—
	inquis	—
	inquit	inquiunt
Fut.	—	—
	inquiēs	—
	inquiet	—
Perf. 3d Sing.	inquit	

135   Ajō, *I say*

INDICATIVE MOOD		
	SINGULAR	PLURAL
Pres.	ajō	—
	aīs	—
	ait	ajunt
Fut.	ajēbam	ajēbāmus
	ajēbās	ajēbātis
	ajēbat	ajēbant
Perf. 3d Sing.	aït	

SUBJUNCTIVE
Pres 3d Sing.   ajat

NOTE—For **aīsne**, *do you mean?* **aīn** is common.

136 Fārī, *to speak*

This is inflected regularly in the perfect tenses. In the Present System it has—

INDICATIVE MOOD		
	SINGULAR	PLURAL
Pres.	—	—
	—	—
	fátur	—
Fut.	fábor	—
	—	—
	fábitur	—
Impv.	fáre	
Inf.	fárī	
Pres. Partic.	fantis, fantī, *etc.*	
Gerund, G.	fandī; *D. and Abl.*, fandō	
Gerundive	fandus	

NOTE—Forms of **fārī** are rare. More frequent are its compounds; as, **affātur**, *he addresses*; **praefāmur**, *we say in advance.*

137 Other Defective Forms

1. **Queō, quīre, quīvī,** *to be able,* and **nequeō, nequīre, nequīvī,** *to be unable,* are inflected like **eō**, but occur chiefly in the Present Tense, and there only in special forms.

2. **Quaesō,** *I entreat*; **quaesumus,** *we entreat.*

3. **Cedo** (2d sing. Impv.), **cette** (2d plu.); *give me, tell me.*

4. **Salvē, salvēte,** *hail.* Also Infinitive, **salvēre.**

5. **Havē (avē), havēte,** *hail.* Also Infinitive, **havēre.**

Impersonal Verbs

138 Impersonal Verbs correspond to the English, *it snows, it seems, etc.* They have no personal subject, but may take an Infinitive, a Clause, or a Neuter Pronoun; as, **mē pudet hōc fēcisse,** lit. *it shames me to have done this*; **hōc decet,** *this is fitting.* Here belong—

I. Verbs denoting operations of the weather; as,—

fulget	fulsit	*it lightens*
tonat	tonuit	*it thunders*
grandinat	—	*it hails*
ningit	ninxit	*it snows*
pluit	pluit	*it rains*

II. Special Verbs

paenitet	paenitēre	paenituit	*it repents*
piget	pigēre	piguit	*it grieves*
pudet	pudēre	puduit	*it causes shame*
taedet	taedēre	taeduit	*it disgusts*
miseret	miserēre	miseruit	*it causes pity*
libet	libēre	libuit	*it pleases*
licet	licēre	licuit	*it is lawful*
oportet	oportēre	oportuit	*it is fitting*
decet	decēre	decuit	*it is becoming*
dēdecet	dēdecēre	dēdecuit	*it is unbecoming*
rēfert	rēferre	rētulit	*it concerns*

III. Verbs Impersonal only in Special Senses

cōnstat	cōnstāre	cōnstitit	*it is evident*
praestat	praestāre	praestitit	*it is better*
juvat	juvāre	jūvit	*it delights*
appāret	appārēre	appāruit	*it appears*
placet	placēre	placuit	*it pleases*
		(placitum est)	
accēdit	accēdere	accessit	*it is added*
accidit	accidere	accidit	*it happens*
contingit	contingere	contigit	*it happens*
ēvenit	ēvenīre	ēvēnit	*it turns out*
interest	interesse	interfuit	*it concerns*

IV. The Passive of Intransitive Verbs; as,—

ītur	lit. *it is gone*	*i.e. some one goes*
curritur	lit. *it is run*	*i.e. some one runs*
ventum est	lit. *it has been come*	*i.e. some one has come*
veniendum est	lit. *it must be come*	*i.e. somebody must come*
pugnārī potest	lit. *it can be fought*	*i.e. somebody can fight*

Part III:
Particles

139 Particles are the four Parts of Speech that do not admit of inflection, namely Adverbs, Prepositions, Conjunctions, Interjections.

Adverbs

140 Adverbs denote manner, place, time, or degree Most adverbs are in origin case-forms which have become stereotyped by usage. The common adverbial terminations have already been given above (§ 76). The following Table of Correlatives is important:—

RELATIVE AND INTERROGATIVE	DEMONSTRATIVE	INDEFINITE
ubi *where; where?*	**hīc**, *here* **ibi**, **illīc**, **istīc**, *there*	**alicubī, ūsquam, ūspiam**, *somewhere*
quō *whither; whither?*	**hūc**, *hither* **eō**, **istūc**, **illūc**, *thither*	**aliquō**, *to some place*
unde *whence; whence?*	**hinc**, *hence* **inde**, **istinc**, **illinc**, *thence*	**alicunde**, *from somewhere*
quā *where; where?*	**hāc**, *by this way* **eā**, **istāc**, **illāc**, *by that way*	**aliquā**, *by some way*
cum, *when.* **quandō**, *when?*	**nunc**, *now* **tum**, **tunc**, *then*	**aliquandō, umquam**, *sometime, ever*
quotiēns, *as often as; how often?*	**totiēns**, *so often*	**aliquotiēns**, *some number of times*
quam, *as much as; how much?*	**tam**, *so much*	**aliquantum**, *somewhat*

Prepositions

141 Prepositions show relations of words. The following Prepositions govern the Accusative:—

ad, *to*	contrā, *against*	post, *after*
adversus, *against*	ergā, *toward*	praeter, *past*
adversum, *toward, against*	extrā, *outside*	prope, *near*
ante, *before*	īnfrā, *below*	propter, *on account of*
apud, *with, near*	inter, *between*	secundum, *after*
circā, *around*	intrā, *within*	subter, *beneath*
circiter, *about*	jūxtā, *near*	super, *over*
circum, *around*	ob, *on account of*	suprā, *above*
cis, *this side of*	penes, *in the hands of*	trāns, *across*
citrā, *this side of.*	per, *through*	ultrā, *beyond*
	pōne, *behind*	versus, *toward*

1. **Ūsque** is often prefixed to **ad**, in the sense of *even*; as,—

   ūsque ad urbem, *even to the city*

2. **Versus** always follows its case; as,—

   Rōmam versus, *toward Rome*

   It may be combined with a preceding Preposition; as,—

   ad urbem versus, *toward the city*

3. Like **prope**, the Comparatives **propior, propius**, and the Superlatives **proximus, proximē**, sometimes govern the Accusative; as,—

   Ubiī proximē Rhēnum incolunt, *the Ubii dwell next to the Rhine*

   propius castra hostium, *nearer the camp of the enemy*

142

The following Prepositions govern the Ablative:—

ā, ab, abs, *from, by*	cum, *with*	prō, *in front of, for*
absque, *without*	dē, *from, concerning*	sine, *without*
cōram, *in the presence of*	ē, ex, *from out of*	tenus, *up to*
	prae, *before*	

1. **Ā, ab, abs**. Before vowels or **h**, **ab** must be used; before consonants we find sometimes **ā**, sometimes **ab** (the latter usually not before the labials **b, p, f, v, m**; nor before **c, g, q**, or **t**); **abs** occurs only before **tē**, and **ā** is admissible even there.

2. **Ē, ex**. Before vowels or **h, ex** must be used; before consonants we find sometimes **ē**, sometimes **ex**.

3. **Tenus** regularly follows its case, as, **pectoribus tenus**, *up to the breast*. It sometimes governs the Genitive, as, **labrōrum tenus**, *as far as the lips*.

4. **Cum** is appended to the Pronouns of the First and Second Persons, and to the Reflexive Pronoun; usually also to the Relative and Interrogative. Thus:—

mēcum	**nōbīscum**	**quōcum** *or* **cum quō**
tēcum	**vōbīscum**	**quācum** *or* **cum quā**
sēcum		**quibuscum** *or* **cum quibus**

On **quīcum**, see § 89, Footnote 27.

143 Two Prepositions, **in**, *in*, *into*, and **sub**, *under*, govern both the Accusative and the Ablative. With the Accusative they denote **motion**; with the Ablative, **rest**; as,—

> **in urbem**, *into the city*
>
> **in urbe**, *in the city*

1. **Subter** and **super** are also occasionally construed with the Ablative.

144 **Relation of Adverbs and Prepositions**

1. Prepositions were originally Adverbs, and many of them still retain their adverbial meaning; as, **post**, *afterwards*; **ante**, *previously*; **contrā**, *on the other hand*, etc.

2. Conversely several words, usually adverbs, are occasionally employed as prepositions; as,—

> **clam**, **prīdiē**, with the Accusative
>
> **procul**, **simul**, **palam**, with the Ablative

3. **Anástrophe.** A Preposition sometimes follows its case. This is called Anástrophe; as,—

> **eī, quōs inter erat**, *those among whom he was*

Anastrophe occurs chiefly with dissyllabic prepositions.

Conjunctions and Interjections

145 1. Conjunctions are used to connect ideas. For Coördinate Conjunctions, see §§ 341 ff. Subordinate Conjunctions are treated in connection with Subordinate Clauses.

2. Interjections express emotion. Thus:—

    a. Surprise; as, **ēn, ecce, ō**

    b. Joy; as, **iō, euoe**

    c. Sorrow and Pain; as, **heu, ēheu, vae, prō**

    d. Calling; as, **heus, eho**

Part IV:
Word-Formation

DERIVATIVES

146 Derivatives are formed by appending certain terminations called Suffixes to stems of verbs, nouns, or adjectives.

Nouns

Nouns derived from Verbs

147 1. The suffix **-tor** (**-sor**), Fem. **-trīx**, denotes *the agent*; as,—

> **victor, victrīx,** *victor*   **dēfēnsor,** *defender*

NOTE—The suffix **-tor** is occasionally appended to noun stems; as,— **gladiātor,** *gladiator* (from **gladius**).

---

2. The suffix **-or** (originally **-ōs**) denotes *an activity or a condition*; as,—

> **amor,** *love*   **timor,** *fear*   **dolor,** *pain*

3. The suffixes **-tiō** (**-siō**), Gen. **-ōnis**, and **-tus** (**-sus**), Gen. **-ūs**, denote *an action as in process*; as,—

> **vēnātiō,** *hunting*   **obsessiō,** *blockade*
> **gemitus,** *sighing*   **cursus,** *running*

NOTE—Rarer endings with the same force are:—
  a) **-tūra, -sūra**; as,—
      sepultūra, *burial*; **mēnsūra,** *measuring*
  b) **-ium**; as,—
      gaudium, *rejoicing*
  c) **-īdō**; as,—
      cupīdō, *desire*

---

4. The suffixes -**men**, -**mentum**, -**crum**, -**trum**, -**bulum**, -**culum**, denote *the means* or *place* of an action; as,—

lūmen (lūc-s-men), *light*	**vocābulum**, *word*
ōrnāmentum, *ornament*	**documentum**, *proof*
sepulcrum, *grave*	**arātrum**, *plough*
vehiculum, *carriage*	

Nouns derived from Nouns

148　1. Diminutives end in—

-**ulus**,	(-**ula**,	-**ulum**)
-**olus**,	(-**ola**,	-**olum**), after a vowel
-**culus**,	(-**cula**,	-**culum**)
-**ellus**,	(-**ella**,	-**ellum**)
-**illus**,	(-**illa**,	-**illum**)

as,—

nīdulus,	*little nest*	(**nīdus**)
virgula,	*wand*	(**virga**)
oppidulum,	*little town*	(**oppidum**)
fīliolus,	*little son*	(**fīlius**)
opusculum,	*little work*	(**opus**)
tabella,	*tablet*	(**tabula**)
lapillus,	*pebble*	(**lapis**)

NOTE 1—It will be observed that in gender the Diminutives follow the gender of the words from which they are derived.

NOTE 2—The endings -**ellus**, -**illus** contain the primitive form of the diminutive suffix, -**lo**-. Thus:—

agellus,	*field*	for **ager-lus**
lapillus,	*pebble*	for **lapid-lus**

---

2. The suffix -**ium** appended to nouns denoting persons designates either *a collection* of such persons or *their function*; as,—

collēgium, *a corporation, body of colleagues* (**collēga**)
sacerdōtium, *priestly function* (**sacerdōs**)

3. The suffixes -**ārium**, -**ētum**, -**īle** designate a place where objects *are kept* or *are found in abundance*; as,—

columbārium,	*dove-cote*	(**columba**)
olīvētum,	*olive-orchard*	(**olīva**)
ovīle,	*sheep-fold*	(**ovis**).

4. The suffix -**ātus** denotes *official position* or *honor*; as,—

    cōnsulātus, *consulship* (**cōnsul**)

5. The suffix -**īna** appended to nouns denoting persons designates *a vocation* or *the place where it is carried on*; as,—

    doctrīna, *teaching* (**doctor**, *teacher*)
    medicīna, *the art of healing* (**medicus**, *physician*)
    sūtrīna, *cobbler's shop* (**sūtor**, *cobbler*)

6. Patronymics are Greek proper names denoting *son of ...*, *daughter of ....* They have the following suffixes:—

    a) Masculines: -**idēs**, -**adēs**, -**īdēs**; as, **Priamidēs**, *son of Priam*; **Aeneadēs**, *son of Aeneas*; **Pēlīdēs**, *son of Peleus*.

    b) Feminines: -**ēis**, -**is**, -**ias**; as, **Nērēis**, *daughter of Nereus*; **Atlantis**, *daughter of Atlas*; **Thaumantias**, *daughter of Thaumas*.

Nouns derived from Adjectives

149 The suffixes -**tās** (-**itās**), -**tūdō** (-**itūdō**), -**ia**, -**itia** are used for the formation of abstract nouns *denoting qualities*; as,—

    bonitās, *goodness*   **celeritās**, *swiftness*
    magnitūdō, *greatness*   **audācia**, *boldness*
    amīcitia, *friendship*

Adjectives

Adjectives derived from Verbs

150 1. The suffixes -**bundus** and -**cundus** give nearly the force of a present participle; as,—

    tremebundus, *trembling*   **jūcundus** (**juvō**), *pleasing*

2. The suffixes -**āx** and -**ulus** denote *an inclination* or *tendency*, mostly a faulty one; as,—

    loquāx, *loquacious*   **crēdulus**, *credulous*

3. The suffix -**idus** denotes *a state*; as,—

    calidus, *hot*   **timidus**, *timid*   **cupidus**, *eager*

4. The suffixes -**ilis** and -**bilis** denote *capacity* or *ability*, usually in a passive sense; as,—

    fragilis, *fragile* (*i.e.* capable of being broken)
    docilis, *docile*

Adjectives derived from Nouns

From Common Nouns

151

1. The suffixes **-eus** and **-inus** are appended to names of substances or materials; as,—

aureus, *of gold*   **ferreus,** *of iron*   **fāginus,** *of beech*

2. The suffixes **-ius, -icus, -īlis, -ālis, -āris, -ārius, -nus, -ānus, -īnus, -īvus, -ēnsis** signify *belonging to, connected with*; as,—

ōrātōrius, *oratorical*	**legiōnārius,** *legionary*
bellicus, *pertaining to war*	**paternus,** *paternal*
cīvīlis, *civil*	**urbānus,** *of the city*
rēgālis, *regal*	**marīnus,** *marine*
cōnsulāris, *consular*	
aestīvus, *pertaining to summer*	
circēnsis, *belonging to the circus*	

3. The suffixes **-ōsus** and **-lentus** denote *fullness*; as,—

perīculōsus, *full of danger, dangerous*
glōriōsus, *glorious*   **opulentus,** *wealthy*

4. The suffix **-tus** has the force of *provided with*; as,—

barbātus, *bearded*   **stellātus,** *set with stars*

From Proper Names

152

1. Names of *persons* take the suffixes: **-ānus, -iānus, -īnus**; as,—

Catōniānus, *belonging to Cato*
Plautīnus, *belonging to Plautus*

2. Names of *nations* take the suffixes **-icus, -ius**; as,—

Germānicus, *German*   **Thrācius,** *Thracian*

3. Names of *places* take the suffixes **-ānus, -īnus, -ēnsis, -aeus, -ius**; as,—

Rōmānus, *Roman*	**Athēniēnsis,** *Athenian*
Amerīnus, *of Ameria*	**Smyrnaeus,** *of Smyrna*
Corinthius, *Corinthian*	

NOTE   **-ānus** and **-ēnsis**, appended to names of countries, designate something *stationed in* the country or *connected with* it, but not indigenous; as,—

bellum Āfricānum, *a war (of Romans with Romans) in Africa*
bellum Hispāniēnse, *a war carried on in Spain*
legiōnēs Gallicānae, *(Roman) legions stationed in Gaul*

Adjectives derived from Adjectives

153 Diminutives in **-lus** sometimes occur; as,—

> **parvolus,** *little*
> **misellus (passer),** *poor little (sparrow)*
> **pauperculus,** *needy*

Adjectives derived from Adverbs

154 These end in **-ernus, -ternus, -tīnus, -tǐnus**; as,—

hodiernus	*of today*	(**hodiē**)
hesternus	*of yesterday*	(**herī**)
intestīnus	*internal*	(**intus**)
diūtinus	*long-lasting*	(**diū**)

Verbs

Verbs derived from Verbs

155 1. **Inceptives or Inchoatives.** These end in **-scō**, and are formed from Present Stems. They denote *the beginning of an action*; as,—

labāscō	*begin to totter*	(from **labō**)
horrēscō	*grow rough*	(from **horreō**)
tremēscō	*begin to tremble*	(from **tremō**)
obdormīscō	*fall asleep*	(from **dormiō**)

2. **Frequentatives or Intensives.** These denote *a repeated or energetic action.* They are formed from the Participial Stem, and end in **-tō** or **-sō**. Those derived from verbs of the First Conjugation end in **-itō** (not **-ātō**, as we should expect). Examples of Frequentatives are—

jactō	*toss about, brandish*	(from **jaciō,** *hurl*)
cursō	*run hither and thither*	(from **currō,** *run*)
volitō	*flit about*	(from **volō,** *fly*)

a. Some double Frequentatives occur; as,—

cantitō	*sing over and over*	(**cantō**)
cursitō	*keep running about*	(**cursō**)
ventitō	*keep coming*	

b. **agitō,** *set in motion*, is formed from the Present Stem.

3. **Desideratives.** These denote *a desire to do something.* They are formed from the Participial Stem, and end in **-uriō**; as,—

ēsuriō	*desire to eat, am hungry*	**(edō)**
parturiō	*want to bring forth, am in labor*	**(pariō)**

Verbs derived from Nouns and Adjectives (Denominatives)

156 Denominatives of the First Conjugation are mostly transitive; those of the Second exclusively intransitive. Those of the Third and Fourth Conjugations are partly transitive, partly intransitive. Examples are—

a) From Nouns:—

fraudō	*defraud*	**(fraus)**
vestiō	*clothe*	**(vestis)**
flōreō	*bloom*	**(flōs)**

b) From Adjectives:—

līberō	*free*	**(līber)**
saeviō	*be fierce*	**(saevus)**

Adverbs

157 1. Adverbs derived from verbs are formed from the Participial Stem by means of the suffix **-im**; as,—

certātim	*emulously*	**(certō)**
cursim	*in haste*	**(currō)**
statim	*immediately*	**(stō)**

2. Adverbs derived from nouns and adjectives are formed:—

a) With the suffixes **-tim** (**-sim**), **-ātim**; as,—

gradātim, *step by step*

paulātim, *gradually*

virītim, *man by man*

b) With the suffix **-tus**; as,—

antīquitus, *of old*

rādīcitus, *from the roots*

c) With the suffix **-ter**; as,—

breviter, *briefly*

COMPOUNDS

158

1. Compounds are formed by the union of simple words. The second member usually contains the *essential meaning* of the compound; the first member expresses *some modification* of this.

2. Vowel changes often occur in the process of composition. Thus:—

   a. In the second member of compounds. (See § 7, 1.)

   b. The final vowel of the stem of the first member of the compound often appears as ĭ where we should expect ŏ or ă; sometimes it is dropped altogether, and in case of consonant stems ĭ is often inserted; as,—

   > **signifer**, *standard-bearer*
   > **tubicen**, *trumpeter*
   > **magnanimus**, *high-minded*
   > **mātricīda**, *matricide*

159

Examples of Compounds

1. Nouns:—

   a) Preposition + Noun; as,—
   > **dē-decus**, *disgrace*
   > **pro-avus**, *great-grandfather*

   b) Noun + Verb Stem; as,—
   > **agri-cola**, *farmer*
   > **frātri-cīda**, *fratricide*

2. Adjectives:—

   a) Preposition + Adjective (or Noun); as,—
   > **per-magnus**, *very great*
   > **sub-obscūrus**, *rather obscure*
   > **ā-mēns**, *frantic*

   b) Adjective + Noun; as,—
   > **magn-animus**, *great-hearted*
   > **celeri-pēs**, *swift-footed*

   c) Noun + Verb Stem; as,—
   > **parti-ceps**, *sharing*
   > **morti-fer**, *death-dealing*

3. Verbs:—

The second member is always a verb. The first may be—

a) A Noun; as,—

   aedi-ficō, *build*

b) An Adjective; as,—

   ampli-ficō, *enlarge*

c) An Adverb; as,—

   male-dīcō, *rail at*

d) Another Verb; as,—

   cale-faciō, *make warm*

e) A Preposition; as,—

   ab-jungō, *detach*
   re-ferō, *bring back*
   dis-cernō, *distinguish*
   ex-spectō, *await*

NOTE—Here belong the so-called Inseparable Prepositions:
   ambi- (amb-), *around*
   dis- (dir-, di-), *apart, asunder*
   por-, *forward*
   red- (re-), *back*
   sēd- (sē-), *apart from*
   vē-, *without*

---

4. Adverbs:—

These are of various types; as,—

   anteā, *before*
   īlīcō (in locō), *on the spot*
   imprīmīs, *especially*
   obviam, *in the way*

Part V:
Syntax

160 Syntax treats of the use of words in sentences

SENTENCES

Classification of Sentences

161 Sentences may be classified as follows:—

1. Declarative, which state something; as,—

   puer scrībit, *the boy is writing*

2. Interrogative, Which ask a question; as,—

   quid puer scrībit, *what is the boy writing?*

3. Exclamatory, which are in the form of an exclamation; as,—

   quot librōs scrībit, *how many books he writes!*

4. Imperative, which express a command or an admonition; as,—

   scrībe, *write!*

Form of Interrogative Sentences

162 Questions may be either Word-Questions or Sentence-Questions.

1. **Word-Questions.** These are introduced by the various interrogative pronouns and adverbs, such as—**quis, quī, quālis, quantus, quot, quotiēns, quō, quā**, *etc.* Thus:—

   quis venit, *who comes?*

   quam diū manēbit, *how long will he stay?*

2. **Sentence-Questions.** These are introduced—

   a) By **nōnne** implying the answer 'yes'; as,—

      nōnne vidētis, *do you not see?* (Sest. 47)[42]

   b) By **num** implying the answer 'no'; as,—

      num exspectās, *do you expect?* (*i.e. you don't expect, do you?*) (Phil. ii. 86)

   c) by the enclitic **-ne**, appended to the emphatic word (which usually stands first), and simply asking for information; as,—

      vidēsne, *do you see?* (Vatin. 30)

      A question introduced by **-ne** may receive a special implication from the context; as,—

      sēnsistīne, *did you not perceive?* (Cat. 1.8)

   d) Sometimes by no special word, particularly in expressions of *surprise* or *indignation*; as,—

      tū in jūdicum cōnspectum venīre audēs, *do you dare to come into the presence of the judges?*

3. **Rhetorical Questions.** These are questions merely in form, being employed to express an emphatic assertion; as, **quis dubitat**, *who doubts?* (= *no one doubts*).

4. **Double Questions.** Double Questions are introduced by the following particles:—

      utrum ... an   **-ne ... an**   **— ... an**

If the second member is negative, **annōn** (less often **necne**) is used. Examples:—

      utrum honestum est an turpe ⎫
      honestumne est an turpe   ⎬ *is it honorable*
      honestum est an turpe   ⎭ *or base?*

      suntne dī annōn, *are there gods or not?*

   a. **An** was not originally confined to double questions, but introduced single questions, having the force of **-ne**, **nōnne**, or **num**. Traces of this use survive in classical Latin; as,—

      Ā rēbus gerendīs abstrahit senectūs. Quibus? An eīs quae juventūte geruntur et vīribus? *Old age (it is alleged) withdraws men from active pursuits. From what pursuits? Is it not merely from those which are carried on by the strength of youth?* (de Sen. 15)

---

42   See the list of abbreviations used in the illustrative examples, p. 156

5. **Answers**

a. The answer YES is expressed by **ita, etiam, vērō, sānē**, or by repetition of the verb; as,—

'vīsne locum mūtēmus?' 'sānē'.

'Shall we change the place?' 'Certainly.' (Leg. ii.1)

'estīsne vōs lēgatī?' 'sumus.'

'Are you envoys?' 'Yes.' (Liv. i.38.2)

b. The answer NO is expressed by **nōn, minimē, minimē vērō**, or by repeating the verb with a negative; as,—

'jam ea praeteriit?' 'nōn.'

'Has it passed?' 'No.' (Ter. Phor. 525)

'estne frāter intus?' 'nōn est.'

'Is your brother within?' 'No.' (Ter. Ad. 569)

Subject and Predicate

163 The two essential parts of a sentence are the **Subject** and **Predicate**.

The Subject is that *concerning which something is said, asked, etc.* The Predicate is that *which is said, asked, etc., concerning* the Subject.

Simple and Compound Sentences

164 Sentences containing but one Subject and one Predicate are called **Simple Sentences**, those containing more are called **Compound Sentences**. Thus **puer librōs legit**, *the boy reads books*, is a Simple Sentence; but **puer librōs legit et epistulās scrībit**, *the boy reads books and writes letters*, is a Compound Sentence. The different members of a Compound Sentence are called Clauses.

165 **Coördinate and Subordinate Clauses.** Clauses which stand upon an equality are called Coördinate; a Clause dependent on another is called Subordinate. Thus in **puer librōs legit et epistulās scrībit** the two clauses are Coördinate; but in **puer librōs legit quōs pater scrībit**, *the boy reads the books which his father writes*, the second clause is Subordinate to the first.

SYNTAX OF NOUNS

Subject

166 The Subject of a Finite Verb (*i.e.* any form of the Indicative, Subjunctive, or Imperative) is in the Nominative Case.

    1. The Subject may be—

      a) A Noun or Pronoun; as,—

          puer scrībit, *the boy writes*

          hīc scrībit, *this man writes*

      b) An Infinitive; as,—

          decōrum est prō patriā morī, *to die for one's county is a noble thing.* (Hor. Od. iii.2.13)

      c) A Clause; as,—

          opportūnē accīdit quod vīdistī, *it happened opportunely that you saw* (Att. i.17.2)

    2. A Personal Pronoun as Subject is usually implied in the Verb and is not separately expressed; as,—

          scrībō, *I write*   **videt**, *he sees*

      a) But for the purpose of emphasis or contrast the Pronoun is expressed; as,—

          ego scrībō et tū legis, *I write, and you read*

    3. The verb is sometimes omitted when it can be easily supplied from the context, especially the auxiliary **sum**; as,—

          rēctē ille (*sc.* **facit**), *he does rightly*

          consul profectus (*sc.* **est**), *the consul set out*

Predicate Nouns

167 A **Predicate Noun** is one connected with the Subject by some form of the verb **Sum** or a similar verb.

168 A Predicate Noun agrees with its Subject in Case;[43] as,—

          Cicerō ōrātor fuit, *Cicero was an orator*

          Numa creātus est rēx, *Numa was elected king.* (Eut. i.3)

---

43   For the Predicate Genitive, see §§ 198, 3; 203, 5.

1. When possible, the Predicate Noun usually agrees with its Subect in Gender also; as,—

> **philosophia est vītae magistra**, *philosophy is the guide of life* (*Tusc. Disp.* ii.16)

2. Besides **sum**, the verbs most frequently accompanied by a Predicate Noun are—

   a) **fiō, ēvādō, exsistō; maneō; videor**; as,—

   > **Croesus nōn semper mānsit rēx**, *Croesus did not always remain king*

   b) Passive verbs of *making, calling, regarding, etc.*; as, **creor, appellor, habeor**; as,—

   > **Rōmulus rēx appellatus est**, *Romulus was called king*
   >
   > **habitus est deus**, *he was regarded as a god*

Appositives

169

1. An Appositive is a Noun explaining or defining another Noun denoting the same person or thing; as,—

   > **Cicerō cōnsul**, *Cicero, the Consul*
   >
   > **urbs Rōma**, *the city Rome*

   The Appositive is said to be *in apposition* to the other noun.

2. An Appositive agrees with its Subject in Case; as,—

   > **opera Cicerōnīs ōrātōris**, *the works of Cicero, the orator*
   >
   > **apud Hērodotum, patrem historiae**, *in the works of Herodotus, the father of history.*

3. When possible, the Appositive agrees with its Subject in Gender also; as,—

   > **assentātiō adjūtrīx vitiōrum**, *flattery, the promoter of evils* (*Lael.* 89)

4. A Locative may take in Apposition the Ablative of **urbs** or **oppidum**, with or without a preposition; as,—

   > **Corinthī, Achāiae urbe**, or **in Achāiae urbe**, *at Corinth, a city of Greece* (Tac. H. ii.1)

5. **Partitive Apposition.** A Noun denoting a whole is frequently followed by an Appositive denoting a part; as,—

   > **mīlitēs, fortissimus quisque, hostibus restitērunt**, *the soldiers, all the bravest of them, resisted the enemy*

The Cases

The Nominative

170 The Nominative is confined to its use as Subject, Appositive, or Predicate Noun, as already explained. See §§ 166-169.

The Vocative

171 The Vocative is the Case of direct address; as,—

>   **crēdite mihi, jūdicēs**, *believe me, judges*

1. By a species of attraction, the Nominative is occasionally used for the Vocative, especially in poetry and formal prose; as, **audī tū, populus Albānus**, *hear ye, Alban people!* (Liv. i.24)

2. Similarly the Appositive of a Vocative may, in poetry, stand in the Nominative; as, **nāte, mea magna potentia sōlus**, *O son, alone the source of my great power (Aen.* i.664)

The Accusative

172 The Accusative is the Case of the Direct Object.

173 The Direct Object may express either of the two following relations:—

1. **The Person or Thing Affected** by the action; as,—

>   **cōnsulem interfēcit**, *he slew the consul*
>   **legō librum**, *I read the book*

2. **The Result Produced** by the action; as,—

>   **librum scrīpsī**, *I wrote a book* (*i.e.* produced one)
>   **templum struit**, *he constructs a temple*

174 Verbs that admit a Direct Object of either of these two types are **Transitive Verbs**.

  a) Verbs that regularly take a Direct Object are sometimes used without it. They are then said to be employed *absolutely*; as,—

>   **rūmor est meum gnātum amāre**, *it is rumored that my son is in love* (Ter. *And.* 185)

Accusative of the Person or Thing Affected

175 1. This is the most frequent use of the Accusative; as in—

> **parentēs amāmus,** *we love our parents*
> **mare aspicit,** *he gazes at the sea*

2. The following classes of Verbs taking an Accusative of this kind are worthy of note:—

   a) Many Intransitive Verbs, when compounded with a Preposition, become Transitive. Thus:—

      1) Compounds of **circum, praeter, trāns**; as,—

> **hostēs circumstāre,** *to surround the enem*
> **urbem praeterīre,** *to pass by the city*
> **mūrōs trānscendere,** *to climb over the walls*

      2) Less frequently, compounds of **ad, per, in, sub**; as,—

> **adīre urbem,** *to visit the city*
> **peragrāre Italiam,** *to travel through Italy*
> **inīre magistrātum,** *to take office*
> **subīre perīculum,** *to undergo danger*

   b) Many Verbs expressing emotions, regularly Intransitive, have also a Transitive use; as,—

> **queror fātum,** *I lament my fate*
> **doleō ejus mortem,** *I grieve at his death*
> **rīdeō tuam stultitiam,** *I laugh at your folly*

   So also **lūgeō, maereō,** *mourn*; **gemō,** *bemoan*; **horreō,** *shudder,* and others.

   c) The impersonals **decet,** *it becomes*; **dēdecet,** *it is unbecoming*; **juvat,** *it pleases,* take the Accusative of the Person Affected; as,—

> **mē decet haec dīcere,** *it becomes me to say this*

   d) In poetry many Passive Verbs, in imitation of Greek usage, are employed as Middles (§ 256, 1; 2), and take the Accusative as Object; as,—

> **galeam induitur,** *he puts on his helmet* (*Aen.* ii.392)
> **cīnctus tempora hederā,** *having bound his temples with ivy* (*Ov. Am.* iii.9.61)
> **nōdō sinus collēcta,** *having gathered her dress in a knot* (*Aen.* i.320)

Accusative of the Result Produced

176   1. The ordinary type of this Accusative is seen in such expressions as—

> **librum scrībō**, *I write a book*
>
> **domum aedificō**, *I build a house*

2. Many Verbs usually Intransitive take a *Neuter Pronoun*, or *Adjective*, as an Accusative of Result. Thus:—

     a)   A Neuter Pronoun; as,—

> **haec gemēbat**, *he made these moans*
>
> **idem glōriārī**, *to make the same boast* (*de Sen.* 32)
>
> **eadem peccat**, *he makes the same mistakes* (*N.D.* i.31)

     b)   A Neuter Adjective,—particularly *Adjectives of number* or *amount*,—**multum, multa, pauca,** *etc.*; also **nihil**; as,—

> **multa egeō**, *I have many needs* (Gell. xiii.24)
>
> **pauca studet**, *he has few interests*
>
> **multum valet**, *he has great strength* (Hor. *Epp.* i.6.52)
>
> **nihil peccat**, *he makes no mistake* (Stat. 161)

NOTE—In poetry other Adjectives are freely used in this construction; as—

> **minitantem vāna**, *making vain threats* (Sil. i.306)
>
> **acerba tuēns**, *giving a fierce look* (Lucr. v.33)
>
> **dulce loquentem**, *sweetly talking* (Hor. *Od.* i.22.24)

---

3. The adverbial use of several Neuter Pronouns and Adjectives grows out of this Accusative; as,—

> **multum sunt in vēnātiōne**, *they are much engaged in hunting* (*B.G.* iv.1.8).

     a) So also **plūrimum**, *very greatly*; **plērumque**, *generally*; **aliquid**, *somewhat*; **quid**, *why?* **nihil**, *not at all*; *etc.*

4. Sometimes an Intransitive Verb takes an Accusative of Result which is of kindred etymology with the Verb. This is called a Cognate Accusative, and is usually modified by an Adjective; as,—

> **sempiternam servitūtem serviat**, *let him serve an everlasting slavery* (Pl. *Pers.* 34a)
>
> **vītam dūram vīxī**, *I have lived a hard life* (Ter. *Ad.* 859)

a) Sometimes the Cognate Accusative is not of kindred etymology, but merely of kindred meaning; as,—

stadium currit, *he runs a race (Off.* iii.10.42)

Olympia vincit, *he wins an Olympic victory (de Sen.* 14).

5. The Accusative of Result occurs also after Verbs of *tasting* and *smelling*; as,—

> **piscis mare sapit**, *the fish tastes of the sea (Sen. N.Q.* iii.18.2)

> **ōrātiōnēs antīquitātem redolent**, *the speeches smack of the past (Brut.* 82)

Two Accusatives—Direct Object and Predicate Accusative

177

1. Many Verbs of *Making, Choosing, Calling, Showing,* and the like, take two Accusatives, one of the Person or Thing Affected, the other a Predicate Accusative; as,—

> **mē hērēdem fēcit**, *he made me heir.*

Here **mē** is Direct Object, **hērēdēm** Predicate Accusative. So also—

> **eum jūdicem cēpēre**, *they took him as judg*
> **urbem Rōmam vocāvit**, *he called the city Rome*
> **sē virum praestitit**, *he showed himself a man*

2. The Predicate Accusative may be an Adjective as well as a Noun; as,—

> **hominēs caecōs reddit cupiditās**, *covetousness renders men blind (Rosc. Am.* 101)

> **Apollō Sōcratem sapientissimum jūdicāvit**, *Apollo adjudged Socrates the wisest man*

a) Some Verbs, as **reddō**, usually admit only an Adjective as the Predicate Accusative.

3. In the Passive the Direct Object becomes the Subject, and the Predicate Accusative becomes Predicate Nominative (§ 168, 2, b): as,—

> **urbs Rōma vocāta est**, *the city was called Rome*

a) Not all Verbs admit the Passive construction; **reddō** and **efficiō**, for example, never take it.

Two Accusatives—Person and Thing

178   1. Some Verbs take two Accusatives, one of the Person Affected, the other of the Result Produced. Thus:—

a) Verbs of *requesting* and *demanding*; as,—

ōtium dīvōs rogat, *he asks the gods for rest* (Hor. *Od.* ii.16.1)

mē duās ōrātiōnēs postulās, *you demand two speeches of me* (*Att.* ii.7.1)

So also **ōrō, poscō, reposcō, exposcō, flāgitō**, though some of these prefer the Ablative with **ab** to the Accusative of the Person; as,—

opem ā tē poscō, *I demand aid of you*

b) Verbs of *teaching* (**doceō** and its compounds); as,—

tē litterās doceō, *I teach you your letters (Pis. 73)/*

c) Verbs of *inquiring*; as,—

tē haec rogō, *I ask you this*
tē sententiam rogō, *I ask you your opinion*

d) Several Special Verbs: **moneō, admoneō, commoneō, cōgō, accūsō, arguō**, and a few others. These admit only a Neuter Pronoun or Adjective as Accusative of the Thing; as,—

hōc tē moneō, *I give you this advice* (Ter. *Hec.* 766)
mē id accūsās, *you bring this accusation against me* (Pl. *Tr.* 96)
id cōgit nōs nātūra, *nature compels us (to) this*

e) One Verb of *concealing*, **cēlō**; as,—

nōn tē cēlāvī sermōnem, *I have not concealed the conversation from you (Fam. ii.16.3)*

2. In the Passive construction the Accusative of the Person becomes the Subject, and the Accusative of the Thing is retained; as,—

omnēs artēs ēdoctus est, *he was taught all accomplishments* (Liv. xxv.37)
rogātus sum sententiam, *I was asked my opinion (de Dom. 16)*
multa ādmonēmur, *we are given many admonitions (N.D. ii.166)*

a) Only a few Verbs admit the Passive construction.

Two Accusatives with Compounds

179

1. Transitive compounds of **trāns** may take two Accusatives, one dependent upon the Verb, the other upon the Preposition, as,—

mīlitēs flūmen trānsportat, *he leads his soldiers across the river (B.C.* i.54)

2. With other compounds this construction is rare.

3. In the Passive the Accusative dependent upon the preposition is retained; as,—

mīlitēs flūmen trādūcēbantur, *the soldiers were led across the river*

Synecdochical (or Greek) Accusative

180

1. The Synecdochical (or Greek) Accusative denotes the *part* to which an action or quality refers; as,—

tremit artūs, literally, *he trembles as to his limbs, i.e.* his limbs tremble (Lucr. iii.489)
nūda genū, lit. *bare as to the knee, i.e.* with knee bare *(Aen. i.320)*
manūs revinctus, lit. *tied as to the hands, i.e.* with hands tied *(Aen. ii.57)*

2. Note that this construction—

a) Is borrowed from the Greek.

b) Is chiefly confined to poetry.

c) Usually refers to a part of the body.

d) Is used with Adjectives as well as Verbs.

Accusative of Time and Space

181

1. *Duration of Time* and *Extent of Space* are denoted by the Accusative; as,—

quadrāgintā annōs vīxit, *he lived forty years*
hīc locus passūs sescentōs aberat, *this place was six hundred paces away (B.G.* i.49)
arborēs quīnquāgintā pedēs altae, *trees fifty feet high*
abhinc septem annōs, *seven years ago*

2. Emphasis is sometimes added by using the Preposition **per**; as,

per biennium labōrāvī, *I toiled throughout two years*

Accusative of Limit of Motion

182 1. The Accusative of Limit of Motion is used—

a) With names of *Towns, Small Islands,* and *Peninsulas*; as,—

Rōmam vēnī, *I came to Rome.*
Athēnās proficīscitur, *he sets out for Athens.*
Dēlum pervēnī, *I arrived at Delos.*

b) With **domum, domōs, rūs**; as,—

domum revertitur, *he returns home.*
rūs ībō, *I shall go to the country.*

NOTE—When **domus** means *house* (*i.e.* building), it takes a preposition; as,—

in domum veterem remigrāre, *to move back to an old house (Ac.* i.13).

---

2. Other designations of place than those above mentioned require a Preposition to denote Limit of Motion; as,—

ad Italiam vēnit, *he came to Italy*

a) The Preposition is also customary with the Accusatives **urbem** or **oppidum** when they stand in apposition with the name of a town; as,—

Thalam, in oppidum magnum, *to Thala, a large town (Sall. Jug. 75.1)*
Genavam ad oppidum, *to the town Geneva*

b) The name of a town denoting limit of motion may be combined with the name of a country or other word dependent upon a preposition; as,—

Thūriōs in Italiam pervectus, *carried to Thurii in Italy (Nep. Alc. 4)*
cum Acēn ad exercitum vēnisset, *when he had come to the army at Ace* (Nep. *Dat.* 5)

3. To denote *toward, to the vicinity of, in the vicinity of,* **ad** is used; as,—

ad Tarentum vēnī, *I came to the vicinity of Tarentum.*
ad Cannās pugna facta est, *a battle was fought near Cannae.*

4. In poetry the Accusative of any noun denoting a place may be used without a preposition to express the limit of motion; as,—

> **Italiam vēnit**, *he came to Italy (Aen.* i.2)

5. The *goal* notion seems to represent the original function of the Accusative Case. Traces of this primitive force are recognizable in the phrase **īnfitiās īre**, *to deny* (lit. *to go to a denial*), and a few other similar expressions.

Accusative in Exclamations

183 The Accusative, generally modified by an Adjective, is used in Exclamations; as,—

> **mē miserum**, *ah, wretched me!*
> **Ō fallācem spem**, *oh, deceptive hope!*

Accusative as Subject of the Infinitive

184 The Subject of the Infinitive is put in the Accusative; as,—

> **videō hominem abīre**
> *I see that the man is going away*

Other Uses of the Accusative

185 Here belong—

1. Some Accusatives which were originally Appositives, namely,—

> **id genus**, *of that kind*; as, **hominēs id genus**, *men of that kind* (originally **hominēs, id genus hominum**, *men, that kind of men*)
> **virīle secus, muliebre secus**, *of the male sex, of the female sex*
> **meam vicem, tuam vicem**, *etc., for my part, etc.*
> **bonam partem, magnam partem**, *in large part*
> **maximam partem**, *for the most part*

2. Some phrases of doubtful origin; as,—

> | | |
> |---|---|
> | **id temporis**, *at that time* | **quod si**, *but if* |
> | **id aetātis**, *at that time* | **cētera**, *in other respects* |

The Dative

186 The Dative case, in general, expresses relations which are designated in English by the prepositions *to* and *for*.

Dative of Indirect Object

187 The commonest use of the Dative is to denote the person *to whom* something is *given*, *said*, or *done*. Thus:—

I.   With transitive verbs in connection with the Accusative; as,—

hanc pecūniam mihi dat, *he gives me this money*
haec nōbīs dīxit, *he said this to us*

a) Some verbs which take this construction (particularly **dōnō** and **circumdō**) admit also the Accusative of the person along with the Ablative of the thing. Thus:—

Either **Themistoclī mūnera dōnāvit**, *he presented gifts to Themistocles*, or

Themistoclem mūneribus dōnāvit, *he presented Themistocles with gifts.*

urbī mūrōs circumdat, *he builds walls around the city*, or

urbem mūrīs circumdat, *he surrounds the city with walls.*

II. With many intransitive verbs; as,—

nūllī labōrī cēdit, *he yields to no labor*

a) Here belong many verbs signifying *favor*,[44] *help, injure, please, displease, trust, distrust, command, obey, serve, resist, indulge, spare, pardon, envy, threaten, be angry, believe, persuade,* and the like; as,—

Caesar populāribus favet, *Caesar favors (i.e. is favorable to) the popular party*

amīcīs cōnfīdō, *I trust (to) my friends* (Sall. C. 16.4)

Orgetorīx Helvētiīs persuāsit, *Orgetorix persuaded (made it acceptable to) the Helvetians* (B.G. i.2)

bonīs nocet quī malīs parcit, *he injures (does harm to) the good, who spares the bad*

---

44   Many such verbs were originally intransitive in English also, and once governed the Dative.

NOTE—It is to be borne in mind that these verbs do not take the Dative by virtue of their apparent English equivalence, but simply because they are *intransitive*, and adapted to an indirect object. Some verbs of the same apparent English equivalence are *transitive* and govern the Accusative; as, **juvō, laedō, dēlectō**. Thus: **audentēs deus juvat**, *God helps the bold*; **nēminem laesit** *he injured no one*.

b) Verbs of this class are used in the passive only impersonally; as,—

tibi parcitur, *you are spared*
mihi persuādētur, *I am being persuaded*
eī invidētur, *he is envied*

c) Some of the foregoing verbs admit also a Direct Object in connection with the Dative; as,—

mihi mortem minitātur, *he threatens me with death* (*threatens death to me*)

III. With many verbs compounded with the prepositions: **ad, ante, circum, com,**[45] **in, inter, ob, post, prae, prō, sub, super.**

These verbs fall into two main classes,—

1. Many simple verbs which cannot take a Dative of the indirect object become capable of doing so when compounded with a preposition; as,—

afflīctīs succurrit, *he helps the aflicted*
exercituī praefuit, *he was in command of the army*
intersum cōnsiliīs, *I share in the deliberations*

2. Many transitive verbs which take only a direct object become capable, when compounded, of taking a dative also as indirect object; as,—

pecūniae pudōrem antepōnit, *he puts honor before money*
inicere spem amīcīs, *to inspire hope in one's friends*
mūnītiōni Labiēnum praefēcit, *he put Labienus in charge of the fortifications* (*B.G.* i.10)

---

45   This was the original form of the preposition **cum.**

Dative of Reference

188

1. The Dative of Reference denotes the person *to whom a statement refers, of whom it is true,* or *to whom it is of interest;* as,—

mihi ante oculōs versāris, *you hover before my eyes* (lit. *hover before the eyes to me*) (*Verr.* v.123);

illī sevēritās amōrem nōn dēminuit, *in his case severity did not diminish love* (lit. *to him severity did not diminish*) (Tac. *Ag.* 9);

interclūdere inimīcīs commeātum, *to cut of the supplies of the enemy* (Pl. *M.G.* 223).

a) Note the phrase **alicui interdīcere aquā et īgnī,** *to interdict one from fire and water.*

NOTE—The Dative of Reference, unlike the Dative of Indirect Object, does not modify the verb, but rather the sentence as a whole. It is often used where, according to the English idiom, we should expect a Genitive; so in the first and third of the above examples.

---

2. Special varieties of the Dative of Reference are—

a) **Dative of the Local Standpoint.** This is regularly a participle; as,—

oppidum prīmum Thessaliae venientibus ab Ēpīrō, *the first town of Thessaly as you come from Epirus* (lit. *to those coming from Epirus*) (*B.C.* iii.80)

b) **Ethical Dative.** This name is given to those Dative constructions of the personal pronouns in which the connection of the Dative with the rest of the sentence is of the very slightest sort; as,—

tū mihi istīus audāciam dēfendis? *tell me, do you defend that man's audacity?* (*Verr.* iii.213)

quid mihi Celsus agit? *what is my Celsus doing?* (Hor. *Epp.* i.3.15)

c) **Dative of Person Judging;** as,—

erit ille mihi semper deus, *he will always be a god to me* (*i.e.* in my opinion) (*Ecl.* i.7)

quae ista servitūs tam clārō hominī, *how can that be slavery to so illustrious a man* (*i.e.* to his mind)! (*Par. 41*)

d) **Dative of Separation.** Some verbs of *taking away*, especially compounds of **ab, dē, ex, ad**, govern a Dative of the person, less often of the thing; as,—

> **honōrem dētrāxērunt hominī,** *they took away the honor from the man (Verr.* iv.25)

> **Caesar rēgī tetrarchiam ēripuit,** *Caesar took the tetrarchy away from the king (Div.* ii.79)

> **silicī scintillam excūdit,** *he struck a spark from the flint (Aen.* i.174)

Dative of Agency

189 The Dative is used to denote *agency*—

1. Regularly with the Gerundive; as,—

> **haec nōbīs agenda sunt,** *these things must be done by us*
> **mihi eundum est,** *I must go* (lit. *it must be gone by me*)

a) To avoid ambiguity, **ā** with the Ablative is sometimes used with the Gerundive; as,—

> **hostibus ā nōbīs parcendum est,** *the enemy must be spared by us.*

2. Much less frequently with the compound tenses of the passive voice and the perfect passive participle; as,—

> **disputātiō quae mihi nūper habita est,** *the discussion which was recently conducted by me (Tusc. Disp.* ii.2).

3. Rarely with the uncompounded tenses of the passive; as,—

> **honesta bonīs virīs quaeruntur,** *noble ends are sought by good men (Off.* iii.38).

Dative of Possession

190 The Dative of Possession occurs with the verb **esse** in such expressions as:—

> **mihi est liber,** *I have a book*
> **mihi nōmen est Mārcus,** *I have the name Marcus.*

1. But with **nōmen est** the name is more commonly attracted into the Dative; as, **mihi Mārcō nōmen est**.

Dative of Purpose or Tendency

191 The Dative of Purpose or Tendency designates *the end toward which an action is directed* or *the direction in which it tends*. It is used—

1. Unaccompanied by another Dative; as,—

   castrīs locum dēligere, *to choose a place for a camp*
   (B.G. vii.16)

   legiōnēs praesidiō relinquere, *to leave the legions as a*
   guard (lit. *for a guard*) *(B.C.* ii.22)

   receptuī canere, *to sound the signal for a retreat (B.G.*
   vii.47).

2. Much more frequently in connection with another Dative
   of the person:—

   a) Especially with some form of esse; as,—

      fortūnae tuae mihi cūrae sunt, *your fortunes are a*
      care to me (lit. *for a care*) *(Fam.* vi.5.1)

      quibus sunt odiō, *to whom they are an object of*
      hatred (Flac. 19)

      cui bonō? *to whom is it of advantage?*

   b) With other verbs; as,—

      hōs tibi mūnerī mīsit, *he has sent these to you for a*
      present (Nep. *Paus.* 2)

      Pausaniās Atticīs vēnit auxiliō, *Pausanias came to*
      the aid of the Athenians (lit. *to the Athenians for*
      aid).

3. In connection with the Gerundive; as,—

   decemvirī lēgibus scrībundīs, *decemvirs for codifying*
   the laws

   mē gerendō bellō ducem creāvēre, *me they have made*
   leader for carrying on the war (Liv. i.23)

NOTE—This construction with the gerundive is not common till
Livy.

Dative with Adjectives

192 The use of the Dative with Adjectives corresponds very
closely to its use with verbs. Thus:—

1. Corresponding to the Dative of Indirect Object it occurs
   with adjectives signifying: *friendly, unfriendly, similar,*
   dissimilar, equal, near, related to, etc.; as,—

   mihi inimīcus, *hostile to me*
   sunt proximī Germānis, *they are next to the Germans*
   noxiae poena pār estō, *let the penalty be equal to the*
   damage (Leg. iii.11)

a) For **propior** and **proximus** with the Accusative, see §
141, 3.

2. Corresponding to the Dative of Purpose, the Dative occurs
with adjectives signifying: *suitable, adapted, fit*; as,—

castrīs idōneus locus, *a place fit for a camp*
apta diēs sacrificiō, *a day suitable for a sacrifice*

NOTE—Adjectives of this last class often take the Accusative with
ad.

Dative of Direction

193 In the poets the Dative is occasionally used to denote the
direction of motion; as,—

it clāmor caelō, *the shout goes heavenward* (Aen. v.451)
cinerēs rīvō fluentī jace, *cast the ashes toward a flowing
stream*

1. By an extension of this construction the poets sometimes
use the Dative to denote the *limit of motion*; as,—

dum Latiō deōs īnferret, *till he should bring his gods to
Latium* (Aen. i.6)

The Genitive

194 The Genitive is used with Nouns, Adjectives, and Verbs.

Genitive with Nouns

195 With Nouns the Genitive is *the case which defines the
meaning of the limited noun more closely.* This relation is
generally indicated in English by the preposition **of**. There
are the following varieties of the Genitive with Nouns:—

Genitive of Origin	Objective Genitive
Genitive of Material	Genitive of the Whole
Genitive of Possession	Appositional Genitive
Subjective Genitive	Genitive of Quality

196 **Genitive of Origin**; as,—

Mārcī fīlius, *the son of Marcus*

197 **Genitive of Material**; as,—

talentum aurī, *a talent of gold*
acervus frūmentī, *a pile of grain*

198

Genitive of Possession or Ownership; as,—

domus Cicerōnis, *Cicero's house*

1. Here belongs the Genitive with **causā** and **grātiā**. The Genitive always precedes; as,—

   hominum causā, *for the sake of men*
   meōrum amīcōrum grātiā, *for the sake of my friends*

2. The Possessive Genitive is often used predicatively, especially with **esse** and **fierī**; as,—

   domus est rēgis, *the house is the king's*

   stultī est in errōre manēre, *it is (the part) of a fool to remain in error*

   dē bellō jūdicium imperātōris est, nōn mīlitum, *the decision concerning war belongs to the general, not to the soldiers*

   a) For the difference in force between the Possessive Genitive and the Dative of Possession, see § 359, 1.

199

Subjective Genitive. This denotes *the person who makes or produces something or who has a feeling*; as,—

dicta Platōnis, *the utterances of Plato*
timōrēs līberōrum, *the fears of the children*

200

Objective Genitive. This denotes *the object of an action or feeling*; as,—

metus deōrum, *the fear of the gods*
amor lībertātis, *love of liberty*
cōnsuētūdō bonōrum hominum, *intercourse with good men*

1. This relation is often expressed by means of prepositions; as,—

   amor ergā parentēs, *love toward one's parents*

201

Genitive of the Whole. This designates the *whole* of which a part is taken. It is used—

1. With Nouns, Pronouns, Comparatives, Superlatives, and Ordinal Numerals; as,—

   magna pars hominum, *a great part of mankind*
   duo mīlia peditum, *two thousand foot-soldiers*
   quis mortālium, *who of mortals?*

major frātrum, *the elder of the brothers*

gēns maxima Germānōrum, *the largest tribe of the Germans*

prīmus omnium, *the first of all*

a) Yet instead of the Genitive of the Whole we often find **ex** or **dē** with the Ablative, regularly so with Cardinal numbers and **quīdam**; as,—

   fidēlissimus dē servīs, *the most trusty of the slaves*

   quīdam ex amīcīs, *certain of his friends*

   ūnus ex mīlitibus, *one of the soldiers*

b) In English we often use *of* where there is no relation of whole to part. In such cases the Latin is more exact, and does not use the Genitive; as,—

   quot vōs estis, *how many of you are there?*

   trecentī conjūrāvimus, *three hundred of us have conspired (i.e.* we, three hundred in number)

2. The Genitive of the Whole is used also with the Nominative or Accusative Singular Neuter of Pronouns, or of Adjectives used substantively; also with the Adverbs **parum, satis,** and **partim** when used substantively; as,—

   quid cōnsilī, *what purpose?*

   tantum cibī, *so much food*

   plūs auctōritātis, *more authority*

   minus labōris, *less labor*

   satis pecūniae, *enough money*

   parum industriae, *too little industry*

a) An Adjective of the second declension used substantively may be employed as a Genitive of the Whole; as, **nihil bonī**, *nothing good.*

b) But Adjectives of the third declension agree directly with the noun they limit; as, **nihil dulcius**, *nothing sweeter.*

3. Occasionally we find the Genitive of the Whole dependent upon Adverbs of place; as,—

   ubi terrārum? ubi gentium? *where in the world?*

a) By an extension of this usage the Genitive sometimes occurs in dependence upon **prīdiē** and **postrīdiē**, but only in the phrases **prīdiē ejus diēī**, *on the day before that*; **postrīdiē ejus diēī**, *on the day after that.*

202 **Appositional Genitive.** The Genitive sometimes has the force of an appositive; as,—

> **nōmen rēgis,** *the name of king*
> **poena mortis,** *the penalty of death*
> **ars scrībendī,** *the art of writing*

203 **Genitive of Quality.** The Genitive modified by an Adjective is used to denote quality. This construction presents several varieties. Thus it is used—

1. To denote some internal or permanent characteristic of a person or thing; as,—

   > **vir magnae virtūtis,** *a man of great virtue*
   > **ratiōnēs ejus modī,** *considerations of that sort*

   a) Only a limited number of Adjectives occur in this construction, chiefly **magnus, maximus, summus, tantus,** along with **ejus.**

2. To denote measure (*breadth, length, etc.*); as,—

   > **fossa quīndecim pedum,** *a trench fifteen feet wide* (or *deep*)
   > **exsilium decem annōrum,** *an exile of ten years*

3. Equivalent to the Genitive of Quality (though probably of different origin) are the Genitives **tantī, quantī, parvī, magnī, minōris, plūris, minimī, plūrimī, maximī.** These are used predicatively to denote *indefinite value*; as,—

   > **nūlla studia tantī sunt,** *no studies are of so much value*
   > **magnī opera ejus exīstimāta est,** *his assistance was highly esteemed* (Nep. *Cat.* 1.2)

4. By an extension of the notion of *value*, **quantī, tantī, plūris,** and **minōris** are also used with verbs of *buying* and *selling*, to denote *indefinite price*; as,—

   > **quantī aedēs ēmistī,** *at how high a price did you purchase the house?*

5. Any of the above varieties of the Genitive of Quality may be used predicatively; as,—

   > **tantae mōlis erat Rōmānam condere gentem,** *of so great difficulty was it to found the Roman race* (Aen. i.33)

Genitive with Adjectives

204 The Genitive is used with many Adjectives *to limit the extent of their application.* Thus:—

1. With adjectives signifying *desire, knowledge, familiarity, memory, participation, power, fullness,* and their opposites; as,—

   studiōsus discendī, *desirous of learning*
   perītus bellī, *skilled in war*
   īnsuētus labōris, *unused to toil*
   immemor mandātī tuī, *unmindful of your commission*
   plēna perīculōrum est vīta, *life is full of dangers*

   a) Some participles used adjectively also take the Genitive; as,—

      diligēns vēritātis, *fond of truth*
         amāns patriae, *devoted to one's country*

2. Sometimes with **proprius** and **commūnis;** as,—

   virī propria est fortitūdō, *bravery is characteristic of a man (Tusc. Disp.* ii.43)

   memoria est commūnis omnium artium, *memory is common to all professions (Or.* 54)

   a) **proprius** and **commūnis** are also construed with the Dative.

3. With **similis** the Genitive is the commoner construction in Cicero, when the reference is to living objects; as,—

   fīlius patris simillimus est, *the son is exactly like his father*

   meī similis, *like me;* **vestrī similis,** *like you*

   When the reference is to things, both Genitive and Dative occur; as,—

   mors somnō (or **somnī**) **similis est,** *death is like sleep*

4. In the poets and later prose writers the use of the Genitive with Adjectives is extended far beyond earlier limits; as, **atrōx animī,** *fierce of temper;* **incertus cōnsilī,** *undecided in purpose.*

Genitive with Verbs

205 The Genitive is used with the following classes of Verbs:—

MEMINI, REMINĪSCOR, OBLĪVĪSCOR

206

1. **When Referring to Persons—**

a) **meminī** always takes the Genitive of personal or reflexive pronouns; as,—

    meī memineris, *remember me!*
    nostrī meminit, *he remembers us*

With other words denoting persons **meminī** takes the Accusative, rarely the Genitive; as,—

    Sullam meminī, *I recall Sulla*
    vīvōrum meminī, *I remember the living*

b) **oblīvīscor** regularly takes the Genitive; as,—

    Epicūrī nōn licet oblīvīscī, *we mustn't forget*
    Epicurus (F. v.3)

2. **When Referring to Things, meminī, reminīscor, oblīvīscor** take sometimes the Genitive, sometimes the Accusative, without difference of meaning; as,—

    animus praeteritōrum meminit, *the mind remembers the past (Div. i.63)*

    meministīne nōmina, *do you remember the names?* (Pl. *Poen.* 1062)

    reminīscere veteris incommodī, *remember the former disaster (B.G. i.13)*

    reminīscēns acerbitātem, *remembering the bitterness* (Nep. *Alc.* 6).

a) But neuter pronouns, and adjectives used substantively, regularly stand in the Accusative; as,—

    haec meminī, *I remember this*
    multa reminīscor, *I remember many things*

3. The phrase **mihi** (**tibi**, *etc.*) **in mentem venit**, following the analogy of **meminī**, takes the Genitive; as,—

    mihi patriae veniēbat in mentem, *I remembered my country (Sull. 19)*

ADMONEŌ, COMMONEŌ, COMMONEFACIŌ

207

These verbs, in addition to an Accusative of the person, occasionally take a Genitive of the thing; as,—

    tē veteris amīcitiae commonefaciō, *I remind you of our old friendship (ad Her. iv.24.33)*

a) But more frequently (in Cicero almost invariably) these
verbs take **dē** with the Ablative; as,—

> **mē admonēs dē sorōre**, *you remind me of your sister*
> *(ad Att.* v.1.3)

b) A neuter pronoun or adjective used substantively
regularly stands in the Accusative (§ 178, 1, d); as,—

> **tē hōc admoneō**, *I give you this warning*

Verbs of Judicial Action

208 1. Verbs of *Accusing, Convicting, Acquitting* take the
Genitive of the *charge*; as,—

> **mē fūrtī accūsat**, *he accuses me of theft*
> **Verrem avāritiae coarguit**, *he convicts Verres of avarice*
> **impietātis absolūtus est**, *he was acquitted of blasphemy*

2. Verbs of *Condemning* take—

a) The Genitive of the *charge*; as,—

> **pecūniae pūblicae condemnātus**, *condemned (on*
> *the charge) of embezzlement* (lit. *public money*)
> *(Flacc.* 43)

> **capitis damnātus**, *condemned on a capital charge*
> (lit. *on a charge involving his head*)

b) The Ablative of the *penalty*; as,—

> **capite damnātus est**, *he was condemned to death*
> **mīlle nummīs damnātus est**, *he was condemned*
> *(to pay) a thousand sesterces* (lit. *by a thousand*
> *sesterces*, Abl. of Means)

3. Note the phrases:—

> **vōtī damnātus, vōtī reus**, *having attained one's prayer*
> (lit. *condemned on the score of one's vow*)
> **dē vī**, *(accused, convicted, etc.) of assault*
> **inter sīcāriōs**, *(accused, convicted, etc.) of murder*

Genitive with Impersonal Verbs

209 1. The Impersonals **pudet, paenitet, miseret, taedet,
piget** take the Accusative of *the person affected*, along
with the Genitive *of the person or thing toward whom
the feeling is directed*; as,—

> **pudet mē tuī**, *I am ashamed of you* (lit. *it shames me of
> you*)
> **paenitet mē hūjus factī**, *I repent of this act*
> **eum taedet vītae**, *he is weary of life*
> **pauperum tē miseret**, *you pity the poor*

a) Instead of the Genitive of the thing we often find an Infinitive or Neuter Pronoun used as subject of the verb. Thus;—

mē paenitet hōc fēcisse, *I repent of having done this*
mē hōc pudet, *I am ashamed of this*

2. **Misereor** and **miserēscō** also govern the Genitive; as,—

miserēminī sociōrum, *pity the allies (Verr. i.72)*

Interest, Rēfert

210 With **interest**, *it concerns*, three points enter into consideration: —

a) the *person concerned*;

b) the *thing about which* he is concerned;

c) the *extent* of his concern.

211 1. The *person concerned* is regularly denoted by the Genitive; as,—

patris interest, *it concerns the father*

a) But instead of the Genitive of the personal pronouns, **meī**, **tuī**, **nostrī**, **vestrī**, the Latin uses the Ablative Singular Feminine of the Possessive: **meā**, **tuā**, *etc.*; as,—

meā interest, *it concerns me*

2. The *thing about which* a person is concerned is denoted—

a) by a Neuter Pronoun as subject; as,—

hōc reī pūblicae interest, *this concerns the state*

b) by an Infinitive; as,—

omnium interest valēre, *it concerns all to keep well*

c) by an Indirect Question; as,—

meā interest quandō veniās, *I am concerned as to when you are coming*

3. The *degree of concern* is denoted—

a) by the Genitive (cf. § 203, 3): magnī, parvī, etc.; as,—

meā magnī interest, *it concerns me greatly*

b) by the Adverbs, **magnopere, magis, maximē**, *etc.*; as,—

cīvium minimē interest, *it concerns the citizens very little*

c) by the Neuters, **multum, plūs, minus**, *etc.*; as,—

multum vestrā interest, *it concerns you much*

4. **Rēfert** follows **interest** in its construction, except that it rarely takes the Genitive of the person. Thus:—

meā rēfert, *it concerns me*

but rarely **illīus rēfert**, *it concerns him*

Genitive with Other Verbs

212

1. Verbs of *Plenty* and *Want* sometimes govern the Genitive; as,—

    pecūniae indigēs, *you need money*

    a) These verbs more commonly take the Ablative (§ 214, 1); indigeō is the only verb which has a preference for the Genitive.

2. **Potior**, though usually followed by the Ablative, sometimes takes the Genitive, almost always so in Sallust; and regularly in the phrase **potīrī rērum**, *to get control of affairs.*

3. In poetry some verbs take the Genitive in imitation of the Greek; as,—

    dēsine querellārum, *cease your complaints* (Hor. *Od.* ii.9.17)

    operum solūtī, *freed from their tasks* (Hor. *Od.* iii.17.16)

The Ablative

213

The Latin Ablative unites in itself three cases which were originally distinct both **in form** and **in meaning**, specifically:

The Ablative or **from**-case

The Instrumental or **with**-case

The Locative or **where**-case

The uses of the Latin Ablative accordingly fall into Genuine Ablative uses, Instrumental uses, and Locative uses.

Genuine Ablative Uses

Ablative of Separation

214

The Ablative of Separation is construed sometimes with, sometimes without, a preposition.

1. The following words regularly take the Ablative without a preposition:—

    a) The Verbs of *freeing*: **līberō, solvō, levō**;

    b) The Verbs of *depriving*: **prīvō, spoliō, exuō, fraudō, nūdō**;

    c) The Verbs of *lacking*: **egeō, careō, vacō**;

d) The corresponding Adjectives, **līber, inānis, vacuus, nūdus,**

and some others of similar meaning.

Thus:—

cūrīs līberātus, *freed from cares (Marc. 34)*

Caesar hostēs armīs exuit, *Caesar stripped the enemy of their arms (B.G. 5.51)*

caret sēnsū commūnī, *he lacks common sense* (Hor. *Sat.* i.3.66)

auxiliō eget, *he needs help*

bonōrum vīta vacua est metū, *the life of the good is free from fear*

NOTE 1—Yet Adjectives and **līberō** may take the preposition **ab,**—regularly so with the Ablative of persons; as,—

urbem ā tyrannō līberārunt, *they freed the city from the tyrant* (Nep. *Thras.* 1).

NOTE 2—**Indigeō** usually takes the Genitive. See § 212, 1, a.

---

2. Of Verbs signifying *to keep from, to remove, to withdraw,* some take the preposition, others omit it. The same Verb often admits both constructions. Examples:—

abstinēre cibō, *to abstain from food* (Plin. *Epp.* i.12.9)

hostēs fīnibus prohibuērunt, *they kept the enemy from their borders (B.G.* i.1.4)

praedōnēs ab īnsulā prohibuit, *he kept the pirates from the island (Verr.* iv.144).

3. Other Verbs of separation usually take the Ablative with a Prepositon, particularly compounds of **dis-** and **sē-**; as,—

dissentiō ā tē, *I dissent from you (Planc. 9)*

sēcernantur ā nōbīs, *let them be separated from us (Cat.* i.32)

4. The Preposition is freely omitted in poetry.

ABLATIVE OF SOURCE

215 The Ablative of Source is used with the participles **nātus** and **ortus** (in poetry also with **ēditus, satus,** and some others), to designate *parentage* or *station*; as,—

Jove nātus, *son of Jupiter*
summō locō nātus, *high-born* (lit. *born from a very high place*)
nōbilī genere ortus, *born of a noble family*

1. Pronouns regularly (nouns rarely) take **ex**; as,
   ex mē nātus, *sprung from me*

2. To denote remoter descent, **ortus ab**, or **oriundus** (with or without **ab**), is used; as,—
   ab Ulixe oriundus, *descended from Ulysses* (Liv. i.49.9)

ABLATIVE OF AGENT

216

The Ablative accompanied by **ā** (**ab**) is used with passive verbs to denote the *personal agent*; as,—

ā Caesare accūsātus est, *he was arraigned by Caesar*

1. Collective nouns referring to persons, and abstract nouns when personified, may be construed as the personal agent. Thus:—
   hostēs ā fortūnā dēserēbantur, *the enemy were deserted by Fortune* (B.G. v.34.2)
   ā multitūdine hostium mōntēs tenēbantur, *the mountains were held by a multitude of the enemy* (B.G. iii.2.1)

2. Names of animals sometimes admit the same construction. Thus:—
   ā canibus laniātus est, *he was torn to pieces by dogs*

ABLATIVE OF COMPARISON

217

1. The Ablative is often used with Comparatives in the sense of *than*; as,—
   melle dulcior, *sweeter than honey* (de Sen. 31)
   patria mihi vītā cārior est, *my country is dearer to me than life* (Cat. i.27)

2. This construction, as a rule, occurs only as a substitute for **quam** (*than*) with the Nominative or Accusative. In other cases **quam** must be used; as,—
   tuī studiōsior sum quam illīus, *I am fonder of you than of him.*
   —**Studiōsior illō** would have meant, *I am fonder of you than he is.*

Plūs, minus, amplius, longius are often employed as the equivalents of **plūs quam, minus quam,** *etc.* Thus:—

amplius vīgintī urbēs incenduntur, *more than twenty cities are burned (B.G.* vii.15.1)

minus quīnque mīlia prōcessit, *he advanced less than five miles*

3. Note the use of **opīniōne** with Comparatives; as,—

opīniōne celerius venit, *he comes more quickly than expected* (lit. *than opinion*) (*B.G.* ii.3.1)

Instrumental Use of the Ablative

ABLATIVE OF MEANS

218 The Ablative is used to denote *means* or *instrument*; as,—

Alexander sagittā vulnerātus est, *Alexander was wounded by an arrow.*

There are the following special varieties of this Ablative:—

1. **Ūtor, fruor, fungor, potior, vescor,** and their compounds take the Ablative; as,—

dīvitiīs ūtitur, *he uses his wealth* (lit. *he benefits himself by his wealth*)

vītā fruitur, *he enjoys life* (lit. *he enjoys himself by life*)

mūnere fungor, *I perform my duty* (lit. *I busy myself with duty*) (*Aen.* vi.885)

carne vescuntur, *they eat flesh* (lit. *feed themselves by means of*) (*Sall. Jug.* 89)

castrīs potītus est, *he got possession of the camp* (lit. *made himself powerful by the camp*) (*B.G.* ii.26.4)

   a) **Potior** sometimes governs the Genitive. See § 212, 2.

2. With **opus est** (rarely **ūsus est**), *there is need*; as,—

duce nōbīs opus est, *we need a leader*

   a) A Neuter Pronoun or Adjective often stands as subject with **opus** as predicate. Thus:—

hōc mihi opus est, *this is necessary for me*

   b) An ordinary substantive rarely stands as subject. Thus **dux nōbīs opus est** is a rare form of expression.

   c) Note the occasional use of a perfect passive participle with **opus est**; as,—

opus est properātō, *there is need of haste (Mil.* 49)

3. With **nītor, innīxus,** and **frētus;** as,—

nītitur hastā, *he rests on a spear* (lit. *supports himself by a spear*) (*Aen.* vi.760) frētus virtūte, *relying on virtue* (lit. *supported by virtue*)

4. With continērī, cōnsistere, cōnstāre, *consist of*; as,—

nervīs et ossibus continentur, *they consist of sinews and bones* (lit. *they are held together by sinews and bones*) (*N.D.* ii.59)

mortālī cōnsistit corpore mundus, *the world consists of mortal substance* (lit. *holds together by means of, etc.*) (Lucr. v.65)

6. In expressions of the following type:—

quid hōc homine faciās, *what can you do with this man? (Sest. 29)*

quid meā Tulliolā fīet, *what will become of my dear Tullia?* (lit. *what will be done with my dear Tullia?*) (*Fam.* xiv.4.3)

7. In the following special phrases at variance with the ordinary English idiom:—

proeliō contendere, vincere, *to contend, conquer in battle*
proeliō lacessere, *to provoke to battle*
currū vehī, *to ride in a chariot*
pedibus īre, *to go on foot*
castrīs sē tenēre, *to keep in camp*

8. With Verbs of *filling* and Adjectives of *plenty*; as,—

fossās virgultīs complērunt, *they filled the trenches with brush* (*B.G.* iii.18)

a) But plēnus more commonly takes the Genitive. See § 204, 1.

9. Under 'Means' belongs also the Ablative of the Way by Which; as,—

vīnum Tiberī dēvectum, *wine brought down (by) the Tiber* (*Juv.* vii.121)

10. The means may be a person as well as a thing. Thus:—

mīlitibus ā lacū Lemannō ad montem Jūram mūrum perdūcit, *with* (*i.e.* by means of) *his troops he runs a wall from Lake Geneva to Mt. Jura* (*B.G.* i.8.1)

ABLATIVE OF CAUSE

219 The Ablative is used to denote cause; as,—

multa glōriae cupiditāte fēcit, *he did many things on account of his love of glory*

1. So especially with verbs denoting mental states; as, **dēlector, gāudeō, laetor, glōrior, fīdō, cōnfīdō**. Also with **contentus; as,—**

   > **fortūnā amīcī gaudeō,** *I rejoice at the fortune of my friend (i.e. on account of it)*
   >
   > **victōriā suā glōriantur,** *they exult over their victory (B.G. i.14.4)*
   >
   > **nātūrā locī cōnfīdēbant,** *they trusted in the character of their country* (lit. *were confident on account of the character*) *(B.G. iii.9.3)*

   a) **fīdō** and **cōnfīdō** always take the Dative of the person (§ 187, II, a); sometimes the Dative of the thing.

2. As Ablatives of Cause are to be reckoned also such Ablatives as **jussū**, by order of, **injussū**, *without the order*, **rogātū**, *etc.*

ABLATIVE OF MANNER

220 The Ablative with **cum** is used to denote manner; as,—

> **cum gravitāte loquitur,** *he speaks with dignity*

1. The preposition may be absent when the Ablative is modified by an adjective; as,—

   > **magnā gravitāte loquitur,** *he speaks with great dignity*

2. The preposition is regularly absent in the expressions **jūre, injūriā, jocō, vī, fraude, voluntāte, fūrtō, silentiō**.

3. A special variety of the Ablative of Manner denotes that *in accordance with which* or *in pursuance of which* anything is or is done. It is generally used without a preposition. Thus:—

   > **meā sententiā,** *according to my opinion*
   > **suīs mōribus,** *in accordance with their custom*
   > **suā sponte,** *voluntarily, of his (their) own accord*
   > **eā condiciōne,** *on these terms*

ABLATIVE OF ATTENDANT CIRCUMSTANCE

221 The Ablative is often used to denote an *attendant circumstance* of an action or an event; as,—

> **bonīs auspiciīs,** *under good auspices*
>
> **nūlla est altercātiō clāmōribus umquam habita majōribus,** *no debate was ever held under circumstances of greater applause (Brut. 164)*

exstinguitur ingentī lūctū prōvinciae, *he dies under circumstances of great grief on the part of the province* (Tac. A. ii.72)

longō intervāllō sequitur, *he follows at a great distance (Aen.* v.320)

ABLATIVE OF ACCOMPANIMENT

222 The Ablative with **cum** is used with verbs of motion to denote *accompaniment*; as,—

cum comitibus profectus est, *he set out with his attendants*

cum febrī domum rediit, *he returned home with a fever (de Or.* iii.6)

1. In military expressions the Ablative may stand without **cum** when modified by any adjective except a numeral; as,—

omnibus cōpiīs, ingentī exercitū, magnā manū; but usually **cum exercitū, cum duābus legiōnibus**

ABLATIVE OF ASSOCIATION

222^A The Ablative is often used with verbs of *joining, mixing, clinging, exchanging*; also with **assuēscō, cōnsuēscō, assuēfaciō,** and some others to denote *association*; as,—

improbitās scelere jūncta, *badness joined with crime (de Or.* ii.237)

āēr calōre admixtus, *air mixed with heat (N.D.* ii.27);

assuētus labōre, *accustomed to* (lit. *familiarized with) toil (de Or.* iii.58)

pācem bellō permūtant, *they change peace for* (lit. *with) war*

ABLATIVE OF DEGREE OF DIFFERENCE

223 The Ablative is used with comparatives and words involving comparison (as **post, ante, īnfrā, suprā**) to denote the *degree of difference*; as,—

dimidiō minor, *smaller by a half*
tribus pedibus altior, *three feet higher*
paulō post, *a little afterwards*
quō plūra habēmus, eō cupimus ampliōra, *the more we have, the more we want*

ABLATIVE OF QUALITY

224 The Ablative, modified by an adjective, is used to denote *quality;* as,—

> **puella eximiā fōrmā,** *a girl of exceptional beauty*
> (Pl. *Merc.* 13)
>
> **vir singulārī industriā,** *a man of singular industry*
> (Pl. *Vid.* 41)

1. The Ablative of Quality may also be used predicatively; as,—

> **est magnā prūdentiā,** *he is (a man) of great wisdom*
> **bonō animā sunt,** *they are of good courage*

2. In place of the Adjective we sometimes find a limiting Genitive; as,—

> **sunt speciē et colōre taurī,** *they are of the appearance and color of a bull (B.G.* vi.28.1)

3. In poetry the Ablative of Quality sometimes denotes *material;* as,—

> **scopulīs pendentībus antrum,** *a cave of arching rocks (Aen. i.166)*

ABLATIVE OF PRICE

225 With verbs of *buying* and *selling*, price is designated by the Ablative; as—

> **servum quīnque minīs ēmit,** *he bought the slave for five minae*

1. The Ablatives **magnō, plūrimō, parvō, minimō** (by omission of **pretiō**) are used to denote *indefinite price*; as,—

> **aedēs magnō vēndidīt,** *he sold the house for a high price*

2. For the Genitive of Indefinite Price, see § 203, 4.

ABLATIVE OF SPECIFICATION

226 The Ablative of Specification is used to denote that *in respect to which* something is or is done; as,—

> **Helvētiī omnibus Gallīs virtūte praestābant,** *the Helvetians surpassed all the Gauls in valor (B.G.* i.2.2)
> **pede claudus,** *lame in his foot*

1. Note the phrases:—

> **major nātū,** *older* (lit. *greater as to age*)
> **minor nātū,** *younger*

2. Here belongs the use of the Ablative with **dignus**, *worthy*, **indignus**, *unworthy*, and **dignor**, *deem worthy of*; as,—

> **dignī honōre**, *worthy of honor (i.e. in point of honor)*
> **fidē indignī**, *unworthy of confidence*
> **mē dignor honōre**, *I deem myself worthy of honor*
> *(Aen.* i.335)

ABLATIVE ABSOLUTE

227 The Ablative Absolute is grammatically independent of the rest of the sentence. In its commonest form it consists of a noun or pronoun limited by a participle; as,—

> **urbe captā, Aenēās fūgit**, *when the city had been captured, Aeneas fled* (lit. *the city having been captured*)

1. Instead of a participle we often find an adjective or noun; as,—

> **vīvō Caesare rēs pūblica salva erat**, *while Caesar was alive the state was safe* (lit. *Caesar being alive*)
>
> **Tarquiniō rēge, Pythagorās in Italiam vēnit**, *in the reign of Tarquin Pythagoras came into Italy* (lit. *Tarquin being king*)
>
> **Cn. Pompejō, M. Crassō cōnsulibus**, *in the consulship of Gnaeus Pompey and Marcus Crassus* (lit. *P. and C. being consuls*) *(B.G.* iv.1)

2. The Ablative Absolute is generally used in Latin where in English we employ subordinate clauses. Thus the Ablative Absolute may correspond to a clause denoting—

a) Time, as in the foregoing examples.

b) Condition; as,—

> **omnēs virtūtēs jacent, voluptāte dominante**, *all virtues lie prostrate, if pleasure is master* (*Fin.* ii.117)

c) Opposition; as,—

> **perditīs omnibus rēbus, virtūs sē sustentāre potest**, *though everything else is lost, yet Virtue can maintain herself* (*Fam.* vi.1.4)

d) Cause; as,—

> **nūllō adversante rēgnum obtinuit**, *since no one opposed him, he secured the throne* (Tac. *A.* i.2)

e) Attendant circumstance; as,—

> **passīs palmīs pācem petīvērunt**, *with hands outstretched, they sued for peace (B.C. iii.98)*

3. An Infinitive or clause sometimes occurs in the Ablative Absolute construction, especially in Livy and later writers; as,—

> **audītō eum fūgisse**, *when it was heard that he had fled* (Liv. xxviii.7)

4. A noun or pronoun stands in the Ablative Absolute construction only when it denotes a different person or thing from any in the clause in which it stands. Exceptions to this principle are extremely rare.

Locative Uses of the Ablative

ABLATIVE OF PLACE

PLACE WHERE

228 The place where is regularly denoted by the *Ablative with a preposition*; as,—

> **in urbe habitat**, *he dwells in the city*

1. But certain words stand in the Ablative without a preposition: —

a) Names of towns,—except Singulars of the First and Second Declensions (see § 232, 1); as,—

> **Carthāginī**, *at Carthage*
> **Athēnis**, *at Athens*
> **Vejīs**, *at Veii*

b) The general words **locō**, **locīs**, **parte**; also many words modified by **tōtus** or even by other Adjectives; as,—

> **hōc locō**, *at this place*
> **tōtīs castrīs**, *in the whole camp*

c) The special words: **forīs**, *out of doors*; **rūrī**, *in the country*, **terrā marīque**, *on land and sea.*

d) The poets freely omit the preposition with any word denoting place; as,—

> **stant lītore puppēs**, *the sterns rest on the beach* (Aen. vi.901)

PLACE FROM WHICH[46]

229 Place from which is regularly denoted by the *Ablative with a preposition*; as,—

> **ab Italiā profectus est**, *he set out from Italy*
> **ex urbe rediit**, *he returned from the city*

1. But certain words stand in the Ablative without a preposition: —

   a) Names of towns and small islands; as,—

   > **Rōma profectus est**, *he set out from Rome*
   > **Rhodō revertit**, *he returned from Rhodes*

   b) **domō**, *from home*; **rūre**, *from the country.*

   c) Freely in poetry; as,—

   > **Italiā dēcessit**, *he withdrew from Italy*

2. With names of towns, **ab** is used to mean *from the vicinity of*, or to denote the point *whence distance is measured;* as,—

   > **ā Gergoviā discessit**, *he withdrew from the vicinity of Gergovia (B.G.* vii.59.1)

   > **ā Rōmā X mīlia aberat**, *he was ten miles distant from Rome*

   Urbe and **oppidō**, when standing in apposition with a town name, are accompanied by a preposition; as,—

   > **Curibus ex oppidō Sabīnōrum**, *from Cures, a town of the Sabines*

ABLATIVE OF TIME

TIME AT WHICH

230 The Ablative is used to denote the time *at which*; as,—

> **quārtā hōrā mortuus est**, *he died at the fourth hour*
> **annō septuāgēsimō cōnsul creātus**, *elected consul in his seventieth year*

1. Any word denoting a period of time may stand in this construction, particularly **annus**, **vēr**, **aestās**, **hiems**, **diēs**, **nox**, **hōra**, **comitia** (*Election Day*), **lūdī** (*the Games*), *etc.*

2. Words not denoting time require the preposition **in**, unless accompanied by a modifier. Thus:—

   > **in pāce**, *in peace*; **in bellō**, *in war*
   > but **secundō bellō Pūnicō**, *in the second Punic War*

---

46   Place from which, though strictly a Genuine Ablative use, is treated here for sake of convenience.

3. Expressions like **in eō tempore, in summa senectūte**, take the preposition because they denote *situation* rather than *time*.

231 Time *within which* is denoted by the Ablative either *with* or *without a preposition*; as,—

stella Sāturnī trīgintā annīs cursum cōnficit, *the planet Saturn completes its orbit within thirty years* (*N.D.* ii.52)

ter in annō, thrice in the course of the year

1. Occasionally the Ablative denotes *duration of time*; as,—

bienniō prōsperās rēs habuit, *for two years he had a prosperous administration* (Tac. *Agr.* 14)

The Locative

232 The Locative case occurs chiefly in the following words:—

1. Regularly in the Singular of names of towns and small islands of the first and second declensions, to denote the place *in which*; as,—

Rōmae, *at Rome*   **Corinthī,** *at Corinth*
Rhodī, *at Rhodes*

2. In the following special forms:—

domī, *at home*   **humī**, *on the ground*
bellī, *in war*   **mīlitiae**, *in war*
vesperī, *at evening*   **herī**, *yesterday*

3. Note the phrase **pendēre animī**, lit. *to be in suspense in one's mind.*

4. For **urbs** and **oppidum** in apposition with a Locative, see § 169, 4.

SYNTAX OF ADJECTIVES

233
1. The word with which an Adjective agrees is called its Subject.

2. **Attributive and Predicate Adjectives**. An Attributive Adjective is one that limits its subject directly; as,—

> **vir sapiēns,** *a wise man*

A Predicate Adjective is one that limits its subject through the medium of a verb (usually **esse**); as,—

> **vir est sapiēns,** *the man is wise*
> **vir vidēbātur sapiēns,** *the man seemed wise*
> **vir jūdicātus est sapiēns,** *the man was judged wise*
> **hunc virum sapientem jūdicāvimus,** *we adjudged this man wise*

3. Participles and Adjective Pronouns have the construction of Adjectives.

Agreement of Adjectives

234
Agreement with One Noun. When an Adjective limits one noun it agrees with it in Gender, Number, and Case.

1. Two Adjectives in the Singular may limit a noun in the Plural, as; **prīma et vīcēsima legiōnēs,** *the first and twentieth legions* (Tac. A. i.37).

2. A Predicate Adjective may stand in the Neuter when its Subject is Masculine or Feminine and denotes a thing; as,—

> **omnium rērum mors est extrēmum,** *death is the end of all things (Fam.* vi.21.1)

235
Agreement with Two or More Nouns

Agreement as to Number

1. When the Adjective is Attributive, it regularly agrees in number with the nearest noun; as,—

> **pater tuus et māter,** *your father and mother*
> **eadem alacritās et studium,** *the same eagerness and zeal (B.G.* iv.24.4)

2. When the Adjective is Predicative, it is regularly Plural; as,—

> **pāx et concordia sunt pulchrae**, *peace and concord are glorious*

Agreement as to Gender

1. When the Adjective is Attributive, it regularly agrees in gender with the nearest noun; as,—

> **rēs operae multae ac labōris**, *a matter of much effort and labor (B.G. v.11.5)*

2. When the Adjective is Predicative—

    a) If the nouns are of the same gender, the Adjective agrees with them in gender; as,—

> **pater et fīlius captī sunt**, *father and son were captured*

    Yet with feminine abstract nouns, the Adjective is more frequently Neuter; as,—

> **stultitia et timiditās fugienda sunt**, *folly and cowardice must be shunned (F. iii.39)*

    b) If the nouns are of different gender; then,—

      i) In case they denote persons, the Adjective is Masculine; as,—

> **pater et māter mortuī sunt**, *the father and mother have died*

      ii) In case they denote things, the Adjective is Neuter; as,—

> **honōrēs et victōriae fortuīta sunt**, *honors and victories are accidental*

      iii) In case they include both persons and things, the Adjective is,—

      iv) Sometimes Masculine; as,—

> **domus, uxor, līberī inventī sunt**, *home, wife, and children are secured (Ter. And. 891)*

      v) Sometimes Neuter; as,—

> **parentēs, līberōs, domōs vīlia habēre**, *to hold parents, children, houses cheap*

      vi) Sometimes it agrees with the nearest noun; as,—

> **populī prōvinciaeque līberātae sunt**, *nations and provinces were liberated*

c) **Construction according to Sense.** Sometimes an Adjective does not agree with a noun according to strict grammatical form, but according to sense; as,—

> **pars bēstiīs objectī sunt,** *part (of the men) were thrown to beasts* (Sall. *Jug.* 14.15)

Adjectives Used Substantively

236 1. **Plural Adjectives Used Substantively.** Adjectives are quite freely used as Substantives in the Plural. The Masculine denotes persons; the Neuter denotes things; as,—

doctī, *scholars*	**parva,** *small things*
malī, *the wicked*	**magna,** *great things*
Graecī, *the Greeks*	**ūtilia,** *useful things*
nostrī, *our men*	

2. Neuter Plural Adjectives thus used are confined mainly to the Nominative and Accusative cases. Such forms as **magnōrum, omnium; magnīs, omnibus,** would ordinarily lead to ambiguity; yet where there is no ambiguity, they sometimes occur; as,—

> **parvīs compōnere magna,** *to compare great things with small*

Otherwise the Latin says: **magnārum rērum, magnīs rēbus,** *etc.*

237 **Singular Adjectives Used Substantively.** Adjectives are less freely used as Substantives in the Singular than in the Plural.

1. Masculine Adjectives occur only occasionally in this use; as,—

> **probus invidet nēminī,** *the honest man envies nobody*

a) Usually **vir, homō,** or some similar word is employed; as,—

> **homō doctus,** *a scholar*
> **vir Rōmānus,** *a Roman*

b) But when limited by a pronoun any adjective may be so used; as,—

> **hīc doctus,** *this scholar*
> **doctus quīdam,** *a certain scholar*

2. Neuters are likewise infrequent; as,—

vērum, *truth*
jūstum, *justice*
honestum, *virtue*

a) This substantive use of Neuter Singulars is commonest in the construction of the Genitive of the Whole, and after Prepositions; as,—

aliquid vērī, *something true*
nihil novī, *nothing new*
in mediō, *in the midst*

238 From Adjectives which, like the above, occasionally admit the substantive use, must be carefully distinguished certain others which have become nouns; as,—

adversārius, *opponent*	**hīberna**, *winter quarters*
aequālis, *contemporary*	**propinquus**, *relative*
amīcus, *friend*	**socius**, *partner*
cognātus, *kinsman*	**sodālis**, *comrade*
vīcīnus, *neighbor*; *etc.*	

Adjectives with the Force of Adverbs

239 The Latin often uses an Adjective where the English idiom employs an Adverb or an adverbial phrase; as,—

senātus frequēns convēnit, *the senate assembled in great numbers*
fuit assiduus mēcum, *he was constantly with me*

Comparatives and Superlatives

240 1. The Comparative often corresponds to the English Positive with 'rather,' 'somewhat,' 'too'; as,—

senectūs est loquācior, *old age is rather talkative (de Sen. 55)*

2. So the Superlative often corresponds to the Positive with 'very'; as,—

vir fortissimus, *a very brave man*

3. **Strengthening Words. Vel** and **quam** are often used with the Superlative as strengthening particles, **vel** with the force of 'very,' and **quam** with the force of 'as possible'; as,—

vel maximus, *the very greatest*
quam maximae cōpiae, *as great forces as possible*

4. Phrases of the type '*more rich than brave*' regularly take the Comparative in both members; as,—

> **exercitus erat dītior quam fortior,** *the army was more rich than brave* (Liv. xxxix.1)

Other Special Uses

241

1. Certain Adjectives may be used to denote *a part of an object*, chiefly **prīmus, extrēmus, summus, medius, īnfimus, īmus**; as,—

> **summus mōns,** *the top of the mountain*
> **extrēmā hieme,** *in the last part of the winter*

2. **Prior, prīmus, ultimus,** and **postrēmus** are frequently equivalent to a relative clause; as,—

> **prīmus eam vīdī,** *I was the first who saw her*
> **ultimus dēcessit,** *he was the last who withdrew*

3. When **multus** and another adjective both limit the same noun **et** is generally used; as,—

> **multae et magnae cōgitātiōnēs,** *many (and) great thoughts*

SYNTAX OF PRONOUNS

Personal Pronouns

242

1. The Personal Pronouns as subjects of verbs are, as a rule, not expressed except for the purpose of *emphasis, contrast,* or *clearness.* Thus ordinarily:—

> **videō,** *I see;* **amat,** *he loves*

But **ego tē videō, et tū mē vidēs,** *I see you, and you see me.*

2. The Genitives **meī, tuī, nostrī, vestrī** are used only as Objective Genitives; **nostrum** and **vestrum** as Genitives of the Whole. Thus:—

> **memor tuī,** *mindful of you*
> **dēsīderium vestrī,** *longing for you*
> **nēmō vestrum,** *no one of you*

   a) But **nostrum** and **vestrum** are regularly used in the place of the Possessive in the phrases **omnium nostrum, omnium vestrum.**

3. The First Plural is often used for the First Singular of Pronouns and Verbs. Compare the Eng. editorial 'we.'

4. When two Verbs govern the same object, the Latin does not use a pronoun with the second, as is the rule in English. Thus:—

> **virtūs amīcitiās conciliat et cōnservat**, *virtue establishes friendships and maintains them* (not **eās cōnservat**) *(Lael. 100)*

Possessive Pronouns

243 1. The Possessive Pronouns, as a rule, are not employed except for the purpose of *clearness*. Thus:—

> **patrem amō**, *I love my father*
> **dē fīliī morte flēbās**, *you wept for the death of your son*

But—

> **dē morte fīliī meī flēbās**, *you wept for the death of my son*

a) When expressed merely for the sake of clearness, the possessive usually stands after its noun; but in order to indicate emphasis or contrast, it precedes; as,—

> **suā manū līberōs occīdit**, *with his own hand he slew his children*
>
> **meā quidem sententiā**, *in my opinion at least*

2. Sometimes the Possessive Pronouns are used with the force of an Objective Genitive; as,—

> **metus vester**, *fear of you*
> **dēsīderium tuum**, *longing for you*

3. For special emphasis, the Latin employs **ipsīus** or **ipsōrum**, in apposition with the Genitive idea implied in the Possessive; as,—

> **meā ipsīus operā**, *by my own help*
> **nostrā ipsōrum operā**, *by our own help*

a) So sometimes other Genitives; as,—

> **meā ūnīus operā**, *by the assistance of me alone*

Reflexive Pronouns

244 1. The Reflexive Pronoun **sē** and the Possessive Reflexive **suus** have a double use:—

I. They may refer to the subject of the clause (either principal or subordinate) in which they stand,—'Direct Reflexives'; as,—

sē amant, *they love themselves*

suōs amīcōs adjuvāt, *he helps his own friends*

eum ōrāvī, ut sē servāret, *I besought him to save himself*

II. They may stand in a subordinate clause and refer to the subject of the principal clause,—'Indirect Reflexives'; as,—

mē ōrāvit ut sē dēfenderem, *he besought me to defend him* (lit. *that I defend himself*) (*Phil.* ii.45);

mē ōrāvērunt, ut fortūnārum suārum dēfēnsiōnem susciperem, *they besought me to undertake the defense of their fortunes* (*Div. Caec.* 2).

a) The Indirect Reflexive is mainly restricted to those clauses which express the thought, not of the author, but of the subject of the principal clause.

2. The Genitive **suī** is regularly employed, like **meī** and **tuī**, as an Objective Genitive, *e.g.* **oblītus suī**, *forgetful of himself*; but it occasionally occurs—particularly in post-Augustan writers—in place of the Possessive **suus**; as, **fruitur fāmā suī**, *he enjoys his own fame.*

3. **Sē** and **suus** are sometimes used in the sense, *one's self, one's own*, where the reference is not to any particular person; as,—

sē amāre, *to love one's self*

suum genium propitiāre, *to propitiate one's own genius* (Tac. *Dial.* 9)

4. **Suus** sometimes occurs in the meaning *his own, their own,* etc., referring not to the subject but to an oblique case; as,—

Hannibalem suī cīvēs ē cīvitāte ējēcērunt, *his own fellow-citizens drove out Hannibal* (*Sest.* 142)

a) This usage is particularly frequent in combination with **quisque**; as,—

suus quemque error vexat, *his own error troubles each* (*Rosc. Am.* 67)

5. The Reflexives for the first and second persons are supplied by the oblique cases of **ego** and **tū** (§ 85); as,—

vōs dēfenditis, *you defend yourselves*

Reciprocal Pronouns

245
1. The Latin has no special reciprocal pronoun ('each other'), but expresses the reciprocal notion by the phrases: **inter nōs, inter vōs, inter sē**; as,—

Belgae obsidēs inter sē dedērunt, *the Belgae gave each other hostages* (lit. *among themselves*) (*B.G.* ii.1.1);

amāmus inter nōs, *we love each other;*

Gallī inter sē cohortātī sunt, *the Gauls exhorted each other* (*B.G.* vi.8.1).

a) Note that the Object is not expressed in sentences of this type.

Demonstrative Pronouns

Hīc, Ille, Iste

246
1. Where **hīc** and **ille** are used in contrast, **hīc** usually refers to the latter of two objects, and **ille** to the former.

2. **Hīc** and **ille** are often used in the sense of 'the following'; as,—

Themistoclēs hīs verbīs epistulam mīsit, *Themistocles sent a letter (couched) in the following words (Nep. Them. 9)*

illud intellegō, omnium ōra in mē conversa esse, *I understand this, that the faces of all are turned toward me* (Sall. *Jug.* 85.5)

3. **Ille** often means *the famous*; as, **Solōn ille,** *the famous Solon.*

4. **Iste** frequently involves contempt; as, **iste homō,** *that fellow!*

5. The above pronouns, along with **is,** are usually attracted to the gender of a predicate noun; as, **hīc est honor, meminisse officium suum,** *this is an honor, to be mindful of one's duty* (*Pl. Tr.* 697).

Is

247

1. **Is** often serves as the antecedent of the relative **quī**. Thus:—

> **Maximum, eum quī Tarentum recēpit, dīlēxī**, *I loved Maximus, the man who retook Tarentum (de Sen.* 10).

a) Closely akin to this usage is **is** in the sense of *such* (= **tālis**); as,—

> **nōn sum is quī terrear**, *I am not such a person as to be frightened (B.G.* v.30.2)

b) Note the phrase **id quod**, where **id** stands in apposition with an entire clause; as,—

> **nōn suspicābātur (id quod nunc sentiet) satis multōs testēs nōbīs reliquōs esse**, *he did not suspect (a thing which he will now perceive) that we had witnesses enough left (Verr.* i.36)

Yet **quod** alone, without preceding **id**, sometimes occurs in this use.

2. **Is** also in all cases serves as the personal pronoun of the third person, '*he*,' '*she*,' '*it*,' '*they*,' '*them*.'

3. When the English uses '*that of*,' '*those of*,' to avoid repetition of the noun, the Latin omits the pronoun: as,—

> **in exercitū Sullae et posteā in Crassī fuerat**, *he had been in the army of Sulla and afterward in that of Crassus*

> **nūllae mē fābulae dēlectant nisi Plautī**, *no plays delight me except those of Plautus*

4. Note the phrases **et is**, **et ea**, *etc.*, in the sense: *and that too;* as,—

> **vincula, et ea sempiterna**, *imprisonment, and that too permanently (Cat.* iv.7)

Īdem

248

1. **Īdem** in apposition with the subject or object often has the force of *also, likewise*; as,—

> **quod idem mihi contigit**, *which likewise happened to me* (lit. *which, the same thing*) (*Ac.* ii.52)

> **bonus vir, quem eundem sapientem appellāmus**, *a good man, whom we call also wise (Lael.* 65)

For **īdem atque (ac)**, *the same as*, see § 341, 1. c.

Ipse

249

1. **Ipse**, literally *self*, acquires its special force from the context; as,—

    eō ipsō diē, *on that very day*
    ad ipsam rīpam, *close to the bank*
    ipsō terrōre, *by mere fright* (B.G. iv.33.1)
    valvae sē ipsae aperuērunt, *the doors opened of their own accord* (*Div.* i.74)
    ipse aderat, *he was present in person*

2. The reflexive pronouns are often emphasized by the addition of **ipse**, but ipse in such cases, instead of standing in apposition with the reflexive, more commonly agrees with the subject; as,—

    sēcum ipsī loquuntur, *they talk with themselves*
    sē ipse continēre nōn potest, *he cannot contain himself*

3. **Ipse** is also used as an Indirect Reflexive for the purpose of *marking a contrast or avoiding an ambiguity*; as,—

    Persae pertimuērunt nē Alcibiadēs ab ipsīs dēscīsceret et cum suīs in grātiam redīret, *the Persians feared that Alcibiades would break with them and become reconciled with his countrymen* (Nep. *Alc.* 5)

    ea molestissimē ferre dēbent hominēs quae ipsōrum culpā contrācta sunt, *men ought to chafe most over those things which have been brought about by their own fault* (as opposed to the fault of others) (Q.Fr. i.1.2)

Relative Pronouns

250 Agreement

1. The Relative Pronoun agrees with its antecedent in Gender, Number, and Person, but its case is determined by its construction in the clause in which it stands; as,—

    mulier quam vidēbāmus, *the woman whom we saw*
    bona quibus fruimur, *the blessings which we enjoy*

2. Where the antecedent is compound, the same principles for number and gender prevail as in case of predicate adjectives under similar conditions (see § 235, B, 2). Thus:—

    pater et fīlius, qui captī sunt, *the father and son who were captured*

stultitia et timiditās quae fugienda sunt, *folly and cowardice which must be shunned*

honōrēs et victōriae quae sunt fortuīta, *honors and victories, which are accidental*

3. The Relative regularly agrees with a predicate noun (either Nominative or Accusative) instead of its antecedent; as,—

carcer, quae lautumiae vocantur, *the prison, which is called Lautumiae (Verr. v.143)*

Belgae, quae est tertia pars, *the Belgians, who are the third part (B.G. ii.1.1)*

4. Sometimes the Relative takes its gender and number from the meaning of its antecedent; as,—

pars quī bēstiīs objectī sunt, *a part (of the men) who were thrown to beasts*

5. Occasionally the Relative is attracted into the case of its antecedent; as,—

nātus eō patre quō dīxī, *born of the father that I said*

251 Antecedent

1. The antecedent of the Relative is sometimes omitted; as,—

quī nātūram sequitur sapiēns est, *he who follows Nature is wise*

2. The antecedent may be implied in a possessive pronoun (or rarely an adjective); as,—

nostra quī remānsimus caedēs, *the slaughter of us who remained (Cat. i.7)*

servīlī tumultū, quōs ūsus ac disciplīna sublevārunt, *at the uprising of the slaves, whom experience and discipline assisted* (**servīlī** = **servōrum**) *(B.G. i.40)*

3. Sometimes the antecedent is repeated with the Relative; as,—

erant itinera duo, quibus itineribus, *there were two routes, by which (routes) (B.G. i.6)*

4. Incorporation of Antecedent in Relative Clause. The antecedent is often incorporated in the relative clause. Thus:—

a) When the relative clause stands first; as,—

quam quisque nōvit artem, in hāc sē exerceat, *let each one practice the branch which he knows (Tusc. Disp. i.41)*

b) When the antecedent is an appositive; as,—

nōn longē ā Tolōsātium fīnibus absunt, quae cīvitās est in prōvinciā, *they are not far from the borders of the Tolosates, a state which is in our province (B.G. i.10.1)*

c) When the logical antecedent is a superlative; as,—

Themistoclēs dē servīs suīs, quem habuit fidēlissimum, mīsit, *Themistocles sent the most trusty slave he had* (Nep. *Them.* 4.3)

d) In expressions of the following type—

quā es prūdentiā; quae tua est prūdentia, *such is your prudence* (lit. *of which prudence you are; which is your prudence*)

5. The Relative is never omitted in Latin as it is in English. Thus *the boy I saw* must be **puer quem vīdī**.

6. The Relative is used freely in Latin, particularly at the beginning of a sentence, where in English we employ a demonstrative; as,—

quō factum est, *by this it happened*
quae cum ita sint, *since this is so*
quibus rēbus cognitīs, *when these things became known*

7. The Relative introducing a subordinate clause may belong grammatically to a clause which is subordinate to the one it introduces; as,—

numquam dignē satis laudārī philosophia poterit, cui quī pāreat, omne tempus aetātis sine molestiā possit dēgere, *philosophy can never be praised enough, since he who obeys her can pass every period of life without annoyance* (lit. *he who obeys which, etc.*) (*de Sen.* 2)

Here **cui** introduces the subordinate clause **possit** and connects it with **philosophia**; but **cui** is governed by **pāreat**, which is subordinate to **possit**.

Indefinite Pronouns

252

1. **Quis,** *any one,* is the weakest of the Indefinites, and stands usually in combination with **sī, nisi, nē, num**; as,—

sī quis putat, *if any one thinks*

2. **Aliquis** (adj. **aliquī**) is more definite than **quis**, and corresponds usually to the English *some one, somebody, some*; as,—

> **nunc aliquis dīcat mihī**, *now let somebody tell me*
> **utinam modo agātur aliquid**, *oh that something may be done*

3. **Quīdam**, *a certain one*, is still more definite than **aliquis**; as,—

> **homō quīdam**, *a certain man (i.e., one whom I have in mind)*

a) **Quīdam** (with or without **quasi**, *as if*) is sometimes used in the sense: *a sort of, kind of*; as,—

> **cognātiō quaedam**, *a sort of relationship (Arch. 2)*
> **mors est quasi quaedam migrātiō**, *death is a kind of transfer as it were (Tusc. Disp. i.27)*

4. **Quisquam**, *any one, any one whoever* (more general than **quis**), and its corresponding adjective **ūllus**, *any*, occur mostly in negative and conditional sentences, in interrogative sentences implying a negative, and in clauses of comparison; as,—

> **jūstitia numquam nocet cuiquam**, *justice never harms anybody (F. i.50)*
> **sī quisquam, Catō sapiēns fuit**, *if anybody was ever wise, Cato was (Lael. 9)*
> **potestne quisquam sine perturbātiōne animī īrāscī**, *can anybody be angry without excitement? (Tusc. Disp. iv.54)*
> **sī ūllō modō poterit**, *if it can be done in any way (Att. xii.23.1)*
> **taetrior hīc tyrannus fuit quam quisquam superiōrum**, *he was a viler tyrant than any of his predecessors (Verr. iv.123)*

5. **Quisque**, *each one*, is used especially under the following circumstances:—

a) In connection with **suus**. See § 244, 4, a.

b) In connection with a Relative or Interrogative Pronoun; as,—

> **quod cuique obtigit, id teneat**, *what falls to each, that let him hold (Off. i.21)*

c) In connection with superlatives; as,—

optimus quisque, *all the best* (lit. *each best one*)

d) With ordinal numerals; as,—

quīntō quōque annō, *every four years* (lit. *each fifth year*) (*Verr.* ii.139)

6. **Nēmō**, *no one*, in addition to its other uses, stands regularly with adjectives used substantively; as,—

nēmō mortālis, *no mortal*

nēmō Rōmānus, *no Roman* (Liv. viii.30.3)

Pronominal Adjectives

253

1. **Alius**, *another*, and **alter**, *the other*, are often used correlatively; as,—

aliud loquitur, aliud sentit, *he says one thing, he thinks another*

aliī resistunt, aliī fugiunt, *some resist, others flee*

alter exercitum perdidit, alter vēndidit, *one ruined the army, the other sold it* (*Planc.* 86)

alterī sē in montem recēpērunt, alterī ad impedīmenta sē contulērunt, *the one party retreated to the mountain, the others betook themselves to the baggage* (*B.G.* i.26.1)

2. Where the English says *one does one thing, another another*, the Latin uses a more condensed form of statement; as,—

alius aliud amat, *one likes one thing, another another*

aliud aliīs placet, *one thing pleases some, another others*

a) So sometimes with adverbs; as,—

aliī aliō fugiunt, *some flee in one direction, others in another*

3. The Latin also expresses the notion '*each other*' by means of **alius** repeated; as,—

Gallī alius alium cohortātī sunt, *the Gauls encouraged each other*

4. **Cēterī** means *the rest, all the others*; as,—

cēterīs praestāre, *to be superior to all the others*

5. **Reliquī** means *the others* in the sense of *the rest, those remaining*,—hence is the regular word with numerals; as,—

reliquī sex, *the six others*

6. **Nescio quis** forms a compound indefinite pronoun with the force of *some one or other*; as,—

> **causidicus nescio quis,** *some pettifogger or other (de Or.* i.202)
> **mīsit nescio quem,** *he sent some one or other*
> **nescio quō pactō,** *somehow or other*

SYNTAX OF VERBS

Agreement

With One Subject

254 1. **Agreement in Number and Person.** A Finite Verb agrees with its subject in Number and Person; as,—

> **vōs vidētis,** *you see*
> **pater fīliōs īnstituit,** *the father trains his sons*

2. **Agreement in Gender.** In the compound forms of the verb the participle regularly agrees with its subject in gender; as,—

> **sēditiō repressa est,** *the mutiny was checked*

3. But when a predicate noun is of different gender or number from its subject, the verb usually agrees with its nearest substantive; as,—

> **Tarquiniī māterna patria erat,** *Tarquinii was his native country on his mother's side* (Liv. i.34.7)
> **nōn omnis error stultitia est dīcenda,** *not every error is to be called folly (Div.* ii.90)

a) Less frequently the verb agrees with an appositive; as,—

> **Coriolī, oppidum Volscōrum, captum est,** *Corioli, a town of the Volsci, was captured* (Liv. ii.33.8)

4. **Construction according to Sense.** Sometimes the verb agrees with its subject according to sense instead of strict grammatical form. Thus:—

a) In Number; as,—

> **multitūdō hominum convēnerant,** *a crowd of men had gathered*

b) In Gender; as,—

> **duo mīlia crucibus adfīxī sunt**, *two thousand (men) were crucified* (Curt. iii.2.5)

With Two or More Subjects

255

1. **Agreement in Number**. With two or more subjects the verb is regularly plural; as,—

> **pater et fīlius mortuī sunt**, *the father and son died*

2. But sometimes the verb agrees with the nearest subject, namely: —

   a) When the verb precedes both subjects or stands between them; as,—

   > **mortuus est pater et fīlius**
   > **pater mortuus est et fīlius**

   b) When the subjects are connected by **aut; aut ... aut; vel ... vel; neque ... neque**; as,—

   > **neque pater neque fīlius mortuus est**, *neither father nor son died*

3. When the different subjects are felt together as constituting a whole, the singular is used; as,—

   > **temeritās ignōrātiōque vitiōsa est**, *rashness and ignorance are bad* (F. iii.72)

   a) This is regularly the case in **senātus populusque Rōmānus**.

4. **Agreement in Person**. With compound subjects of different persons the verb always takes the *first* person rather than the *second*, and the *second* rather than the *third*; as,—

   > **sī tū et Tullia valētis, ego et Cicerō valēmus**, *if you and Tullia are well, Cicero and I are well* (Fam. xiv.5.1)

5. **Agreement in Gender**. With subjects of different genders the participle in the compound tenses follows the same principles as laid down for predicate adjectives. See § 235, B, 2.

Voices

256

1. The Passive Voice sometimes retains traces of its original middle or reflexive meaning; as,—

> **ego nōn patiar eum dēfendī**, *I shall not allow him to defend himself*

2. In imitation of Greek usage many perfect passive participles are used by the poets as indirect middles, *i.e.* the subject is viewed as acting not upon itself, but as doing something *in his own interest*; as,—

> **vēlātus tempora**, *having veiled his temples* (Ov. *Met.* v.110)

a) Occasionally finite forms of the verb are thus used; as,—

> **tunicā indūcitur artūs**, *he covers his limbs with a tunic (Aen.* viii.457)

3. Intransitive Verbs may be used impersonally in the passive; as,—

> **curritur**, *people run* (lit. *it is run*)
>
> **ventum est**, *he (they, etc.) came* (lit. *it was come*)

Tenses

Tenses of the Indicative

257

1. The Latin tenses express two distinct notions:—

a) The *period of time* to which the action belongs: Present, Past, or Future.

b) The *kind of action*: Undefined, Going on, or Completed.

The Latin with its six tenses is able to express each of the three kinds of action for each of the three periods of time (making practically nine tenses). It does this by employing certain tenses in more than one way, as may be seen by the following table:—

KIND OF ACTION	PERIOD OF TIME		
	PRESENT	PAST	FUTURE
UNDEFINED	Present: **scrībō** *I write.*	Historical Perfect: **scrīpsī** *I wrote.*	Future: **scrībam** *I shall write.*
GOING ON	Present: **scrībō** *I am writing.*	Imperfect: **scrībēbam** *I was writing.*	Future: **scrībam** *I shall be writing.*
COMPLETED	Present Perfect: **scrīpsī** *I have written.*	Pluperfect: **scrīpseram** *I had written.*	Future Perfect: **scrīpserō** *I shall have written.*

2. It will be seen that the Present may express Undefined action or action Going on; so also the Future. The Perfect likewise has a double use, according as it denotes action Completed in present time (Present Perfect) or Undefined action belonging to past time (Historical Perfect).

Principal and Historical Tenses

258 Tenses which denote Present or Future time are called **Principal** (or Primary) Tenses, those which denote Past time are called **Historical** (or Secondary).

The Principal Tenses of the Indicative are: Present, Future, Present Perfect, Future Perfect.

The Historical Tenses are: Imperfect, Historical Perfect, Pluperfect.

Present Indicative

259 Besides the two uses indicated in the table, the Present Indicative presents the following peculiarities:—

1. It is used to denote *a general truth*, *i.e.* something true not merely in the present but at all times ('Gnomic Present'); as,—

   virtūs conciliat amīcitiās et cōnservat, *virtue establishes ties of friendship and maintains them* (*i.e.* always does so) *(Lael.* 100)

2. It is used of an attempted action ('Conative Present'); as,—

   dum vītant vitia, in contrāria currunt, *while they try to avoid* (**vītant**) *vices, they rush into opposite ones* (Hor. *Sat.* i.2.24)

3. In lively narration the Present is often used of a past action ('Historical Present'); as,—

   Caesar imperat magnum numerum obsidum, *Caesar demanded a large number of hostages* (lit. *demands*) (*B.G.* vii.90.2)

4. In combination with **jam, jam diū, jam prīdem**, and similar words, the Present is frequently used of an action originating in the past and continuing in the present; as,—

   jam prīdem cupiō tē vīsere, *I have long been desiring to visit you* (*i.e.* I desire and have long desired) *(Att.* ii.5.1)

Imperfect Indicative

260

1. The Imperfect primarily denotes action *going on in past time*; as,—

   librum legēbam, *I was reading a book.*

   a) This force makes the Imperfect especially adapted to serve as the tense of *description* (as opposed to mere *narration*).

2. From the notion of action *going on*, there easily develops the notion of *repeated* or *customary* action; as,—

   lēgātōs interrogābat, *he kept asking the envoys*

   C. Duīlium vidēbam puer, *as a boy I often used to see Gaius Duilius (de Sen.* 44)

3. The Imperfect often denotes an attempted action ('Conative Imperfect') or an action as beginning ('Inceptive Imperfect'); as,—

   hostēs nostrōs intrā mūnītiōnēs prōgredī prohibēbant, *the enemy tried to prevent* (**prohibēbant**) *our men from advancing within the fortifications* ('Conative') (*B.G.* v.9.6)

   ad proelium sē expediēbant, *they were beginning to get ready for battle* ('Inceptive')

4. The Imperfect, with **jam, jam diū, jam dūdum**, *etc.*, is sometimes used of an action which had been continuing some time; as,—

   domicilium Rōmae multōs jam annōs habēbat, *he had had his residence at Rome for many years* (*i.e.* he had it at this time and had long had it) (*Arch.* 7)

Future Indicative

261

1. The Latin is much more exact in the use of the Future than is the English. We say: '*If he comes, I shall be glad,*' where we really mean: '*If he shall come,*' *etc.* In such cases the Latin rarely admits the Present, but generally employs the Future.

2. Sometimes the Future has Imperative force; as, **dīcēs**, *say!*

Perfect Indicative

262 A. **Present Perfect**. Several Present Perfects denote the *state resulting from a completed act*, and so seem equivalent to the Present; as,—

nōvī, cognōvī, *I know* (lit. *I have become acquainted with*)
cōnsuēvī, *I am wont* (lit. *I have become accustomed*)

B. **Historical Perfect**. The Historical Perfect is the tense of *narration* (as opposed to the Imperfect, the tense of *description*); as,—

Rēgulus in senātum vēnit, mandāta exposuit, reddī captivōs negāvit esse ūtile, *Regulus came into the Senate, set forth his commission, said it was useless for captives to be returned (Off.* iii.100).

1. Occasionally the Historical Perfect is used of a general truth ('Gnomic Perfect').

Pluperfect Indicative

263 The Latin Pluperfect, like the English Past Perfect, denotes an act *completed in the past*; as,—

Caesar Rhēnum trānsīre dēcrēverat, sed nāvēs deerant, *Caesar had decided to cross the Rhine, but had no boats (B.G.* vii.4.4).

a) In those verbs whose Perfect has Present force (§ 262, A), the Pluperfect has the force of an Imperfect; as,—

nōveram, *I knew.*

Future Perfect Indicative

264 The Future Perfect denotes an action *completed in future time*. Thus:—

scrībam epistulam, cum redieris, *I will write the letter when you have returned* (lit. *when you shall have returned*).

a) The Latin is much more exact in the use of the Future Perfect than the English, which commonly employs the Present Perfect instead of the Future Perfect.

b) In those verbs whose Perfect has Present force (§ 262, A) the Future Perfect has the force of a Future; as,—

nōverō, *I shall know.*

Epistolary Tenses

265 In letters the writer often uses tenses which are not appropriate at the time of writing, but which will be so at the time when his letter is received; he thus employs the Imperfect and the Perfect for the Present, and the Pluperfect for the Present Perfect; as,—

> **nihil habēbam quod scrīberem, neque enim novī quidquam audieram et ad tuās omnēs epistulās jam rescrīpseram,** *I have nothing to write, for I have heard no news and have already answered all your letters (Att. ix.10.1).*

Tenses of the Subjunctive

266 A. **In Independent sentences**. See §§ 272-280.

B. **In Dependent Sentences**. In dependent sentences the tenses of the subjunctive usually conform to the so-called

Sequence of Tenses

267 1. In the Subjunctive the Present and Perfect are Principal tenses, the Imperfect and Pluperfect, Historical.

2. By the Sequence of Tenses Principal tenses are followed by Principal, Historical by Historical. Thus:—

PRINCIPAL SEQUENCE,—

videō quid faciās, *I see what you are doing.*
vidēbō quid faciās, *I shall see what you are doing.*
vīderō quid faciās, *I shall have seen what you are doing.*
videō quid fēcerīs, *I see what you have done.*
vidēbō quid fēcerīs, *I shall see what you have done.*
vīderō quid fēcerīs, *I shall have seen what you have done.*

HISTORICAL SEQUENCE,—

vidēbam quid facerēs, *I saw what you were doing.*
vīdī quid facerēs, *I saw what you were doing.*
vīderam quid facerēs, *I had seen what you were doing.*
vidēbam quid fēcissēs, *I saw what you had done.*
vīdī quid fēcissēs, *I saw what you had done.*
vīderam quid fēcissēs, *I had seen what you had done.*

Principal sequence is also called **primary sequence** and historical sequence is also called **secondary sequence**.

3. The Present and Imperfect Subjunctive denote incomplete action, the Perfect and Pluperfect completed action, exactly as in the Indicative.

Peculiarities of Sequence

268

1. The Perfect Indicative is usually an historical tense (even when translated in English as a Present Perfect), and so is followed by the Imperfect and Pluperfect Subjunctive; as,—

> **dēmōnstrāvī quārē ad causam accēderem,** *I have shown why I took the case* (lit. *I showed why, etc.*).

2. A dependent Perfect Infinitive is treated as an historical tense wherever, if resolved into an equivalent Indicative, it would be historical; as,—

> **videor ostendisse quālēs deī essent,** *I seem to have shown of what nature the gods are* (**ostendisse** here corresponds to an Indicative, **ostendī,** *I showed*) *(N.D. ii.72).*

3. The Historical Present is sometimes regarded as a principal tense, sometimes as historical. Thus:—

> **Sulla suōs hortātur ut fortī animō sint,** *Sulla exhorts his soldiers to be stout-hearted*
>
> **Gallōs hortātur ut arma caperent,** *he exhorted the Gauls to take arms (B.G. vii.4.4).*

4. Conditional sentences of the 'contrary-to-fact' type are not affected by the principles for the Sequence of Tenses; as,—

> **honestum tāle est ut, vel sī ignōrārent id hominēs, suā tamen pulchritūdine laudabīle esset,** *virtue is such a thing that even if men were ignorant of it, it would still be worthy of praise for its own loveliness (F. ii.49).*

5. In conditional sentences of the 'contrary-to-fact' type the Imperfect Subjunctive is usually treated as an Historical tense; as,—

> **sī sōlōs eōs dīcerēs miserōs, quibus moriendum esset, nēminem tū quidem eōrum quī vīverent exciperēs,** *if you called only those wretched who must die, you would except no one of those who live (Tusc. Disp. i.9).*

6. In clauses of Result and some others, the Perfect Subjunctive is sometimes used as an historical tense. Thus:—

rēx tantum mōtus est, ut Tissaphernem hostem jūdicārit, *the king was so much moved that he adjudged Tissaphernes an enemy* (Nep. *Con.* 4).

This construction is rare in Cicero, but frequent in Nepos and subsequent historians. The Perfect Subjunctive in this use represents a result simply *as a fact without reference to the continuance of the act,* and therefore corresponds to an Historical Perfect Indicative of direct statement. Thus, **jūdicārit** in the above example corresponds to **adjūdicāvit,** *he adjudged.* To denote a result as *something continuous,* all writers use the Imperfect Subjunctive after historical tenses.

7. Sometimes perspicuity demands that the ordinary principles of Sequence be abandoned altogether. Thus:

a) We may have the Present or Perfect Subjunctive after an historical tense; as,—

> **Verrēs Siciliam ita perdidit ut ea restituī nōn possit,** *Verres so ruined Sicily that it cannot be restored* (Direct statement: **nōn potest restitui**) *(Verr. act. pr.* 12);
>
> **ārdēbat Hortēnsius dīcendī cupiditāte sīc, ut in nūllō flagrantius studium vīderim,** *Hortensius burned so with eagerness to speak that I have seen in no one a greater desire* (Direct statement: **in nūllō vīdī,** *I have seen in no one) (Brut.* 302).

NOTE—This usage is different from that cited under 6. Here, by neglect of Sequence, the Perfect is used, though a principal tense; there the Perfect was used as an historical tense.

---

b) We may have a principal tense followed by the Perfect Subjunctive used historically; as,—

> **nesciō quid causae fuerit cūr nūllās ad mē litterās darēs,** *I do not know what reason there was why you did not send me a letter.*

Here **fuerit** is historical, as is shown by the following Imperfect Subjunctive.

Method of Expressing Future Time in the Subjunctive

269 The Future and Future Perfect, which are lacking to the Latin Subjunctive, are supplied in subordinate clauses as follows:—

1.

    a) The Future is supplied by the Present after principal tenses, by the Imperfect after historical tenses.

    b) The Future Perfect is supplied by the Perfect after principal tenses, by the Pluperfect after historical tenses.

    This is especially frequent when the context clearly shows, by the presence of a future tense in the main clause, that the reference is to future time. Thus:—

        Gallī pollicentur sē factūrōs, quae Caesar imperet, *the Gauls promise they will do what Caesar shall order*

        Gallī pollicēbantur sē factūrōs, quae Caesar imperāret, *the Gauls promised they would do what Caesar should order*

        Gallī pollicentur sē factūrōs quae Caesar imperāverit, *the Gauls promise they will do what Caesar shall have ordered*

        Gallī pollicēbantur sē factūrōs quae Caesar imperāvisset, *the Gauls promised they would do what Caesar should have ordered.*

2. Even where the context does not contain a Future tense in the main clause, Future time is often expressed in the subordinate clauses by the Present and Imperfect Subjunctive. Thus:—

        timeō nē veniat, *I am afraid he will come*

        Caesar exspectābat quid cōnsilī hostēs caperent, *Caesar was waiting to see what plan the enemy would adopt (B.G. iii.24.1).*

3. Where greater definiteness is necessary, the periphrastic forms in **-ūrus sim** and **-ūrus essem** are employed, especially in clauses of Result, Indirect Questions, and after **nōn dubitō quīn**; as,—

        nōn dubitō quīn pater ventūrus sit, *I do not doubt that my father will come*

        nōn dubitābam quīn pater ventūrus esset, *I did not doubt that my father would come.*

4. Where the verb has no Future Active Participle, or where it stands in the passive voice, its Future character may be indicated by the use of the particles **mox, brevī, statim**, *etc.*, in connection with the Present and Imperfect Subjunctive; as,—

> **nōn dubitō quīn tē mox hūjus reī paeniteat,** *I do not doubt that you will soon repent of this thing*
>
> **nōn dubitābam quīn haec rēs brevī cōnficerētur,** *I did not doubt that this thing would soon be fnished.*

Tenses of the Infinitive

270 1. The tenses of the Infinitive denote time not absolutely, but *with reference to the verb on which they depend.* Thus:—

a) The Present Infinitive represents an act as *contemporaneous with* the time of the verb on which it depends; as,—

> **vidētur honōrēs adsequī,** *he seems to be gaining honors*
>
> **vidēbātur honōrēs adsequī,** *he seemed to be gaining honors.*

b) The Perfect Infinitive represents an act as *prior to* the time of the verb on which it depends; as,—

> **vidētur honōrēs adsecūtus esse,** *he seems to have gained honors*
>
> **vīsus est honōrēs adsecūtus esse,** *he seemed to have gained honors.*

c) The Future Infinitive represents an act as *subsequent to* that of the verb on which it depends; as,—

> **vidētur honōrēs adsecūtūrus esse,** *he seems to be about to gain honors*
>
> **vīsus est honōrēs adsecūtūrus esse,** *he seemed to be about to gain honors.*

2. Where the English says *'ought to have done,' 'might have done,'* etc., the Latin uses **dēbuī, oportuit, potuī** (**dēbēbam, oportēbat, poteram**), with the Present Infinitive; as,—

> **dēbuit dīcere,** *he ought to have said* (lit. *owed it to say*)
>
> **opōrtuit venīre,** *he ought to have come*
>
> **potuit vidēre,** *he might have seen*

a) **Oportuit, volō, nōlō** (and in poetry some other verbs), may take a Perfect Infinitive instead of the Present; as,—

> **hōc jam prīdem factum esse oportuit,** *this ought long ago to have been done* (Cat. i.5).

3. **Periphrastic Future Infinitive**. Verbs that have no Participial Stem, express the Future Infinitive Active and Passive by **fore ut** or **futūrum esse ut**, with the Subjunctive; as,—

> **spērō fore ut tē paeniteat levitātis**, *I hope you will repent of your fickleness* (lit. *hope it will happen that you repent*)

> **spērō futūrum esse ut hostēs arceantur**, *I hope that the enemy will be kept off.*

a) The Periphrastic Future Infinitive is often used, especially in the Passive, even in case of verbs which have the Participial Stem; as,—

> **spērō fore ut hostēs vincantur**, *I hope the enemy will be conquered.*

4. Passives and Deponents sometimes form a Future Perfect Infinitive with **fore**; as,—

> **spērō epistulam scrīptam fore**, *I hope the letter will have been written*

> **dīcō mē satis adeptum fore**, *I say that I shall have gained enough (Sull. 27).*

Moods

Moods in Independent Sentences

The Indicative in Independent Sentences

271 The Indicative is used for the *statement of facts*, the *supposition of facts*, or *inquiry after facts*.

1. Note the following idiomatic uses:—

a) With **possum**; as,—

> **possum multa dīcere**, *I might say much*
> **poteram multa dīcere**, *I might have said much* (§ 270, 2).

b) In such expressions as **longum est, aequum est, melius est, difficile est, ūtilius est**, and some others; as,—

> **longum est ea dīcere**, *it would be tedious to tell that*
> **difficile est omnia persequī**, *it would be difficult to enumerate everything.*

The Subjunctive in Independent Sentences

272 The Subjunctive is used in Independent Sentences to express something—

1. **As willed—Volitive Subjunctive**
2. **As desired—Optative Subjunctive**
3. **Conceived of as possible—Potential Subjunctive**

VOLITIVE SUBJUNCTIVE

273 The Volitive Subjunctive represents the action *as willed*. It always implies authority on the part of the speaker, and has the following varieties:—

HORTATORY SUBJUNCTIVE

274 The Hortatory Subjunctive expresses *an exhortation*. This use is confined to the first person plural of the Present. The negative is **nē**. Thus:—

> **eāmus**, *let us go*
> **amēmus patriam**, *let us love our country*
> **nē dēspērēmus**, *let us not despair*

JUSSIVE SUBJUNCTIVE

275 The Jussive Subjunctive expresses a *command*. The Jussive stands regularly in the Present Tense, and is used—

1. Most frequently in the third singular and the third plural; as,—

   > **dīcat**, *let him tell*
   > **dīcant**, *let them tell*
   > **quārē sēcēdant improbī**, *wherefore let the wicked depart! (Cat. i.32)*

2. Less frequently in the second person, often with indefinite force; as,—

   > **istō bonō ūtāre**, *use that advantage (de Sen. 33)*
   > **modestē vīvās**, *live temperately.*

PROHIBITIVE SUBJUNCTIVE

276 The Subjunctive is used in the second and third persons singular and plural, with **nē**, to express *a prohibition*. Both Present and Perfect occur, and without appreciable difference of meaning; as,—

> **nē repugnētis**, *do not resist! (Cluent. 6)*

tū vērō istam nē relīquerīs, *don't leave her!* *(Tusc.Disp.*
i.112)

impiī nē plācāre audeant deōs, *let not the impious dare
to appease the gods!* *(Leg.* ii.41)

a) Neither of these constructions is frequent in classical
prose.

b) A commoner method of expressing a prohibition in
the second person is by the use of **nōlī** (**nōlīte**) with
a following infinitive, or by **cavē** or **cavē nē** with the
Subjunctive; as,—

nōlī hōc facere, *don't do this* (lit. *be unwilling to do*)!

nōlīte mentīrī, *do not lie!*

cavē ignōscās, cavē tē misereat, *do not forgive, do
not pity!* *(Lig.* 14)

cavē nē haec faciās, *do not do this* (lit. *take care lest
you do*)!

DELIBERATIVE SUBJUNCTIVE

277 The Deliberative Subjunctive is used *in questions and
exclamations implying doubt, indignation, the impossibility
of an act, obligation, or propriety.* The Present is used
referring to present time, the Imperfect referring to past.
The negative is **nōn.** Thus:—

quid faciam, *what shall I do?* (Pl. *Curc.* 589)

ego redeam, *I go back!* (Ter. *Eun.* 49)

huic cēdāmus! hūjus condiciōnēs audiāmus! *are we to
bow to him! are we to listen to his terms!*(Phil. *xiii.16*)

quid facerem, *what was I to do?* (Ter. *Eun.* 831)

hunc ego nōn dīligam, *should I not cherish this man?*
(Arch. 18)

a) These Deliberative Questions are usually purely
Rhetorical in character, and do not expect an answer.

CONCESSIVE SUBJUNCTIVE

278 The Subjunctive is used to indicate something *as granted or
conceded for the sake of argument.* The Present is used for
present time, the Perfect regularly for past. The negative is
nē. Thus:—

sit hōc vērum, *I grant that this is true* (lit. *let this be true*)

nē sint in senectūte vīrēs, *I grant there is not strength
in old age* (de Sen. 34)

fuerit malus cīvis aliīs; tibi quandō esse coepit, *I grant that he was a bad citizen to others; when did he begin to be so toward you? (Verr.* i.37)

Optative Subjunctive

279 The Optative Subjunctive occurs in expressions of *wishing.* The negative is regularly **nē**.

1. The Present Tense, often accompanied by **utinam**, is used where the wish is conceived of *as possible.*

   dī istaec prohibeant, *may the gods prevent that!* (Ter. *H.T.* 1038)

   falsus utinam vātēs sim, *oh that I may be a false prophet!* (Liv. xxi.10.10)

   nē veniant, *may they not come!*

2. The Imperfect expresses, in the form of a wish, the *regret that something is not so now;* the Pluperfect that something *was not so in the past.* The Imperfect and Pluperfect are regularly accompanied by **utinam**; as,—

   utinam istud ex animō dīcerēs, *would that you were saying that in earnest (i.e.* I regret that you are not saying it in earnest)

   Pēlīdēs utinam vītāsset Apollinis arcūs, *would that Achilles had escaped the bow of Apollo*

   utinam nē nātus essem, *would that I had not been born.*

Potential Subjunctive

280 The Potential Subjunctive expresses *a possibility.* The negative is **nōn**. The following uses are to be noted:—

1. **The 'May' Potential.**—The Potential Subjunctive may designate *a mere possibility* (English auxiliary *may*). Both Present and Perfect occur, and without appreciable difference of meaning. Thus:—

   dīcat aliquis, *some one may say* (Ter. *And.* 640)
   dīxerit aliquis, *some one may say*

   a) This construction is by no means frequent, and is confined mainly to a few phrases like those given as examples.

2. **'Should'-'Would' Potential.**—The Potential Subjunctive may represent something as *depending upon a condition expressed or understood* (English auxiliary *should, would*). Both Present and Perfect occur, and without appreciable difference of meaning. Thus:—

fortūnam citius reperiās quam retineās, *one would more quickly find Fortune than keep it* (*i.e.* if one should make the trial) (Pub. Syr. 193).

crēdiderim, *I should believe.*

a) Here belongs the use of **velim**, **mālim**, **nōlim**, as softened forms of statement for **volō**, **mālō**, **nōlō**. Thus:—

> **velim mihi ignōscās**, *I wish you would forgive me* (*Fam.* xiii.75.1).
>
> **nōlim putēs mē jocārī**, *I don't want you to think I'm joking* (*Fam.* ix.15.4).

b) When the condition is expressed, we get one of the regular types of Conditional Sentences (see § 303); as,—

> **diēs dēficiat, sī cōner ēnumerāre causās**, *time would fail if I should attempt to enumerate the reasons* (*N.D.* iii.81).

3. **'Can'-'Could' Potential.**—In the Present and Imperfect the Potential occurs in the second person singular (with *indefinite* force; § 356, 3) of a few verbs of perceiving, seeing, thinking, and the like; as,—

> **videās**, **cernās**, *one can see, one can perceive*
> **crēderēs**, *one could believe*
> **vidērēs**, **cernerēs**, *one could see, perceive*
> **putārēs**, *one could imagine*

4. The Imperfect and Pluperfect in the Apodosis of conditional sentences of the contrary-to-fact type (see § 304) are also Potential in character. By omission of the Protasis, such an Apodosis sometimes stands alone, particularly vellem, nōllem, māllem; as,—

> **vellem id quidem**, *I should wish that* (*i.e.* were I bold enough)

The Imperative

281 The Imperative is used in *commands*, *admonitions* and *entreaties* (negative **nē**), as,—

> **ēgredere ex urbe**, *depart from the city* (*Cat.* i.20)
> **mihi ignōsce**, *pardon me*
> **valē**, *farewell*

1. The Present is the tense of the Imperative most commonly used, but the Future is employed—

a) Where there is a distinct reference to future time, especially in the apodosis of conditional sentences; as,—

> **rem vōbīs prōpōnam; vōs eam penditōte**, *I will lay the matter before you; do you (then) consider it (Verr. iv.1)*

> **sī bene disputābit, tribuitō litterīs Graecis**, *if he shall speak well, attribute it to Greek literature (de Sen. 3).*

b) In laws, treaties, wills, maxims, *etc.*; as,—

> **cōnsulēs summum jūs habentō**, *the consuls shall have supreme power (Leg. iii.8)*

> **hominem mortuom in urbe nē sepelītō**, *no one shall bury a dead body in the city (Twelve Tables)*

> **amīcitia rēgī Antiochō cum populō Rōmānō hīs legibus et condiciōnibus estō**, *let there be friendship between Antiochus and the Roman people on the following terms and conditions (Liv. xxxviii.38.1)*

> **quārtae estō partis Mārcus hērēs**, *let Marcus be heir to a fourth (of the property)*

> **ignōscitō saepe alterī, numquam tibi**, *forgive your neighbor often, yourself never.*

2. Except with the Future Imperative the negative is not used in classical prose. Prohibitions are regularly expressed in other ways. See § 276, b.

3. Questions in the Indicative introduced by **quīn** (*why not?*) are often equivalent to an Imperative or to the Hortatory Subjunctive; as,—

> **quīn abīs**, *go away!* (lit. *why don't you go away?*)

> **quīn vōcem continētis**, *keep still!* (lit. *why don't you stop your voices?*)

> **quīn equōs cōnscendimus**, *let us mount our horses* (lit. *why do we not mount our horses?*) (Liv. i.57.7)

Moods in Dependent Clauses

Clauses of Purpose

282 1. Clauses of Purpose are introduced most commonly by **ut (utī), quō** (*that, in order that*), **nē** (*in order that not, lest*), and stand in the Subjunctive, as,—

edimus ut vīvāmus, *we eat that we may live*

adjūtā mē quō hōc fīat facilius, *help me, in order that this may be done more easily (Ter. Eun.* 150)

portās clausit, nē quam oppidānī injūriam acciperent, *he closed the gates, lest the townspeople should receive any injury (B.G.* ii.33.1).

a) **Quō**, as a rule, is employed only when the purpose clause contains a comparative or a comparative idea. Occasional exceptions occur; as,—

> **haec faciunt quō Chremētem absterreant**, *they are doing this in order to frighten Chremes (Ter. And.* 472).

b) **Ut nē** is sometimes found instead of **nē**. Thus:—

> **ut nē quid neglegenter agāmus**, *in order that we may not do anything carelessly (Off.* 1.103)

c) **Ut nōn** (not **nē**) is used where the negation belongs to some single word, instead of to the purpose clause as a whole. Thus:—

> **ut nōn ējectus ad aliēnōs, sed invītātus ad tuōs videāre**, *that you may seem not driven out among strangers, but invited to your own friends (Cat.* i.23).

d) To say '*and that not*' or '*or that not,*' the Latin regularly uses **nēve (neu)**; as,—

> **ut eārum rērum vīs minuerētur, neu pontī nocērent**, *that the violence of these things might be lessened, and that they might not harm the bridge (B.G.* iv.17.10)

> **profūgit, nē caperētur nēve interficerētur**, *he fled, that he might not be captured or killed.*

e) But **neque** (for **nēve**) is sometimes used in a second Purpose Clause when **ut** stands in the first, and, after the Augustan era, even when the first clause is introduced by **nē**.

f) Purpose Clauses sometimes stand in apposition with a preceding noun or pronoun: as,—

> **hāc causā, ut pācem habērent**, *on this account, that they might have peace*

2. A Relative Pronoun (**quī**) or Adverb (**ubi, unde, quō**) is frequently used to introduce a Purpose Clause; as,—

> **Helvētiī lēgātōs mittunt, quī dīcerent**, *the Helvetii sent envoys to say* (lit. *who should say) (B.G.* i.7.3)

haec habuī, dē senectūte quae dīcerem, *I had these
things to say about old age (de Sen.* 85)

nōn habēbant quō sē reciperent, *they had no place
to which to flee* (lit. *whither they might flee*) *(B.G.*
iv.38.2).

a) **Quī** in such clauses is equivalent to **ut is, ut ego,** *etc.*; **ubi**
to **ut ibi; unde** to **ut inde; quō** to **ut eō.**

3. Relative Clauses of purpose follow **dignus**, **indignus**, and
idōneus; as,—

idōneus fuit nēmō quem imitārēre, *there was no one
suitable for you to imitate (cf.* **nēmō fuit quem
imitārēre,** *there was no one for you to imitate) (Verr.*
iii.41)

dignus est quī aliquandō imperet, *he is worthy to rule
sometime (Leg.* iii.5).

4. Purpose Clauses often depend upon something to be
supplied from the context instead of upon the principal
verb of their own sentences; as,—

ut haec omnia omittam, abiimus, *to pass over all this,*
(I will say that) we departed.

Clauses of Characteristic

283 1. A relative clause used *to express a quality or
characteristic of a general or indefinite antecedent* is
called a Clause of Characteristic, and usually stands in
the Subjunctive; as,—

multa sunt, quae mentem acuant, *there are many
things which sharpen the wits (Tusc. Disp.* i.80).

Clauses of Characteristic are opposed to those relative
clauses which are used merely to state some fact about a
definite antecedent, and which therefore take the Indicative;
as,—

Catō, senex jūcundus, quī Sapiēns appellātus est,
Cato, a delightful old man, who was called 'The Wise'

The Clause of Characteristic implies *'a person of the sort
that does something'*; the Indicative relative clause implies
'a particular person who does something.'

2. Clauses of Characteristic are used especially after such
expressions as, **est quī; sunt quī; nēmō est quī; nūllus est
quī; ūnus est quī; sōlus est quī; quis est quī; is quī;** *etc.*
Thus:—

sunt quī dīcant, *there are (some) who say (Inv.* ii.144)

nēmō est quī nesciat, *there is nobody who is ignorant (Fam.* i.4.2)

sapientia est ūna quae maestitiam pellat, *philosophy is the only thing that drives away sorrow (Fin.* i.43)

quae cīvitās est quae nōn ēvertī possit, *what state is there that cannot be overthrown? (Lael.* 23)

nōn is sum quī improbōs laudem, *I am not the sort of man that praises the wicked (B.G.* v.30.2).

a) Sometimes (very rarely in Cicero and Caesar) the clause of characteristic is used after comparatives; as,—

> **nōn longius hostēs aberant quam quō tēlum adigī posset,** *the enemy were not too far off for a dart to reach them* (lit. *further off than [a point] to which a dart could be cast*) *(B.G.* ii.21.3).

3. The Clause of Characteristic often conveys an accessory notion of cause (*since*) or opposition (*although*). Thus:—

a) Cause. The relative is then frequently accompanied by **ut, quīppe, utpote;** as,—

> **ō fortūnāte adulēscēns, quī tuae virtūtis Homērum praecōnem invēnerīs,** *O fortunate man, since you have found a Homer as the herald of your valor (Arch.* 24)

> **ut quī optimō jūre eam prōvinciam obtinuerit,** *since he held that province by excellent right (Phil.* xi.30)

b) Opposition:—

> **egomet quī sērō Graecās litterās attigissem, tamen complūrēs diēs Athēnīs commorātus sum,** *I, although I had taken up Greek literature late in life, nevertheless tarried several days at Athens (de Or.* i.82).

4. Clauses of Characteristic may also be introduced by **quīn =** **quī (quae, quod) nōn;** as,—

> **nēmō est quīn saepe audierit,** *there is no one who has not often heard (Verr.* iv.115)

> **nēmō fuit mīlitum quīn vulnerārētur,** *there was no one of the soldiers who was not wounded (B.C.* iii.53.3).

5. Related to Clauses of Characteristic are also phrases of the type:

quod sciam, *so far as I know*; **quem (quam, quod), audierim**, *so far as I have heard* (Nep. *Ar.* 1.2)

Clauses of Result

284

1. Clauses of Result are usually introduced by **ut** (*that, so that*), negative **ut nōn** (*so that not*), and take the Subjunctive. The main clause often contains **tantus, tālis, tot, is** (= **tālis**), **tam, ita, sīc, adeō**, or some similar word. Thus:—

quis tam dēmēns est ut suā voluntāte maereat, *who is so senseless as to mourn of his own volition? (Tusc. Disp.* iii.71)

Siciliam ita vāstāvit ut restituī in antīquum statum nōn possit, *he so ravaged Sicily that it cannot be restored to its former condition (Verr. act. pr.* 12)

mōns altissimus impendēbat, ut facile perpaucī prohibēre possent, *a very high mountain overhung, so that a very few could easily stop them (B.G.* i.6.1)

nōn is es ut tē pudor umquam ā turpitūdine āvocārit, *you are not so constituted that shame ever called you back from baseness (Cat.* i.22).

2. A Result Clause is often introduced by a Relative Pronoun or Adverb, **quī** (= **ut is**), **quō** (= **ut eō**), *etc.*; as,—

nēmō est tam senex quī sē annum nōn putet posse vīvere, *nobody is so old as not to think he can live a year (de Sen.* 24)

habētis eum cōnsulem quī pārēre vestrīs dēcrētīs nōn dubitet, *you have a consul such as does not hesitate to obey your decrees (Cat.* iv.24).

a) These Relative Clauses of Result are closely related to the Clause of Characteristic, and sometimes it is difficult to distinguish the two constructions. It is best to class the relative clause as one of Characteristic, unless the result idea is clear and unmistakable.

3. Result clauses may also be introduced by **quīn = ut nōn**; as,—

nihil tam difficile est quīn quaerendō invēstīgārī possit, *nothing is so difficult that it cannot be discovered by searching* (Ter. *H.T.* 675)

nēmō est tam fortis quīn reī novitāte perturbētur, *no
one is so steadfast as not to be thrown into confusion
by a strange occurrence* (B.G. vi.39.3).

4. Note the use of **quam ut** (sometimes **quam** alone) to denote
Result after comparatives; as,—

urbs erat mūnītior quam ut prīmō impetū capī
posset, *the city was too strongly fortified to be taken
at the first attack* (lit. *more strongly fortified than [so]
that it could be taken, etc.*).

Causal Clauses

285 Causal clauses are introduced chiefly by the following particles:—

1. **Quod, quia, quoniam**
2. **Cum**
3. **Quandō**

286 The use of moods is as follows:—

1. **Quod, quia, quoniam** take the Indicative when the reason
is *that of the writer or speaker;* they take the Subjunctive
when the reason is viewed *as that of another.* Thus:—

Parthōs timeō quod diffīdō cōpiīs nostrīs, *I fear the
Parthians, because I distrust our troops.*

Themistoclēs, quia nōn tūtus erat, Corcyram
dēmigrāvit, *Themistocles, since he was not safe,
moved to Corcyra* (Nep. *Them.* 8.3).

neque mē vīxisse paenitet, quoniam bene vīxī, *I do not
regret having lived, since I have lived well* (de Sen. 84).

Sōcratēs accūsātus est quod corrumperet juventūtem,
*Socrates was arraigned on the ground that he was
corrupting the young.* (Here the reason is not that of
the writer but of the accuser. Hence the Subjunctive.)

Haeduī Caesarī grātiās ēgērunt quod sē perīculō
līberāvisset, *the Haedui thanked Caesar because he
had delivered them from danger.* (The reason of the
Haedui.)

quoniam Miltiadēs dīcere nōn posset, verba prō eō
fēcit Tīsagorās, *since Miltiades could not speak,
Tisagoras spoke for him.* (The reason of Tisagoras.)
(Nep. *Milt.* 7.5)

noctū ambulābat Themistoclēs, quod somnum capere nōn posset, *Themistocles used to walk at night because (as he said) he couldn't sleep (Tusc. Disp. iv.44).*

a) Verbs of *thinking* and *saying* often stand in the Subjunctive in causal clauses as though the act of thinking or saying, and not the contents of the thought or language, constituted the reason. Thus:—

Bellovacī suum numerum nōn complēvērunt quod sē suō nōmine cum Rōmānīs bellum gestūrōs dīcerent, *the Bellovaci did not furnish their complement, because they said they were going to wage war with the Romans on their own account (B.G. vii.75).*

b) **Nōn quod, nōn quō** (by attraction for **nōn eō quod**), **nōn quia,** *not that, not because;* and **nōn quod nōn, nōn quō nōn, nōn quīn,** *not that ... not; not because ... not; not but that,* are usually employed merely to introduce a hypothetical reason, and hence take the Subjunctive; as,—

id fēcī, nōn quod vōs hanc dēfēnsiōnem dēsīderāre arbitrārer, sed ut omnēs intellegerent, *this I did, not because I thought you needed this defense, but that all might perceive (Caec. 101)*

Crassō commendātiōnem nōn sum pollicitus, nōn quīn eam valitūram apud tē arbitrārer, sed egēre mihi commendātiōne nōn vidēbātur, *I did not promise a recommendation to Crassus, not that I did not think it would have weight with you, but because he did not seem to me to need recommendation (Fam. xiii.16.3).*

c) But clauses introduced by **nōn quod, nōn quīa** take the Indicative *if they state a fact,* even though that fact is denied to be the reason for something; as,—

hōc ita sentiō, nōn quia sum ipse augur, sed quia sīc exīstimāre nōs est necesse, *this I think, not because I am myself an augur (which I really am), but because it is necessary for us to think so (Leg. iii.31).*

2. **Cum** causal regularly takes the Subjunctive; as,—

quae cum īta sint, *since this is so*

cum sīs mortālis, quae mortālia sunt, cūrā, *since you are mortal, care for what is mortal.*

a) Note the phrase **cum praesertim (praesertim cum)**, *especially since;* as,—

> **Haeduōs accūsat, praesertim cum eōrum precibus adductus bellum suscēperit**, *he blamed the Haedui, especially since he had undertaken the war at their entreaties (B.G.* i.16.6).

3. **Quandō** (less frequent than the other causal particles) governs the Indicative; as,—

> **id omittō, quandō vōbīs ita placet**, *I pass over that, since you so wish* (Sall. *Jug.* 110.7).

Temporal Clauses introduced by *Postquam, Ut, Ubi, Simul ac, etc.*

287

1. **Postquam (posteāquam)**, *after;* **ut, ubi**, *when;* **cum prīmum, simul, simul ac (simul atque)**, *as soon as*, when used to refer *to a single past act* regularly take the Perfect Indicative; as,—

> **Epamīnōndās postquam audīvit vīcisse Boeōtiōs, 'Satis' inquit 'vīxī,'** *Epaminondas, after he heard that the Boeotians had conquered, said, 'I have lived enough'* (Nep. *Ep.* 9.4)

> **id ut audīvit, Corcyram dēmigrāvit**, *when he heard this, he moved to Corcyra* (Nep. *Them.* 8.3)

> **Caesar cum prīmum potuit, ad exercitum contendit**, *Caesar, as soon as he could, hurried to the army (B.G.* iii.9.2)

> **ubi dē Caesaris adventū certiōrēs factī sunt, lēgātōs ad eum mittunt**, *when they were informed of Caesar's arrival, they sent envoys to him (B.G.* i.7.3).

a) The Historical Present may take the place of the Perfect in this construction.

2. To denote *the repeated occurrence* of an act, **ut, ubi, simul atque**, *as often as*, when following an historical tense, take the Pluperfect Indicative (compare §§ 288, 3; 302, 3); as,—

> **ut quisque Verris animum offenderat, in lautumiās statim coniciēbātur**, *whenever anybody had offended Verres's feelings, he was forthwith put in the stone-quarry (Verr.* v.143)

> **hostēs, ubi aliquōs ēgredientēs cōnspexerant, adoriēbantur**, *whenever the enemy had seen any men disembarking, they attacked them (B.G.* iv.26.2).

a) In Livy and succeeding historians the Imperfect and
Pluperfect Subjunctive are used to denote this repeated
occurrence of an act ('Indefinite Frequency'); as,—

id ubi dīxisset hastam mittēbat, *whenever he had
said that, he hurled a* spear (Liv. i.32.13).

3. Occasionally the above conjunctions are followed by
the Pluperfect Indicative of a single occurrence. This is
regularly the case with **postquam** in expressions denoting
a definite interval of time (days, months, years, *etc.*), such as
post tertium annum quam, trienniō postquam. Thus:—

**quīnque post diēbus quam Lūcā discesserat, ad
Sardiniam vēnit** *five days after he had departed from
Luca he came to Sardinia*

**postquam occupātae Syrācūsae erant, profectus est
Carthāginem,** *after Syracuse had been seized, he set
out for* Carthage (Liv. xxiv.35.4).

4. The Imperfect Indicative also sometimes occurs, to denote
a continued state; as,—

**postquam Rōmam adventābant, senātus cōnsultus
est,** *after they were on the march toward Rome, the
Senate was consulted* (Sall. *Jug.* 28.2)

postquam strūctī utrimque stābant, *after they had
been drawn up on both sides and were in position*
(Liv. i.23.6)

5. **Rarely postquam, posteāquam,** following the analogy of
cum, take the Subjunctive, but only in the historical tenses;
as,—

**posteāquam sūmptuōsa fieri fūnera coepissent,
lēge sublāta sunt,** *after funerals had begun to be
elaborate, they were done away with by law (Leg.*
ii.64).

Temporal Clauses introduced by *Cum*

Cum Referring to the Past

288   1. **Cum,** when referring to the past, takes,—

A. The Indicative (Imperfect, Historical Perfect, or Pluperfect)
to denote *the point of time at which* something occurs.

B. The Subjunctive (Imperfect or Pluperfect) to denote *the
situation or circumstances under which* something occurs.

Examples:—

INDICATIVE

**an tum erās cōnsul, cum in Palātiō mea domus
ārdēbat**, *or were you consul at the time when my
house burned up on the Palatine? (Pis.* 26)

**crēdō tum cum Sicilia flōrēbat opibus et cōpiīs magna
artificia fuisse in eā īnsulā**, *I believe that at the time
when Sicily was powerful in riches and resources there
were great crafts in that island (Verr.* iv.46)

eō tempore pāruit cum pārēre necesse erat, *he obeyed
at the time when it was necessary to obey (Lig.* 20)

illō diē, cum est lāta lēx dē mē, *on that day when the
law concerning me was passed (Mil.* 38)

SUBJUNCTIVE

**Lysander cum vellet Lycūrgī lēgēs commūtāre,
prohibitus est**, *when Lysander desired to change the
laws of Lycurgus, he was prevented (Div.* i.96);

**Pythagorās cum in geōmetriā quiddam novī
invēnisset, Mūsīs bovem immolāsse dīcitur**,
*when Pythagoras had discovered something new in
geometry, he is said to have sacrificed an ox to the
Muses (N.D.* iii.88).

a) Note that the Indicative is much less frequent in such
clauses than the Subjunctive, and is regularly confined
to those cases where the main clause has **tum, eō diē,
eō annō, eō tempore** or some similar correlative of the
cum. Sometimes it depends entirely upon the point of
view of the writer whether he shall employ the Indicative
or Subjunctive.

2. **Cum Inversum**. When the logical order of the clauses
is inverted, we find **cum** with the Perfect Indicative or
Historical Present, in the sense of *when, when suddenly.*
The main clause in such cases often has **jam, vix, aegrē,
nōndum;** as,—

**jam Gallī ex oppidō fugere apparābant, cum mātrēs
familiae repente prōcurrērunt**, *the Gauls were
already preparing to flee, when suddenly the matrons
rushed forth* (logically, *the matrons rushed forth as
the Gauls were preparing to flee*) *(B.G.* vii.26.3)

**Trēvirī Labiēnum adorīrī parābant, cum duās
legiōnēs vēnisse cognōscunt**, *the Treviri were
preparing to attack, when (suddenly) they learned
that two legions had arrived (B.G.* vi.7.1).

3. To denote a *recurring action* in the past, **cum** is followed by the Indicative, particularly of the Pluperfect (compare §§ 287, 2; 302, 3); as,—

> **cum ad aliquod oppidum vēnerat, eādem lectīcā ad cubiculum dēferēbātur,** *whenever he had arrived at some town, he was (always) carried in the same litter to his room (Verr.* v.27)

> **cum equitātus noster sē in agrōs ējēcerat, essedāriōs ex silvīs ēmittēbat,** *whenever our cavalry had advanced into the fields, he would send his charioteers out from the woods (B.G.* v.19.2).

a) Sometimes the Imperfect or Pluperfect Subjunctive is thus used; as,—

> **saepe cum aliquem vidēret minus bene vestītum, suum amiculum dedit,** *often, wherever he saw some one more poorly clothed, he gave him his own mantle (Nep. Cim.* 4.2)

> **cum prōcucurrissent, Numidae effugiēbant,** *as often as they had advanced, the Numidians ran away (B.C.* ii.41.6).

This construction is frequent in Livy and subsequent historians.

Cum Referring to the Present or Future

289 When **cum** refers to the Present or Future it regularly takes the Indicative; as,—

> **tum tua rēs agitur, pariēs cum proximus ārdet,** *your own interests are at stake when your neighbor's house is burning (Hor. Epp.* i.18.84)

> **cum vidēbis, tum sciēs,** *when you see, then you will know (Pl. Bacch.* 145).

a) The Indicative of the Present or Future may denote also a *recurring action;* as,—

> **stabilitās amīcitiae cōnfirmārī potest, cum hominēs cupīdinibus imperābunt,** *firm friendship can be established whenever men shall control their desires (Lael.* 82).

OTHER USES OF CUM

290 1. **Cum Explicative.** **Cum**, with the Indicative, is sometimes used to indicate the identity of one act with another; as,—

> **cum tacent clāmant,** *their silence is a shout* (lit. *when they are silent, they shout*) *(Cat.* i.21).

2. **Cum ... tum.** When **cum ... tum** mean *both ... and*, the **cum**-clause is in the Indicative; but when **cum** has the force of *while, though*, it may take the Subjunctive; as,—

> **cum tē semper dīlēxerim, tum tuīs factīs incēnsus sum,** *while I have always loved you, at the same time I am stirred by your conduct (Att.* xiv.17a.4).

Clauses introduced by *Antequam* and *Priusquam*

WITH THE INDICATIVE

291 **Antequam** and **priusquam** (often written **ante ... quam, prius ... quam**) take the Indicative to denote *an actual fact.*

1. Sometimes the Present or Future Perfect; as,—

> **prius respondēs quam rogō,** *you answer before I ask* (Pl. *Merc.* 456)

> **nihil contrā disputābō priusquam dīxerit,** *I will say nothing in opposition, before he speaks (Flacc.* 51).

2. Sometimes the Perfect, especially after negative clauses; as,—

> **nōn prius jugulandī fīnis fuit, quam Sulla omnēs suōs dīvitiīs explēvit,** *there was no end of murder until Sulla satisfied all his henchmen with wealth (Sall. Cat.* 51).

WITH THE SUBJUNCTIVE

292 **Antequam** and **priusquam** take the Subjunctive to denote an act as *anticipated.*

1. Thus the Subjunctive may denote—

a) An act in preparation for which the main act takes place; as,—

> **priusquam dīmicārent, foedus īctum est,** *i.e. in anticipation of the fight, a treaty was struck (Liv.* i.24.3).

By an extension of this usage, the Subjunctive is sometimes used of *general truths*, where the anticipatory notion has faded out; as,—

> **tempestās minātur antequam surgat**, *the tempest threatens before it rises* (Sen. *Ep.* 103.2).

b) An act anticipated and forestalled; as,—

> **priusquam tēlum adicī posset, omnis aciēs terga vertit**, *before a spear could be hurled, the whole army fled (B.C. ii.34.6).*

c) An act anticipated and deprecated; as,—

> **animum omittunt priusquam locō dēmigrent**, *they die rather than quit their post (Pl. Amph. 240).*

2. After historical tenses the Imperfect Subjunctive is used, especially by some writers, where the notion of anticipation has practically vanished; as,—

> **sōl antequam sē abderet fugientem vīdit Antōnium**, *the sun before it set saw Antony fleeing (Phil. xiv.27).*

Clauses introduced by *Dum, Dōnec, Quoad*

293 I. **Dum**, *while*, regularly takes the Indicative of the Historical Present; as,—

Alexander, dum inter prīmōrēs pugnat, sagittā ictus est, *Alexander, while he was fighting in the van, was struck by an arrow* (Quint. Curt. iv.6.17)

dum haec geruntur, in fīnēs Venellōrum pervēnit, *while these things were being done, he arrived in the territory of the Venelli (B.G. iii.17.1).*

II. **Dum**, **dōnec**, and **quoad**, *as long as*, take the Indicative; as,—

dum anima est, spēs est, *as long as there is life, there is hope (Att. ix.10.3)*

Lacedaemoniōrum gēns fortis fuit, dum Lycūrgī lēgēs vigēbant, *the race of the Lacedaemonians was powerful, as long as the laws of Lycurgus were in force (Tusc. Disp. i.101)*

Catō, quoad vīxit, virtūtum laude crēvit, *Cato, at long as he lived, increased in the fame of his virtues* (Nep. *Cat.* 2.4).

III. **Dum**, **dōnec**, and **quoad**, *until*, take:—

1. The Indicative, to denote *an actual event*; as,—

> **dōnec rediit, fuit silentium**, *there was silence till he came* (Liv. xxiii.31.9)

ferrum in corpore retinuit, quoad renūntiātum est Boeōtiōs vīcisse, *he kept the iron in his body until word was brought that the Boeotians had conquered* (Nep. *Ep.* 9.3).

a) In Livy and subsequent historians **dum** and **dōnec** in this sense often take the Subjunctive instead of the Indicative; as,—

trepidātiōnis aliquantum ēdēbant dōnec timor quiētem fēcisset, *they showed some trepidation, until fear produced quiet* (Liv. xxi.28.11).

2. The Subjunctive, to denote *anticipation* or *expectancy*; as,—

exspectāvit Caesar dum nāvēs convenīrent, *Caesar waited for the ships to assemble* (B.G. iv.23.4)

dum litterae veniant, morābor, *I shall wait for the letter to come* (*Fam.* xi.23.2).

Substantive Clauses (Noun Clauses)

294 A Substantive Clause or Noun Clause is one which as a whole serves as the Subject or Object of a verb, or stands in some other case relation.

Substantive Clauses developed from the Volitive

295 Substantive Clauses Developed from the Volitive are used with the following classes of verbs:—

1. With verbs signifying *to admonish, request, command, urge, persuade, induce*,[47] etc. (conjunctions **ut, nē**, or **ut nē**); as,—

postulō ut fīat, *I demand that it be done* (dependent form of the Jussive **fīat**, *let it be done!*) (Ter. *And.* 550)

ōrat, nē abeās, *he begs that you will not go away* (Ter. *Ad.* 882)

mīlitēs cohortātus est ut hostium impetum sustinērent, *he exhorted his soldiers to withstand the attack of the enemy* (B.G. ii.21.2)

Helvētiīs persuāsit ut exīrent, *he persuaded the Helvetii to march forth* (B.G. i.2.1).

---

47 Especially: **moneō, admoneō; rogō, ōrō, petō, postulō, precor, flāgitō; mandō, imperō, praecipiō; suādeō, hortor, cohortor; persuādeō, impellō**.

a) **Jubeō**, *command, order,* regularly takes the Infinitive.

2. With verbs signifying *to grant, concede, permit, allow,*[48] etc. (conjunction ut); as,—

> **huic concēdō ut ea praetereat,** *I allow him to pass that by* (dependent form of the Jussive **ea praetereat**, *let him pass that by!*) (*Rosc. Am.* 54)

> **cōnsulī permissum est ut duās legiōnēs scrīberet,** *the consul was permitted to enroll two legions* (Liv. xxxv.20.4).

3. With verbs of *hindering, preventing,*[49] etc. (conjunctions nē, quōminus, quīn); as,—

> **nē lūstrum perficeret, mors prohibuit,** *death prevented him from finishing the lustrum* (dependent form after past tense of **nē lūstrum perficiat**, *let him not finish, etc.*) (Liv. xxiv.43.4)

> **prohibuit quōminus in ūnum coīrent,** *he prevented them from coming together* (Liv. xxv.35.6)

> **nec quīn ērumperet, prohibērī poterat,** *nor could he be prevented from rushing forth* (Liv. xxvi.40.4)

a) **Quīn** is used only when the verb of *hindering* is accompanied by a negative, or stands in a question implying a negative; it is not *necessarily* used even then.

4. With verbs of *deciding, resolving,*[50] etc. (conjunctions ut, nē, or ut nē); as,—

> **cōnstitueram ut prīdiē Īdūs Aquīnī manērem,** *I had decided to remain at Aquinum on the 12th* (*Att.* xiv.10.1)

> **dēcrēvit senātus ut Opīmius vidēret,** *the Senate decreed that Opimius should see to it* (*Cat.* 1.4)

> **convēnit ut ūnīs castrīs miscērentur,** *it was agreed that they should be united in one camp* (Liv. x.27.2).

5. With verbs of *striving,*[51] etc. (conjunctions **ut, nē,** or **ut nē**); as,—

> **fac ut eum exōrēs,** *see to it that you prevail upon him!* (Pl. *Rud.* 1218)

> **cūrā ut vir sīs,** *see to it that you are a man!* (*Cat.* 3.12)

---

48   Especially: **permittō, concēdō, nōn patior.**
49   Especially: **prohibeō, impediō, dēterreō.**
50   Especially: **cōnstituō, dēcernō, cēnseō, placuit, convenit, pacīscor.**
51   Especially: **labōrō, dō operam, id agō, contendō, impetrō.**

> **labōrābat ut reliquās cīvitātēs adjungeret,** *he was
> striving to join the remaining states to him (B.G.
> vii.31.1).*

   a) **Cōnor,** *try,* always takes the Infinitive.

NOTE—Verbs of all the above classes also admit the Infinitive,
especially in poetry.

---

  6. With a few other expressions, such as **necesse est, reliquus
est, sequitur, licet, oportet**; as,—

> **sequitur ut doceam,** *it remains for me to show (N.D. ii.81)*
> **licet redeās,** *you may return*
> **oportet loquāmur,** *we must speak.*

On the absence of **ut** with **licet** and **oportet**, see paragraph 8.

  7. Here also belong phrases of the type: **nūlla causa est cūr,
quīn; nōn est cūr,** *etc.*; **nihil est cūr,** *etc.*; as,—

> **nūlla causa est cūr timeam,** *there is no reason why I
> should fear* (originally Deliberative: *why should I
> fear? There's no reason*)
> **nihil est quīn dīcam,** *there is no reason why I should
> not say.*

  8. Many of the above classes of verbs at times take the simple
Subjunctive without **ut**. In such cases we must not recognize
any omission of **ut**, but simply an earlier form of expression
which existed before the **ut**-clause arose. This is regularly
the case with **necesse est, licet,** and **oportet**; see 6. Other
examples are:—

> **eōs moneō dēsinant,** *I warn them to stop (Cat. 2.20)*
> **huic imperat adeat cīvitātēs,** *he orders him to visit the
> states (B.G. iv.21.8).*

Substantive Clauses developed from the Optative

296

Substantive Clauses Developed from the Optative occur:—

  1. With verbs of *wishing, desiring,* especially **cupiō, optō,
volō, mālō** (conjunctions **ut, nē, ut nē**); as,—

> **optō ut in hōc jūdiciō nēmō improbus reperiātur,**
> *I hope that in this court no bad man may be found*
> (here **ut reperiātur** represents a simple optative of
> direct statement, that is, **reperiātur,** *may no bad
> man be found!*) (*Verr., act. pr., 50*)
> **cupiō nē veniat,** *I desire that he may not come.*

a) The simple Subjunctive (without **ut**) sometimes occurs with verbs of this class. (See § 295, 8.) Examples are: velim scrībās, I wish you would write; vellem scrīpsisset, I wish he had written.

2. With expressions of *fearing* (**timeō, metuō, vereor, etc.**). Here **nē** means *that, lest*, and **ut** means *that not*; as,—

   timeō nē veniat, *I fear that he will come* (originally: *may he not come! I'm afraid* [*he will*])

   timeō ut veniat, *I fear that he will not come* (originally: *may he come! I'm afraid* [*he won't*])

   a) **Nē nōn** sometimes occurs instead of **ut**, especially where the verb of *fearing* has a negative, or where the writer desires to emphasize some particular word in the dependent clause; as,—

      nōn vereor ne hōc nōn fīat, *I am not afraid that this will not happen*

      vereor nē exercitum fīrmum habēre nōn possit, *I fear that he is unable* (**nōn possit**) *to have a strong army (Att. vii.12.2).*

SUBSTANTIVE CLAUSES OF RESULT

297 Substantive Clauses of Result (introduced by **ut, ut nōn**) are a development of pure Result clauses, and occur with the following classes of words:—

1. As object clauses after verbs of *doing, accomplishing* (especially **faciō, efficiō, cōnficiō**). Thus:—

   gravitās morbī facit ut medicīnā egeāmus, *the severity of disease makes us need medicine.*

2. As the subject of several impersonal verbs, particularly **fit, efficitur, accidit, ēvenit, contingit, accēdit, fierī potest, fore, sequitur, relinquitur.** Thus:—

   ex quō efficitur, ut voluptās nōn sit summum bonum, *from which it follows that pleasure is not the greatest good (F. ii.24)*

   ita fit, ut nēmō esse possit beātus, *thus it happens that no one can be happy (Tusc. Disp. ii.16)*

   accēdēbat ut nāvēs deessent, *another thing was the lack of ships* (lit. *it was added that ships were lacking*)

3. As predicate or appositive after expressions like **jūs est, mōs est, cōnsuētūdō est**; also after neuter pronouns, **hōc, illud**, *etc.* Thus:—

est mōs hominum ut nōlint eundem plūribus rēbus excellere, *it is the way of men not to wish the same person to excel in many things (Brut. 84).*

SUBSTANTIVE CLAUSES INTRODUCED BY QUĪN

298 Substantive Clauses introduced by **quīn** (used sometimes as subject, sometimes as object) occur after negative and interrogative expressions of *doubt, omission,* and the like, particularly after **nōn dubitō,** *I do not doubt*; **quis dubitat,** *who doubts?*; **nōn (haud) dubium est,** *there is no doubt.* The mood is the Subjunctive. Examples:—

> **quis dubitat quīn in virtūte dīvitiae sint,** *who doubts that in virtue there are riches? (Par. 48)*
>
> **nōn dubium erat quīn ventūrus esset,** *there was no doubt that he was about to come.*

a) In Nepos, Livy, and post-Augustan writers an Infinitive sometimes takes the place of the **quīn**-clause after **nōn dubitō**; as,—

> **nōn dubitāmus inventōs esse,** *we do not doubt that men were found*

b) **Nōn dubitō,** *I do not hesitate*, is regularly followed by the Infinitive, though sometimes by a **quīn**-clause.

SUBSTANTIVE CLAUSES INTRODUCED BY QUOD

299 1. **Quod,** *the fact that, that,* introduces Substantive Clauses in the Indicative. This construction occurs especially—

a) In apposition with a preceding demonstrative, as **hōc, id, illud, illa, ex eō, inde,** *etc.* Thus:—

> **illud est admīrātiōne dignum, quod captīvōs retinendōs cēnsuit,** *this is especially worthy of admiration, that he thought the prisoners ought to be kept (Off. iii.111)*
>
> **hōc ūnō praestāmus vel maximē ferīs, quod colloquimur inter nōs,** *in this one respect we are especially superior to the beasts, that we talk with each other (de Or. i.32).*

b) After **bene fit, bene accidit, male fit, bene facere, mīror,** *etc.*; as,—

> **bene mihi ēvenit, quod mittor ad mortem,** *it is well for me that I am sent to death (Tusc. Disp. i.97)*
>
> **bene fēcistī quod mānsistī,** *you did well in remaining.*

2. **Quod** at the beginning of the sentence sometimes has the force of *as regards the fact that*. Thus:—

> **quod multitūdinem Germānōrum in Galliam trādūcō, id meī mūniendī causā faciō,** *as regards the fact that I am transporting a multitude of Germans into Gaul, I am doing it for the sake of strengthening myself (B.G. i.44.6)*

> **quod mē Agamemnona aemulārī putās, falleris,** *as regards your thinking that I emulate Agamemnon, you are mistaken (*Nep. *Ep.* 5.6).

INDIRECT QUESTIONS

300 1. Indirect Questions are Substantive Clauses used after verbs of *asking, inquiring, telling,* and the like. They take their verb in the Subjunctive.[52] Like Direct Questions (see § 162) they may be introduced—

a) By Interrogative Pronouns or Adverbs; as,—

> **dīc mihi ubi fuerīs, quid fēcerīs,** *tell me where you were, what you did*

> **oculīs jūdicārī nōn potest in utram partem fluat Arar,** *it cannot be determined by the eye in which direction the Arar flows (B.G. i.12.1)*

> **bis bīna quot essent, nesciēbat,** *he did not know how many two times two were (N.D. ii.49).*

NOTE—Care should be taken to distinguish Indirect Questions from Relative Clauses. The difference between the two appears clearly in the following:—

> **effugere nēmō id potest quod futūrum est,** *no one can escape what is destined to come to pass (N.D. iii.14);* but

> **saepe autem ne ūtile quidem est scīre quid futūrum sit,** *but often it is not even useful to know what is coming to pass (N.D. iii.14).*

---

b) By **num** or **-ne**, without distinction of meaning; as,—

> **Epamīnōndās quaesīvit num salvus esset clipeus,** or **salvusne esset clipeus,** *Epaminondas asked whether his shield was safe (F. ii.97)*

---

52 Exclamations, also, upon becoming indirect, take the Subjunctive, as **cōnsiderā quam variae sint hominum cupīdinēs,** consider how varied are the desires of men. (Direct: **quam variae sunt hominum cupīdinēs!**)

disputātur num interīre virtūs in homine possit, *the question is raised whether virtue can die in a man*

ex Sōcrate quaesītum est nōnne Archelāum beātum putāret, *the question was asked of Socrates whether he did not think Archelaus happy (Tusc. Disp. v.34).*

NOTE—**Nōnne** in Indirect Questions occurs only after **quaerō,** as in the last example above.

---

2. Often the Indirect Question represents a Deliberative Subjunctive of the direct discourse; as,—

nesciō quid faciam, *I do not know what to do.* (Direct: **quid faciam,** *what shall I do!*) (Pl. *Amph.* 1056)

3. After verbs of *expectation* and *endeavor* (**exspectō, cōnor, experior, temptō**) we sometimes find an Indirect Question introduced by **sī;** as,—

cōnantur sī perrumpere possint, *they try whether they can break through (B.G. i.8.4)*

a) Sometimes the governing verb is omitted; as,—

pergit ad proximam spēluncam sī forte eō vēstīgia ferrent, *he proceeded to the nearest cave (to see) if the tracks led thither (Liv. i.7.6).*

4. **Indirect Double Questions** are introduced in the main by the same particles as direct double questions (§ 162, 4); viz.;—

utrum ... an

-ne ... an

— ... an

— ... ne

Examples:—

quaerō utrum vērum an falsum sit
quaerō vērumne an falsum sit 　　　} *I ask whether it*
quaerō vērum an falsum sit 　　　　　*is true or*
quaerō vērum falsumne sit 　　　　　*false?*

a) *'Or not'* in the second member of the double question is ordinarily expressed by **necne,** less frequently by **an nōn;** as,—

dī utrum sint necne, quaeritur, *it is asked whether there are gods or not (N.D. i.61).*

5. **Haud sciō an**, **nesciō an**, by omission of the first member of the double question, occur with the Subjunctive in the sense: *I am inclined to think, probably, perhaps;* as,—

> **haud sciō an ita sit**, *I am inclined to think this is so (Tusc. Disp. ii.41).*

6. In early Latin and in poetry the Indicative is sometimes used in indirect Questions.

Conditional Sentences

301 Conditional Sentences are compound sentences (§ 164) consisting of two parts, the Protasis (or condition), usually introduced by sī, nisi, or sīn, and the Apodosis (or conclusion). There are the following types of Conditional Sentences:—

First Type—Nothing Implied as to the Reality of the Supposed Case

302 1. Here we regularly have the Indicative in both Protasis and Apodosis. Any tense may be used; as,—

> **sī hōc crēdis, errās**, *if you believe this, you are mistaken*
>
> **nātūram sī sequēmur, numquam aberrābimus**, *if we follow Nature, we shall never go astray (Off. i.100)*
>
> **sī hōc dīxistī, errāstī**, *if you said this, you were in error.*

2. Sometimes the Protasis takes the Indefinite Second Person Singular (§ 356, 3) of the Present or Perfect Subjunctive, with the force of the Indicative; as,—

> **memoria minuitur, nisi eam exerceās**, *memory is impaired unless you exercise it (de Sen. 21).*

3. Here belong also those conditional sentences in which the Protasis denotes a repeated action (compare §§ 287, 2; 288, 3); as,—

> **sī quis equitum dēciderat, peditēs circumsistēbant**, *if any one of the horsemen fell, the foot-soldiers gathered about him (B.G. i.48.6).*

a) Instead of the Indicative, Livy and subsequent writers employ the Subjunctive of the Historical tenses in the Protasis to denote repeated action; as,—

> **sī dīcendō quis diem eximeret**, *if (ever) anybody consumed a day in pleading (Tac. Dial. 19)*
>
> **sī quandō adsidēret**, *if ever he sat by*

4. Where the sense demands it, the Apodosis in conditional sentences of the First Type may be an Imperative or one of the Independent Subjunctives (Hortatory, Deliberative, *etc.*); as,—

> **sī hōc crēditis, tacēte**, *if you believe this, be silent*
>
> **sī hōc crēdimus, taceāmus**, *if we believe this, let us keep silent.*

Second Type—'Should'-'Would' Conditions

303 Here we regularly have the Subjunctive (of the Present or Perfect tense) in both Protasis and Apodosis; as,—

> **sī hōc dīcās, errēs**, or **sī hōc dīxerīs, errāverīs**, *if you should say this, you would be mistaken*
>
> **sī velim Hannibalis proelia omnia dēscrībere, diēs mē dēficiat**, *if I should wish to describe all the battles of Hannibal, time would fail me*
>
> **mentiar, sī negem**, *I should lie, if I should deny it (Lael. 10)*
>
> **haec sī tēcum patria loquātur, nōnne impetrāre dēbeat**, *if your country should plead thus with you, would she not deserve to obtain her request? (Cat. 1.19)*

a) The Subjunctive in the Apodosis of conditional sentences of this type is of the Potential variety.

b) Sometimes we find the Indicative in the Apodosis of sentences of the Second Type, where the writer wishes to assert the accomplishment of a result more positively; as,—

> **aliter sī faciat, nūllam habet auctōritātem**, *if he should do otherwise, he has no authority.*

Third Type—Supposed Case Represented as Contrary to Fact

304 1. Here we regularly have the Subjunctive in both Protasis and Apodosis, the Imperfect referring *to present time*, and the Pluperfect referring *to past*; as,—

> **sī amīcī meī adessent, opis nōn indigērem**, *if my friends were here, I should not lack assistance*
>
> **sī hōc dīxissēs, errāssēs**, *if you had said this, you would have erred*

sapientia nōn expeterētur, sī nihil efficeret, *philosophy would not be desired, if it accomplished nothing (F. i.42)*

cōnsilium, ratiō, sententia nisi essent in senibus, nōn summum cōnsilium majōrēs nostrī appellāssent senātum, *unless deliberation, reason, and wisdom existed in old men, our ancestors would not have called their highest deliberative body a senate (de Sen. 19).*

2. Sometimes the Imperfect Subjunctive is found referring to the past, especially to denote *a continued act, or a state of things still existing*; as,—

   Laelius, Fūrius, Catō sī nihil litterīs adjuvārentur, numquam sē ad eārum studium contulissent, *Laelius, Furius, and Cato would never have devoted themselves to the study of letters, unless they had been (constantly) helped by them (Arch. 16)*

   num igitur sī ad centēsimum annum vīxisset, senectūtis eum suae paenitēret, *if he had lived to his hundredth year, would he have regretted (and now be regretting) his old age? (de Sen. 19)*

3. The Apodosis in conditional sentences of this type sometimes stands in the Indicative (Imperfect, Perfect, or Pluperfect), *viz.*—

   a) Frequently in expressions of *ability, obligation,* or *necessity*; as,—

      nisi fēlīcitās in sōcordiam vertisset, exuere jugum potuērunt, *unless their prosperity had turned to folly, they could have thrown off the yoke (Tac. Agr. 31).*

NOTE—In sentences of this type, however, it is not the *possibility* that is represented as-contrary-to-fact, but something to be supplied in thought from the context. Thus in the foregoing sentence the logical apodosis is *et exuissent* understood (*and they would have shaken it off*). When the *possibility* itself is conditioned, the Subjunctive is used.

---

eum patris locō colere dēbēbās, sī ūlla in tē pietās esset, *you ought to revere him as a father, if you had any sense of devotion (Phil. ii.99).*

b) With both the Periphrastic Conjugations; as,—

sī Sēstius occīsus esset, fuistisne ad arma itūrī, *if Sestius had been slain, would you have proceeded to arms? (Sest.* 81)

sī ūnum diem morātī essētis, moriendum omnibus fuit, *if you had delayed one day, you would all have had to die* (Liv. ii.38.5).

Protasis expressed without *Sī*

305 1. The Protasis is not always expressed by a clause with **sī,** but may be implied in a word, a phrase, or merely by the context; as,—

aliōquī haec nōn scrīberentur, *otherwise* (*i.e.* if matters were otherwise) *these things would not be written*

nōn potestis, voluptāte omnia dīrigentēs, retinēre virtūtem, *you cannot retain virtue, if you direct everything with reference to pleasure (F.* ii.71).

2. Sometimes an Imperative, or a Jussive Subjunctive, serves as Protasis. Thus:—

crās petitō, dabitur, *if you ask to-morrow, it shall be given you* (lit. *ask to-morrow, etc.*) (Pl. *Merc.* 770)

haec reputent, vidēbunt, *if they consider this, they will see* (lit. *let them consider, etc.*) *(Tusc. Disp. i.51)*

rogēs Zēnōnem, respondeat, *if you should ask Zeno, he would answer (F.* iv.69).

Use of *Nisi, Sī Nōn, Sīn*

306 1. **Nisi,** *unless,* negatives the entire protasis; **sī nōn** negatives a single word; as,—

ferreus essem, nisi tē amārem, *I should be hard-hearted unless I loved you (Fam.* xv.21.3); but—

ferreus essem, sī tē nōn amārem, *I should be hard-hearted if I did* NOT *love you.*

In the first example, it is the notion of *loving you* that is negatived, in the second, the notion of *loving.*

2. **Sī nōn (sī minus)** is regularly employed:—

a) When an apodosis with **at, tamen, certē** follows; as,—

dolōrem sī nōn potuerō frangere, tamen occultābō, *if I cannot crush my sorrow, yet I will hide it* (Phil. *xii.21*).

b) When an affirmative protasis is repeated in negative form; as,—

> **sī fēceris, magnam habēbō grātiam; sī nōn fēceris, ignōscam,** *if you do it, I shall be deeply grateful; if you do not do it, I shall pardon you (Fam. v.19.2).*

  i) But if the verb is omitted in the repetition, only **si minus** or **sin minus** is admissible; as,—

> **hōc sī assecūtus sum, gaudeō; sī minus, mē cōnsōlor,** *if I have attained this, I am glad; if not, I console myself (Fam. vii.1.6).*

3. **Sīn.** Where one protasis is followed by another opposed in meaning, but affirmative in form, the second is introduced by **sīn**; as,—

> **hunc mihi timōrem ēripe; sī vērus est, nē opprimar, sīn falsus, ut timēre dēsinam,** *relieve me of this fear; if it is well founded, that I may not be destroyed; but if it is groundless, that I may cease to fear (Cat. 1.18).*

4. **Nisi** has a fondness for combining with negatives (**nōn, nēmō, nihil**); as,—

> **nihil cōgitāvit nisi caedem,** *he had no thought but murder (Cat. 2.10).*

  a) **Nōn** and **nisi** are always separated in the best Latinity.

5. **Nisi forte, nisi vērō, nisi sī,** *unless perchance, unless indeed* (often with ironical force), take the Indicative; as,—

> **nisi vērō, quia perfecta rēs nōn est, nōn vidētur pūnienda,** *unless indeed, because an act is not consummated, it does not seem to merit punishment (Mil. 19).*

Conditional Clauses of Comparison

307 1. Conditional Clauses of Comparison are introduced by the particles, **ac sī, ut sī, quasi, quam sī, tamquam sī, velut sī,** or simply by **velut** or **tamquam**. They stand in the Subjunctive mood and regularly involve an ellipsis (see § 374, 1), as indicated in the following examples:—

> **tantus patrēs metus cēpit, velat sī jam ad portās hostis esset,** *as great fear seized the senators as (would have seized them) if the enemy were already at the gates*

> **sed quid ego hīs testibus ūtor quasi rēs dubia aut obscūra sit**, *but why do I use these witnesses, as (I should do) if the matter were doubtful or obscure (Div. Caec. 14)*
>
> **serviam tibi tam quasi ēmerīs mē argentō**, *I will serve you as though you had bought me for money* (Pl. Men. 1101).

2. Note that in sentences of this kind the Latin observes the regular principles for the Sequence of Tenses. Thus after principal tenses the Latin uses the Present and Perfect (as in the second and third examples), where the English uses the Past and Past Perfect.

Concessive Clauses

308 The term 'Concessive' is best restricted to those clauses developed from the Jussive Subjunctive which have the force of *granted that, etc.*; (see § 278) as,—

> **sit fūr, sit sacrilegus, at est bonus imperātor**, *granted that he is a thief and a robber, yet he is a good commander (Verr. v.4)*
>
> **haec sint falsa**, *granted that this is false (Ac. ii.105)*
>
> **nē sit summum malum dolor, malum certē est**, *granted that pain is not the greatest evil, yet it is certainly an evil (Tusc. Disp. ii.14).*

Adversative Clauses with *Quamvīs, Quamquam, etc.*

309 Clauses introduced by **quamvīs, quamquam, etsī, tametsī, cum**, *although*, while often classed as 'Concessive,' are yet essentially different from genuine Concessive clauses. As a rule, they do not *grant* or *concede* anything, but rather state that something is true *in spite of something else*. They accordingly emphasize the adversative idea, and are properly Subordinate Adversative Clauses. The different particles used to introduce these clauses have different meanings and take different constructions, as follows:—

1. **Quamvīs**, *however much, although*, does not introduce a statement of fact, but represents an act merely as conceived. It is followed by the Subjunctive, usually of the present tense; as,—

> **hominēs quamvīs in turbidīs rēbus sint, tamen interdum animīs relaxantur**, *in however stirring*

events men may engage, yet at times they relax their
energies (Phil. ii.39)

nōn est potestās opitulandī reī pūblicae quamvīs ea
premātur perīculīs, *there is no opportunity to succor*
the state, though it be beset by dangers (Rep. 1.10).

2. **Quamquam, etsī, tametsī,** *although,* introduce a statement
   of fact, and are followed by the Indicative (of any tense);
   as,—

   quamquam omnis virtūs nōs allicit, tamen jūstitia
   id maximē efficit, *although all virtue attracts us, yet*
   justice does so especially (Off. i.56)

   Caesar, etsī nōndum cōnsilium hostium cognōverat,
   tamen id quod accidit suspicābātur, *Caesar, though*
   he did not yet know the plans of the enemy, yet was
   suspecting what actually occurred (B.G. iv.31.1).

   a) **Etsī,** *although,* must be distinguished from **etsī,** *even if.*
      The latter is a conditional particle and takes any of the
      constructions admissible for **sī.** (See §§ 302-304.)

3. **Cum,** *although,* is followed by the Subjunctive; as,—

   Atticus honōrēs nōn petiit, cum eī patērent, *Atticus*
   did not seek honors, though they were open to him
   (Nep. *Att.* 6.2).

4. **Licet** sometimes loses its verbal force (see § 295, 6) and sinks
   to the level of a conjunction with the force of although. It
   takes the Subjunctive, Present or Perfect; as,—

   licet omnēs terrōrēs impendeant, succurram, *though all*
   terrors hang over me, (yet) I will lend aid (Rosc. Am. 31).

5. **Quamquam,** with the force *and yet,* is often used to
   introduce principal clauses; as,—

   quamquam quid loquor, *and yet why do I speak? (Cat.*
   i.22)

6. In post-Augustan writers **quamquam** is freely construed
   with the Subjunctive, while **quamvīs** is often used to
   introduce statements of fact, and takes either the Indicative
   or the Subjunctive. Thus:—

   quamquam movērētur hīs vōcibus, *although he was*
   moved by these words (Liv. xxxvi.34.6)

   quamvīs multī opīnārentur, *though many thought*
   (Tac. *Dial.* 2)

   quamvīs īnfēstō animō pervēnerās, *though you had*
   come with hostile intent (Liv. ii.40.7).

Clauses with *Dum, Modo, Dummodo,* denoting a Wish or a Proviso

310 These particles are followed by the Subjunctive (negative nē) and have two distinct uses:—

I.   They are used to introduce clauses *embodying a wish* entertained by the subject of the leading verb; as,—

multī honesta neglegunt dummodo potentiam cōnsequantur, *many neglect honor in their desire to obtain power (if only they may attain) (Off.* iii.82)

omnia postposuī, dum praeceptīs patris pārērem, *I made everything else secondary, in my desire to obey the injunctions of my father (Fam.* xvi.21.6)

nīl obstat tibi, dum nē sit dītior alter, *nothing hinders you in your desire that your neighbor may not be richer than you (Hor. Sat.* i.1.40).

II.   They are used to express a *proviso* ('*provided that*'); as,—

ōderint, dum metuant, *let them hate, provided they fear* (Acc. 204)

manent ingenia senibus, modo permaneat studium et industria, *old men retain their faculties, provided only they retain their interest and vigor (de Sen.* 22)

nūbant, dum nē dōs fiat comes, *let them marry, provided no dowry goes with it* (Pl. *Aul.* 491).

Relative Clauses

311 Relative Clauses are introduced by Relative Pronouns, Adjectives, or Adverbs.

312 1. Relative clauses usually stand in the Indicative Mood, especially clauses introduced by those General Relatives which are doubled or have the suffix **-oumque**; as,—

quidquid id est, timeō Danaōs et dōna ferentēs, *whatever it is, I fear the Greeks even when they offer gifts (Aen.* ii.49)

quidquid oritur, quālecumque est, causam ā nātūrā habet, *whatever comes into being, of whatever sort it is, has its primal cause in Nature (Div.* ii.60).

2. Any simple Relative may introduce a conditional sentence of any of the three types mentioned in §§ 302-304; as,—

quī hōc dīcit, errat, *he who says this is mistaken* (First Type);

quī hōc dīcat, erret, *he would be mistaken who should say this* (Second Type);

quī hōc dīxisset, errāsset, *the man who had said this would have been mistaken.*

Indirect Discourse *(Ōrātiō Oblīqua)*

313   When the language or thought of any person is reproduced without change, that is called Direct Discourse (*Ōrātiō Recta*); as, *Caesar said, 'The die is cast.'* When, on the other hand, one's language or thought is made to depend upon a verb of *saying, thinking, etc.,* that is called Indirect Discourse (*Ōrātiō Oblīqua*); as, *Caesar said that the die was cast; Caesar thought that his troops were victorious.*

a) For the verbs most frequently employed to introduce Indirect Discourse, see § 331.

Moods in Indirect Discourse

Declarative Sentences

314   1. Declarative Sentences upon becoming Indirect change their main clause to the Infinitive with Subject Accusative, while all subordinate clauses take the Subjunctive; as,—

Rēgulus dīxit quam diū jūre jūrandō hostium tenērētur nōn esse sē senātōrem, *Regulus said that as long as he was held by his pledge to the enemy he was not a senator.* (Direct: **quam diū teneor nōn sum senātor.**) *(Off.* iii.100)

2. The verb of *saying, thinking, etc.,* is sometimes to be inferred from the context; as,—

tum Rōmulus lēgātōs circā vīcīnās gentēs mīsit quī societātem cōnūbiumque peterent: urbēs quoque, ut cētera, ex īnfimō nāscī, *then Romulus sent envoys around among the neighboring tribes, to ask for alliance and the right of intermarriage, (saying that) cities, like everything else, start from a modest beginning* (Liv. i.9.2).

3. Subordinate clauses which contain an explanatory statement of the writer and so are not properly a part of the Indirect Discourse, or which emphasize the fact stated, take the Indicative; as,—

> **nūntiātum est Ariovistum ad occupandum Vesontiōnem, quod est oppidum maximum Sēquanōrum contendere**, *it was reported that Ariovistus was hastening to seize Vesontio, which is the largest town of the Sequani (B.G.* i.38.1).

4. Sometimes a subordinate clause is such only in its external form, and in sense is principal. It then takes the Infinitive with Subject Accusative. This occurs especially in case of relative clauses, where quī is equivalent to **et hīc**, **nam hīc**, *etc.*; as,—

> **dīxit urbem Athēniēnsium prōpugnāculum oppositum esse barbarīs, apud quam jam bis classēs rēgiās fēcisse naufragium**, *he said the city of the Athenians had been set against the barbarians like a bulwark, near which (= and near it) the fleets of the King had twice met disaster* (Nep. *Them.* 7.5).

5. The Subject Accusative of the Infinitive is sometimes omitted when it refers to the same person as the subject of the leading verb, or can easily be supplied from the context; as,—

> **cum id nescīre Māgō dīceret**, *when Mago said he did not know this* (for **sē nescīre**).

Interrogative Sentences

315

1. Real questions of the Direct Discourse, upon becoming indirect, are regularly put in the Subjunctive; as,—

> **Ariovistus Caesarī respondit: sē prius in Galliam vēnisse quam populum Rōmānum. Quid sibi vellet? Cūr in suās possessiōnēs venīret**, *Ariovistus replied to Caesar that he had come into Gaul before the Roman people. What did he (Caesar) mean? Why did he come into his domain?* (Direct: **quid tibi vīs? cūr in meās possessiōnēs venīs?**) *(B.G.* i.44.7)

2. Rhetorical questions, on the other hand, being asked merely for effect, and being equivalent in force to emphatic statements, regularly stand in the Infinitive in Indirect Discourse. Thus :—

quid est levius (lit. *what is more trivial*, = nothing is more trivial) of the Direct Discourse becomes **quid esse levius** in the Indirect.

3. Deliberative Subjunctives of the Direct Discourse remain unchanged in mood in the Indirect: as,—

quid faceret, *what was he to do?* (Direct: **quid faciat?**)

Imperative Sentences

316 All Imperatives or Jussive Subjunctives of the Direct Discourse appear as Subjunctives in the Indirect; as,—

mīlitēs certiōrēs fēcit paulisper intermitterent proelium, *he told the soldiers to stop the battle for a little.* (Direct: **intermittite.**) (*B.G.* iii.5.3)

a) The negative in such sentences is **nē**; as,—

nē suae virtūtī tribueret, *let him not attribute it to his own valor!*

Tenses in Indirect Discourse

Tenses of the Infinitive

317 These are used in accordance with the regular principles for the use of the Infinitive as given in § 270.

a) The Perfect Infinitive may represent any past tense of the Indicative of Direct Discourse. Thus:—

sciō tē haec ēgisse may mean—

I know you were doing this.(Direct: **haec agēbās.**)
I know you did this. (Direct: **haec ēgistī.**)
I know you had done this. (Direct: **haec ēgerās.**)

Tenses of the Subjunctive

318 These follow the regular principle for the Sequence of Tenses, being Principal if the verb of *saying* is Principal; Historical if it is Historical. Yet for the sake of vividness, we often find the Present Subjunctive used after an historical tense (*Repraesentātiō*); as,—

Caesar respondit, sī obsidēs dentur, sēsē pācem esse factūrum, *Caesar replied that, if hostages be given, he would make peace* (*B.G.* i.14.6).

a) For the sequence after the Perfect Infinitive, see §268, 2.

Conditional Sentences in Indirect Discourse

Conditional Sentences of the First Type

319 The Apodosis. Any tense of the Indicative is changed to the corresponding tense of the Infinitive (§§ 270; 317, a).

The Protasis. The protasis takes those tenses of the Subjunctive which are required by the Sequence of Tenses.

Examples:—

DIRECT	INDIRECT
sī hōc **crēdis, errās,**	dīcō, sī hōc **crēdās,** tē **errāre;** dīxī, sī hōc **crēderēs,** tē **errāre.**
sī hōc **crēdēs, errābis,**	dīcō, sī hōc **crēdās,** tē **errātūrum esse;** dīxī, sī hōc **crēderēs,** tē **errātūrum esse.**
sī hōc **crēdideris, errābis,**	dīcō, sī hōc **crēderīs,** tē **errātūrum esse;** dīxī, sī hōc **crēdidissēs,** tē **errātūrum esse.**
sī hōc **crēdēbās, errāvistī,**	dīcō, sī hōc **crēderēs,** tē **errāvisse;** dīxī, sī hōc **crēderēs,** tē **errāvisse.**

a) Note that a Future Perfect Indicative of the Direct Discourse regularly appears in the Indirect as a Perfect Subjunctive after a principal tense, and as a Pluperfect Subjunctive after an historical tense.

Conditional Sentences of the Second Type

320 The Apodosis. The Present Subjunctive of the Direct Discourse regularly becomes the Future Infinitive of the Indirect.

The Protasis. The Protasis takes those tenses of the Subjunctive demanded by the sequence of tenses.

Examples:—

sī hōc crēdās, errēs, $\left\{\begin{array}{l}\text{dīcō, sī hōc crēdās, tē errātūrum esse;}\\ \text{dīxī, sī hōc crēderēs, tē errātūrum}\\ \text{esse;}\end{array}\right.$

Conditional Sentences of the Third Type

321 The Apodosis

1. The Imperfect Subjunctive of the Direct Discourse becomes the Future Infinitive.

a) But this construction is rare, being represented in the classical Latinity by a single example (Caesar, V. 29. 2). Some scholars question the correctness of this passage.

2. The Pluperfect Subjunctive of the Direct Discourse becomes:—

a) In the Active Voice the Infinitive in **-ūrus fuisse.**

b) In the Passive Voice it takes the form **futūrum fuisse ut** with the Imperfect Subjunctive.

The Protasis. The protasis in Conditional Sentences of this type always remains unchanged.

Examples:—

sī hōc **crēderēs, errārēs,**	dīcō (dīxī), sī hōc **crēderēs,** tē **errātūrum esse;**
sī hōc **crēdidissēs, errāvissēs,**	dīcō (dīxī), sī hōc **crēdidissēs,** tē **errātūrum fuisse;**
sī hōc **dīxissēs, pūnītus essēs.**	dīcō (dīxī), sī hōc **dīxissēs, futūrum fuisse ut pūnīrēris.**

322 When an apodosis of a conditional sentence of the Third Type referring to the past is at the same time a Result clause or a **quīn**-clause (after **nōn dubitō,** *etc.*), it stands in the Perfect Subjunctive in the form **-ūrus fuerim**; as,—

ita territī sunt, ut arma trāditūrī fuerint,[53] **nisi Caesar subitō advēnisset,** *they were so frightened that they would have given up their arms, had not Caesar suddenly arrived*

nōn dubitō quīn, sī hōc dīxissēs, errātūrus fueris, *I do not doubt that, if you had said this, you would have made a mistake.*

a) This peculiarity is confined to the Active Voice. In the Passive, such sentences, when they become dependent, remain unchanged; as,—

nōn dubitō quīn, sī hōc dīxissēs, vituperātus essēs, *I do not doubt that, if you had said this, you would have been blamed.*

---

53 **Trāditūri fuerint** and **errātūrus fueris** are to be regarded as representing **trāditūri fuērunt** and **errātūrus fuistī** of Direct Discourse. (See §304, 3, b.)

b) When an Indirect Question becomes an apodosis in a
    conditional sentence of the Third Type, **-ūrus fuerim**
    (rarely **-ūrus fuissem**) is used; as,—

> **quaerō, num, sī hōc dīxissēs, errātūrus fuerīs** (or
> **fuissēs**).

c) **Potuī**, when it becomes a dependent apodosis in
    sentences of this Type, usually changes to the Perfect
    Subjunctive; as,—

> **concursū tōtīus civitātis dēfēnsī sunt, ut**
> **frīgidissimōs quoque ōrātōrēs populī studia**
> **excitāre potuerint,** *they were defended before a*
> *gathering of all the citizens, so that the interest of*
> *the people would have been enough to excite even*
> *the most apathetic orators* (Tac. *Dial.* 39).

Implied Indirect Discourse

323 The Subjunctive is often used in subordinate clauses whose
indirect character is *merely implied by the context*; as,—

> **dēmōnstrābantur mihi praetereā, quae Sōcratēs**
> **dē immortālitāte animōrum disseruisset,** *there*
> *were explained to me besides, the arguments which*
> *Socrates had set forth concerning the immortality*
> *of the soul* (*i.e.* the arguments which, it was said,
> Socrates had set forth) (*de Sen.* 78)

> **Paetus omnēs librōs quōs pater suus relīquisset mihi**
> **dōnāvit,** *Paetus gave me all the books which (as he*
> *said) his father had left* (*Att.* ii.1.12).

Subjunctive by Attraction

324 1. Subordinate clauses dependent upon the Subjunctive
        are frequently attracted into the same mood especially
        when they do not express a fact, but constitute *an*
        essential part of one complex idea; as,—

> **nēmō avārus adhūc inventus est, cui, quod habēret,**
> **esset satis,** *no miser has yet been found who was*
> *satisfed with what he had* (*Par.* 52)

> **cum dīversās causās afferrent, dum fōrmam suī**
> **quisque et animī et ingeniī redderent,** *as they*
> *brought forward different arguments, while each*
> *mirrored his own individual type of mind and natural*
> *bent* (Tac. *Dial.* i.4)

> **quod ego fatear, pudeat?** *should I be ashamed of a thing which I admit?* (Pl. *Capt.* 961)

2. Similarly a subordinate clause dependent upon an Infinitive is put in the Subjunctive when the two form one closely united whole; as,—

> **mōs est Athēnīs quotannīs in cōntiōne laudārī eōs quī sint in proeliīs interfectī**, *it is the custom at Athens every year for those to be publicly eulogized who have been killed in battle.* (Here the notion of 'praising those who fell in battle' forms an inseparable whole.) *(Orat.* 151)

Noun and Adjective Forms of the Verb

325 These are the Infinitive, Participle, Gerund, and Supine. All of these partake of the nature of the Verb, on the one hand, and of the Noun or Adjective, on the other. Thus:—

As Verbs,—

a) They may be limited by adverbs;

b) They admit an object;

c) They have the properties of voice and tense.

As Nouns or Adjectives,—

a) They are declined;

b) They take Noun or Adjective constructions.

The Infinitive

Infinitive without Subject Accusative

326 This is used chiefly as Subject or Object but also as Predicate or Appositive.

NOTE—The Infinitive was originally a Dative, and traces of this are still to be seen in the poetical use of the Infinitive to express *purpose*; as, **nec dulcēs occurrent ōscula nātī praeripere**, *and no sweet children will run to snatch kisses.*

As Subject

327

1. The Infinitive without Subject Accusative is used as the Subject of **esse** and various impersonal verbs, particularly **opus est, necesse est, oportet, juvat, dēlectat, placet, libet, licet, praestat, decet, pudet, interest**, *etc.*; as,—

> **dulce et decōrum est prō patriā morī**, *it is sweet and noble to die for one's country* (Hor. *Od.* iii.2.13)

> **virōrum est fortium toleranter dolōrem patī**, *it is the part of brave men to endure pain with patience* (Tusc. Disp. ii.43)

> **senātuī placuit lēgātōs mittere**, *the Senate decided* (lit. *it pleased the Senate) to send envoys.*

2. Even though the Infinitive itself appears without Subject, it may take a Predicate Noun or Adjective in the Accusative; as,—

> **aliud est īrācundum esse, aliud īrātum**, *it is one thing to be irascible, another to be angry* (Tusc. Disp. iv.27)

> **impūne quaelibet facere, id est rēgem esse**, *to do whatever you please with impunity, that is to be a king* (Sall. Jug. 31.26).

a) But when **licet** is followed by a Dative of the person, a Predicate Noun or Adjective with **esse** is attracted into the same case; as, **licuit esse ōtiōsō Themistoclī**, lit. *it was permitted to Themistocles to be at leisure* (Tusc. Disp. i.33). So sometimes with other Impersonals.

As Object

328

1. The Infinitive without Subject Accusative is used as the Object of many verbs, to denote another action of the same subject, particularly after—

volō, cupiō, mālō, nōlō,	**cōgitō, meditor,** *purpose, intend*
dēbeo, *ought*	**neglegō,** *neglect*
statuō, cōnstituō, *decide*	**vereor, timeō,** *fear*
audeō, *dare*	**mātūrō, festīnō, properō,**
studeō, contendō, *strive*	**contendō,** *hasten*
parō, *prepare* (so **parātus**)	**assuēscō, cōnsuēscō,** *accustom*
incipiō, coepī, īnstituō, *begin*	*myself* (so **assuētus,**
pergō, *continue*	**īnsuētus, assuēfactus**)
dēsinō, dēsistō, *cease*	**discō,** *learn*
possum, *can*	**sciō,** *know how*
cōnor, *try*	**soleō,** *am wont*

as,—

> **tū hōs intuērī audēs**, *do you dare to look on these men?*
>
> **Dēmosthenēs ad flūctūs maris dēclāmāre solēbat**, *Demosthenes used to declaim by the waves of the sea (F. v.5).*

2. A Predicate Noun or Adjective with these Infinitives is attracted into the Nominative; as,—

> **beātus esse sine virtūte nēmō potest**, *no one can be happy without virtue (N.D. i.48)*
>
> **Catō esse quam vidērī bonus mālēbat**, *Cato preferred to be good rather than to seem so* (Sall. *Cat. 54.5).*

Infinitive with Subject Accusative

329 This is used chiefly as Subject or Object but also as Predicate or Appositive.

As Subject

330 The Infinitive with Subject Accusative (like the simple Infinitive) is used as Subject with **esse** and Impersonal verbs, particularly with **aequum est, ūtile est, turpe est, fāma est, spēs est, fās est, nefās est, opus est, necesse est, oportet, cōnstat, praestat, licet**, *etc.*; as,—

> **nihil in bellō oportet contemnī**, *nothing ought to be despised in war*
>
> **apertum est sibi quemque nātūrā esse cārum**, *it is manifest that by nature everybody is dear to himself (F. v.34).*

As Object

331 The Infinitive with Subject Accusative is used as Object after the following classes of verbs:

1. Most frequently after verbs of *saying, thinking, knowing, perceiving,* and the like (*Verba Sentiendi et Dēclārandī*). This is the regular construction of Principal Clauses of Indirect Discourse. Verbs that take this construction are, among others, the following: **sentiō, audiō, videō, cognōscō; putō, jūdicō, spērō, cōnfīdō; sciō, meminī; dīcō, affīrmō, negō** (*say that ... not*), **trādō, nārrō, fateor, respondeō, scrībō, prōmittō, glōrior.** Also the phrases: **certiōrem faciō** (*inform*), **memoriā teneō** (*remember*), *etc.*

Examples:—

Epicūrēī putant cum corporibus simul animōs interīre, *the Epicureans think that the soul perishes with the body (Lael.* 13)

Thalēs dīxit aquam esse initium rērum, *Thales said that water was the first principle of the universe (N.D.* 1.25)

Dēmocritus negat quicquid esse sempiternum, *Democritus says nothing is everlasting (N.D. i.29)*

spērō eum ventūrum esse, *I hope that he will come.*

2. With **jubeō,** *order,* and **vetō,** *forbid;* as,—

   Caesar mīlitēs pontem facere jussit, *Caesar ordered the soldiers to make a bridge.*

   a) When the name of the person who is ordered or forbidden to do something is omitted, the Infinitive with **jubeō** and **vetō** is put in the Passive; as, **Caesar pontem fierī jussit.**

3. With **patior** and **sinō,** *permit, allow;* as,—

   nūllō sē implicārī negōtiō passus est, *he did not permit himself to be involved in any difficulty (Lig.* 3).

4. With **volō, nōlō, mālō, cupiō,** when the Subject of the Infinitive is different from that of the governing verb; as,—

   nec mihi hunc errōrem extorquērī volō, *nor do I wish this error to be wrested from me (de Sen.* 85)

   eās rēs jactārī nōlēbat, *he was unwilling that these matters should be discussed (B.G. i.18)*

   tē tuā fruī virtūte cupimus, *we desire that you enjoy your worth (Brut.* 331).

   a) When the Subject of both verbs is the same, the simple Infinitive is regularly used in accordance with § 328, 1. But exceptions occur, especially in case of esse and Passive Infinitives as,—

      cupiō mē esse clēmentem, *I desire to be lenient (Cat.* 1.4)

      Tīmoleōn māluit sē diligī quam metuī, *Timoleon preferred to be loved rather than feared (Nep. Tim.* 3.4).

   b) **Volō** also admits the Subjunctive, with or without **ut;** **nōlō** the Subjunctive alone. (See § 296, 1, a.)

5. With Verbs of *emotion* (*joy, sorrow, regret, etc.*), especially **gaudeō, laetor, doleō; aegrē ferō, molestē ferō, graviter ferō**, *am annoyed, distressed*; **mīror, queror, indignor**; as,—

>**gaudeō tē salvum advenīre**, *I rejoice that you arrive safely* (Pl. *Bacch.* 456)

>**nōn molestē ferunt sē libīdinum vinculīs laxātōs ēsse**, *they are not troubled at being released from the bonds of passion (de Sen. 7)*

>**mīror tē ad mē nihil scrībere**, *I wonder that you write me nothing.*

a) Instead of an Infinitive these verbs also sometimes admit a **quod-** clause as Object. (See § 299.) Thus:—

>**mīror quod nōn loqueris**, *I wonder that you do not speak.*

6. Some verbs which take two Accusatives, one of the Person and the other of the Thing (§ 178, 1), may substitute an Infinitive for the second Accusative; as,—

>**cōgō tē hōc facere**, *I compel you to do this* (*cf.* **tē hōc cōgō**)

>**docuī tē contentum esse**, *I taught you to be content* (*cf.* **tē modestiam docuī**, *I taught you temperance*).

Passive Construction of the Foregoing Verbs

332 Those verbs which in the Active are followed by the Infinitive with Subject Accusative, usually admit the personal construction of the Passive. This is true of the following and of some others:—

a) **jubeor, vetor, sinor**; as,—

>**mīlitēs pontem facere jussī sunt**, *the soldiers were ordered to build a bridge*

>**pōns fierī jussus est**, *a bridge was ordered built*

>**mīlitēs castrīs exīre vetitī sunt**, *the troops were forbidden to go out of the camp*

>**Sēstius Clōdium accūsāre nōn est situs**, *Sestius was not allowed to accuse Clodius (Sest. 95).*

b) **videor**, *I am seen, I seem*; as,—

>**vidētur comperisse**, *he seems to have discovered.*

c) **dīcor, putor, exīstimor, jūdicor** (in all persons); as,—

> **dīcitur in Italiam vēnisse,** *he is said to have come into Italy*

> **Rōmulus prīmus rēx Rōmānōrum fuisse putātur,** *Romulus is thought to have been the first king of the Romans.*

d) **fertur, feruntur, trāditur, trāduntur** (only in the third person); as,—

> **fertur Homērus caecus fuisse,** *Homer is said to have been blind*

> **carmina Archilochī contumēliīs referta esse trāduntur,** *Archilochus's poems are reported to have been full of abuse.*

NOTE—In compound tenses and periphrastic forms, the last two classes of verbs, *c*), *d*), more commonly take the impersonal construction; as—

> **trāditum est Homērum caecum fuisse,** *the story goes that Homer was blind (Tusc. Disp. v.114).*

Infinitive with Adjectives

333 The Infinitive with Adjectives (except **parātus, assuētus,** *etc.*; see § 328, 1) occurs only in poetry and post-Augustan prose writers; as,—

> **contentus dēmōnstrāsse,** *contented to have proved*

> **audāx omnia perpetī,** *bold for enduring everything* (Hor. *Od.* i.3.25).

Infinitive in Exclamations

334 The Infinitive is used in Exclamations implying *scorn, indignation,* or *regret.* An intensive **-ne** is often attached to some word in the clause. Examples:—

> **huncine sōlem tam nigrum surrēxe mihi,** *to think that today's sun rose with such evil omen for me!* (Hor. *Sat.* i.9.72)

> **sedēre tōtōs diēs in vīllā,** *to stay whole days at the villa.*

Historical Infinitive

335 The Infinitive is often used in historical narrative instead of the Imperfect Indicative. The Subject stands in the Nominative; as,—

> **interim cottīdiē Caesar Haeduōs frūmentum**
> **flāgitāre,** *meanwhile Caesar was daily demanding*
> *grain of the Haedui (B.G. i.16.1).*

The Participles

Tenses of the Participle

336

1. The tenses of the Participle, like those of the infinitive (see § 270), express time not absolutely, but with reference to the verb upon which the Participle depends.

2. The Present Participle denotes action *contemporary with* that of the verb. Thus:—

   audiō tē loquentem = *you ARE speaking and I hear you*

   audiēbam tē loquentem = *you WERE speaking and I heard you*

   audiam tē loquentem = *you WILL BE speaking and I shall hear you.*

   a) The Present Participle is sometimes employed with Conative force; as,—

   assurgentem rēgem resupīnat, *as the king was trying to rise, he threw him down (Liv. iv.19).*

3. The Perfect Passive Participle denotes action *prior to* that of the verb. Thus:—

   locūtus taceō = *I HAVE spoken and am silent*

   locūtus tacui = *I HAD spoken and then was silent*

   locūtus tacēbō = *I SHALL speak and then shall be silent.*

4. The absolute time of the action of a participle, therefore, is determined entirely by the finite verb with which it is connected.

5. Certain Perfect Passive Participles of Deponent and Semi-Deponent Verbs are used as Presents; *viz.* **arbitrātus, ausus, ratus, gāvīsus, solitus, ūsus, cōnfīsus, diffīsus, secūtus, veritus.**

Use of Participles

337

As an Adjective the Participle may be used either as an attributive or predicate modifier of a Substantive.

1. Attributive Use. This presents no special peculiarities. Examples are:—

glōria est cōnsentiēns laus bonōrum, *glory is the unanimous praise of the good (Tusc. Disp.* iii.3)

Conōn mūrōs ā Lysandrō dīrutōs reficit, *Conon restored the walls destroyed by Lysander (Nep. Con. 4.5).*

2. Predicate Use. Here the Participle is often equivalent to a subordinate clause. Thus the Participle may denote:—

a) Time; as,—

omne malum nāscēns facile opprimitur, *every evil is easily crushed at birth (Phil. v.31).*

b) A Condition; as,—

mente ūtī nōn possumus cibō et pōtiōne complētī, *if gorged with food and drink, we cannot use our intellects (Tusc. Disp. v.100).*

c) Manner; as,—

Solōn senēscere sē dīcēbat multa in diēs addiscentem, *Solon said he grew old learning many new things daily (de Sen. 26).*

d) Means; as,—

sōl oriēns diem cōnficit, *the sun, by its rising, makes the day.*

e) Opposition ('*though*'); as,—

mendācī hominī nē vērum quidem dīcentī crēdimus, *we do not believe a liar, though he speaks the truth (Div. ii.146).*

f) Cause; as,—

perfidiam veritus ad suōs recessit, *since he feared treachery, he returned to his own troops (B.g. vii.5.5).*

3. **Videō** and **audiō**, besides the Infinitive, take the Present Participle in the Predicate use; as,—

videō tē fugientem, *I see you fleeing.*

a) So frequently **faciō, fingō, indūcō,** *etc.*; as,—

eīs Catōnem respondentem facimus, *we represent Cato replying to them (de Sen. 3);*

Homērus Laërtem colentem agrum facit, *Homer represents Laërtes tilling the field (de Sen. 54).*

4. The Future Active Participle (except **futūrus**) is regularly confined to its use in the Periphrastic Conjugation, but in poets and later writers it is used independently, especially to denote *purpose*; as,—

> **vēnērunt castra oppugnātūrī,** *they came to assault the camp.*

5. The Perfect Passive Participle is often equivalent to a coördinate clause; as,—

> **urbem captam dīruit,** *he captured and destroyed the city* (lit. *he destroyed the city captured) (Liv. xxii.20.4).*

6. The Perfect Passive Participle in combination with a noun is sometimes equivalent to an abstract noun with a dependent Genitive; as,—

> **post urbem conditam,** *after the founding of the city*
> **Quīnctius dēfēnsus,** *the defense of Quinctius*
> **quibus animus occupātus,** *the preoccupation of the mind with which*

7. **Habeō** sometimes takes a Perfect Passive Participle in the Predicate construction with a force not far removed from that of the Perfect or Pluperfect Indicative; as,—

> **equitātus quem coāctum habēbat,** *the cavalry which he had collected (B.G. i.15.1).*

8. The Gerundive denotes *obligation, necessity,* etc. Like other Participles it may be used either as Attributive or Predicate.

   a) Less frequently as Attributive. Thus:—

> **liber legendus,** *a book worth reading*
> **lēgēs observandae,** *laws deserving of observance*

   b) More frequently as Predicate.

      i) In the Passive Periphrastic Conjugation (**amandus est,** etc.). In this use Intransitive Verbs can be used only impersonally, but admit their ordinary case-construction (Gen., Dat., Abl.); as,—

> **veniendum est,** *it is necessary to come*
> **oblīvīscendum est offēnsārum,** *one must forget injuries (Tac.* Hist. *ii.1)*
> **numquam prōditōrī crēdendum est,** *you must never trust a traitor (Verr. i.38)*
> **suō cuique ūtendum est jūdiciō,** *every man must use his own judgment (N.D. iii.1).*

ii) After **cūrō**, *provide for*; **dō, trādō**, *give over*; **relinquō**, *leave*; **concēdō**, *hand over*, and some other verbs, instead of an object clause, or to denote purpose; as,—

> **Caesar pontem in Ararī faciendum cūrāvit,**
> *Caesar provided for the construction of a bridge over the Arar (B.G. i.13.1)*

> **imperātor urbem mīlitibus dīripiendam concessit,** *the general handed over the city to the soldiers to plunder.*

9. For the Gerundive as the equivalent of the Gerund, see § 339, 1.

The Gerund

338 As a verbal noun the Gerund admits noun constructions as follows:—

1. **Genitive.** The Genitive of the Gerund is used—

   a) With Nouns, as objective or Appositional Genitive (see §§ 200, 202); as,—

   > **cupiditās dominandī,** *desire of ruling*
   > **ars scrībendī,** *the art of writing*

   b) With Adjectives; as,—

   > **cupidus audiendī,** *desirous of hearing*

   c) With **causā, grātiā**; as,—

   > **discendī causā,** *for the sake of learning*

2. **Dative.** The Dative of the Gerund is used—

   a) With Adjectives; as,—

   > **aqua ūtilis est bibendō,** *water is useful for drinking.*

   b) With Verbs (rarely); as,—

   > **adfuī scrībendō,** *I was present at the writing (Fam. xv.6.2).*

3. **Accusative.** The Accusative of the Gerund is used only with Prepositions, chiefly **ad** and **in** to denote purpose; as,—

   > **homō ad agendum nātus est,** *man is born for action.*

4. **Ablative.** The Ablative of the Gerund is used—

   a) Without a Preposition, as an Ablative of Means, Cause, etc. (see §§ 218, 219); as,—

   > **mēns discendō alitur et cōgitandō,** *the mind is nourished by learning and reflection (Off. i.105).*

Themistoclēs maritimōs praedōnēs cōnsectandō mare tūtum reddidit, *Themistocles made the sea safe by following up the pirates* (Nep. *Them.* 2.3).

b) After the prepositions **ā, dē, ex, in**; as,—

summa voluptās ex discendō capitur, *the keenest pleasure is derived from learning*

multa dē bene beātēque vīvendō ā Platōne disputāta sunt, *there was much discussion by Plato on the subject of living well and happily (F. i.5).*

5. As a rule, only the Genitive of the Gerund and the Ablative (without a preposition) admit a Direct Object.

Gerundive Construction instead of the Gerund

339 1. Instead of the Genitive or Ablative of the Gerund with a Direct Object, another construction *may be, and very often is,* used. This consists in putting the Direct Object in the case of the Gerund (Gen. or Abl.) and using the Gerundive in agreement with it. This is called the Gerundive Construction. Thus:—

GERUND CONSTRUCTION	GERUNDIVE CONSTRUCTION
cupidus urbem videndī, *desirous of seeing the city.*	**cupidus urbis videndae**
dēlector ōrātōrēs legendō, *I am charmed with reading the orators.*	**dēlector ōrātōribus legendīs**

2. The Gerundive Construction *must be used* to avoid a Direct Object with the Dative of the Gerund, or with a case dependent upon a Preposition; as,—

locus castrīs mūniendīs aptus, *a place adapted to fortifying a camp*

ad pācem petendam vēnērunt, *they came to ask peace* (Liv. xxi.13.1)

multum temporis cōnsūmō in legendīs poētīs, *I spend much time in reading the poets.*

3. In order to avoid ambiguity (see § 236, 2), the Gerundive Construction must not be employed in case of Neuter Adjectives used substantively. Thus regularly—

philosophī cupidī sunt vērum invēstīgandī, *philosophers are eager for discovering truth* (rarely **vērī invēstīgandī**)

studium plūra cognōscendī, *a desire of knowing more*
(not **plūrium cognōscendōrum**)

4. From the nature of the case only Transitive Verbs can be used in the Gerundive construction; but **ūtor, fruor, fungor, potior** (originally transitive) regularly admit it; as,—

    hostēs in spem potiundōrum castrōrum vēnerant, *the enemy had conceived the hope of gaining possession of the camp (B.G. iii.6.2).*

5. The Genitives **meī, tuī, suī, nostrī, vestrī**, when used in the Gerundive Construction, are regularly employed without reference to Gender or Number, since they were originally Neuter Singular Adjectives used substantively. Thus:—

    mulier suī servandī causā aufūgit, *the woman fled for the sake of saving herself*

    lēgātī in castra vēnērunt suī pūrgandī causā, *the envoys came into camp for the purpose of clearing themselves (B.G. iv.13.5).*

So **nostrī servandī causā**, *for the sake of saving ourselves.*

6. Occasionally the Genitive of the Gerundive Construction is used to denote *purpose*; as,—

    quae ille cēpit lēgum ac lībertātis subvertundae, *which he undertook for the purpose of overthrowing the laws and liberty (Sall. Fr. i.77.11).*

7. The Dative of the Gerundive Construction occurs in some expressions which have the character of formulas; as,—

    decemvirī lēgibus scrībundīs, *decemvirs for codifying the laws*

    quīndecimvirī sacrīs faciundīs, *quindecimvirs for performing the sacrifices.*

The Supine

340

1. The Supine in -**um** is used after Verbs of motion to express *purpose*; as,—

    lēgātī ad Caesarem grātulātum convēnērunt, *envoys came to Caesar to congratulate him (B.G. i.30.1).*

a) The Supine in -**um** may take an Object; as,—

    pācem petītum ōrātōrēs Rōmam mittunt, *they send envoys to Rome to ask for peace.*

b) Note the phrase:—

>   **dō (collocō) fīliam nūptum**, *I give my daughter in marriage* (Pl. Tr. 735).

2. The Supine in **-ū** is used as an Ablative of Specification with **facilis, difficilis, incrēdibilis, jūcundus, optimus**, *etc.*; also with **fās est, nefās est, opus est**; as,—

>   **haec rēs est facilis cognitū**, *this thing is easy to learn*
>   **hōc est optimum factū**, *this is best to do* (Att. vii.22.2).

a) Only a few Supines in **-ū** are in common use, chiefly **audītū, cognitū, dictū, factū, vīsū**.

b) The Supine in **-ū** never takes an Object.

PARTICLES

Coördinate Conjunctions

341

Copulative Conjunctions. These *join* one word, phrase, or clause to another.

1.

a) **et** simply connects.

b) **-que** joins more closely than **et**, and is used especially where the two members have an internal connection with each other; as,—

>   **parentēs līberīque**, *parents and children*
>   **cum hominēs aestū febrīque jactantur**, *when people are tossed about with heat and fever*

c) **atque (ac)** usually emphasizes the second of the two things connected,—*and also, and indeed, and in fact.* After words of *likeness* and *difference*, **atque (ac)** has the force of *as, than.* Thus:—

>   **ego idem sentiō ac tū**, *I think the same as you*
>   **haud aliter ac**, *not otherwise than*

d) **neque (nec)** means *and not, neither, nor*

2.

a) **-que** is an enclitic, and is appended always to the second of two words connected. Where it connects phrases or clauses, it is appended to the first word of the second clause; but when the first word of the second clause is a Preposition, **-que** is regularly appended to the next following word; as,—

    ob eamque rem, *and on account of that thing*

b) **atque** is used before vowels and consonants; **ac** never before vowels, and seldom before **c, g, qu.**

c) **et nōn** is used for **neque** when the emphasis of the negative rests upon a special word; as,—

    vetus et nōn ignōbilis ōrātor, *an old and not ignoble orator*

d) For *and nowhere, and never, and none*, the Latin regularly said **nec ūsquam, nec umquam, nec ūllus**, *etc.*

3. **Correlatives.** Copulative Conjunctions are frequently used correlatively; as,—

    et ... et, *both ... and*
    neque (nec) ... neque (nec), *neither ... nor*
    cum ... tum, *while ... at the same time*
    tum ... tum, *not only ... but also*

Less frequently:—

    et ... neque; neque ... et

a) Note that the Latin, with its tendency to emphasize antithetical relations, often uses correlatives, especially **et ... et, et ... neque, neque ... et**, where the English employs but a single connective.

4. **In enumerations—**

a) The different members of a series may follow one another without connectives (Asyndeton; see § 346). Thus:—

    ex cupiditātibus odia, discidia, discordiae, sēditiōnēs, bella nāscuntur, *from covetous desires spring up hatred, dissension, discord, sedition, wars (F. 1.44).*

b) The different members may severally be connected by **et** (Polysyndeton). Thus:—

    hōrae cēdunt et diēs et mēnsēs et annī, *hours and days and months and years pass away (de Sen. 69).*

c) The connective may be omitted between the former members, while the last two are connected by **-que** (rarely **et**); as,—

    Caesar in Carnutēs, Andēs Turonēsque legiōnēs dēdūcit, *Caesar leads his legions into the territory of the Carnutes, Andes, and Turones (B.G. ii.35.3).*

342

Disjunctive Conjunctions indicate an *alternative*.

1.

   a) aut must be used when the alternatives are mutually exclusive; as,—

   > **cita mors venit aut victōria laeta**, *(either) swift death or glad victory comes* (Hor. *Sat.* i.1.8).

   b) **vel, -ve** (enclitic) imply a choice between the alternatives; as,—

   > **quī aethēr vel caelum nōminātur**, *which is called aether or heaven (N.D.* ii.41).

2. **Correlatives.** Disjunctive Conjunctions are often used correlatively; as,—

   > **aut ... aut**, *either ... or*
   > **vel ... vel**, *either ... or*
   > **sīve ... sīve**, *if ... or if*

343

Adversative Conjunctions. These denote *opposition*.

1.

   a) **sed**, *but*, merely denotes opposition.

   b) **vērum**, *but*, is stronger than **sed**, but is less frequently used.

   c) **autem**, *but on the other hand, however*, marks a transition. It is always post-positive.

DEFINITION   A post-positive word is one that cannot begin a sentence, but is placed after one or more words.

---

   d) **at**, *but*, is used especially in disputation, to introduce an opposing argument.

   e) **atquī** means *but yet*.

   f) **tamen**, *yet*, usually stands after the emphatic word, but not always.

   g) **vērō**, *however, indeed, in truth*, is always post-positive.

2. Note the correlative expressions:—

   > **nōn sōlum (nōn modo) ... sed etiam**, *not only ... but also*
   > **nōn modo nōn ... sed nē ... quidem**, *not only not, but not even*; as,—

> **nōn modo tibi nōn īrāscor, sed nē reprehendō quidem factum tuum,** *I not only am not angry with you, but I do not even blame your action.*

a) But when the sentence has but one verb, and this stands with the second member, **nōn modo** may be used for **nōn modo nōn**; as,—

> **adsentātiō nōn modo amīcō, sed nē līberō quidem digne est,** *flattery is not only not worthy of a friend, but not even of a free man (Lael. 89).*

344

Illative Conjunctions. These represent the statement which they introduce as *following from* or as *in conformity with* what has preceded.

1.

    a) **itaque** = *and so, accordingly*

    b) **ergō** = *therefore, accordingly*

    c) **igitur** (regularly post-positive[54]) = therefore, accordingly

2. **Igitur** is never combined with **et, atque, -que,** or **neque.**

345

Causal Conjunctions. These denote *cause,* or *give an explanation.* They are **nam, namque, enim** (post-positive), **etenim,** *for.*

346

Asyndeton. The conjunction is sometimes omitted between coördinate members, particularly in lively or impassioned narration. Thus:—

a) A copulative Conjunction is omitted; as,—

> **avāritia īnfīnīta, īnsatiābilis est,** *avarice is boundless (and) insatiable*

> **Cn. Pompejō, M. Crassō cōnsulibus,** *in the consulship of Gnaeus Pompey (and) Marcus Crassus (B.G. iv.1.1)*

The conjunction is regularly omitted between the names of consuls when the praenomen (*Mārcus, Gaius, etc.*) is expressed.

b) An Adversative Conjunction may be omitted; as,—

> **ratiōnēs dēfuērunt, ūbertās ōrātiōnis nōn dēfuit,** *arguments were lacking, (but) abundance of words was not.*

---

54   Except in Sallust and Silver Latin.

Adverbs

347 1. The following particles, sometimes classed as Conjunctions, are more properly Adverbs:—

etiam, *also, even*

quoque (always post-positive), *also*

quidem (always post-positive) lays stress upon the preceding word. It is sometimes equivalent to the English *indeed, in fact*, but more frequently cannot be rendered, except by vocal emphasis.

nē ... quidem means *not even*; the emphatic word or phrase always stands between; as, **nē ille quidem**, *not even he.*

tamen and **vērō**, in addition to their use as Conjunctions, are often employed as Adverbs.

2. **Negatives.** Two negatives are regularly equivalent to an affirmative as in English, as **nōn nūllī**, *some*; but when **nōn, nēmō, nihil, numquam**, *etc.*, are accompanied by **neque ... neque, nōn ... nōn, nōn modo**, or **nē ... quidem**, the latter particles simply take up the negation and emphasize it; as,—

habeō hīc nēminem neque amīcum neque cognātum, *I have here no one, neither friend nor relative.*

nōn enim praetereundum est nē id quidem, *for not even that must be passed by.*

a) **Haud** in Cicero and Caesar occurs almost exclusively as a modifier of Adjectives and Adverbs, and in the phrase **haud sciō an**. Later writers use it freely with verbs.

WORD ORDER
AND SENTENCE STRUCTURE

Word order

348 In the normal arrangement of the Latin sentence the Subject stands at the beginning of the sentence, the Predicate at the end; as,—

> **Dārīus classem quīngentārum nāvium comparāvit**, *Darius got ready a fleet of five hundred ships* (Nep. *Milt.* 4.1).

349 But for the sake of emphasis the normal arrangement is often abandoned, and the emphatic word is put at the beginning, less frequently at the end of the sentence; as,—

> **magnus in hōc bellō Themistoclēs fuit**, GREAT *was Themistocles in this war* (Nep. *Them.* 6.1)
>
> **aliud iter habēmus nūllum**, *other course we have* NONE.

Special Principles

350 1. **Nouns.** A Genitive or other oblique case regularly follows the word upon which it depends. Thus:—

a) Depending upon a Noun:—

> **tribūnus plēbis**, *tribune of the plebs*
> **fīlius rēgis**, *son of the king*
> **vir magnī animī**, *a man of noble spirit*

Yet always **senātūs cōnsultum**, **plēbis scītum**.

b) Depending upon an Adjective:—

> **ignārus rērum**, *ignorant of affairs*
> **dignī amīcitiā**, *worthy of friendship*
> **plūs aequō**, *more than (what is) fair*

2. **Appositives.** An Appositive regularly follows its Subject; as,—

> **Philippus, rēx Macedonum**, *Philip, king of the Macedonians*
>
> **adsentātiō, vitiōrum adjūtrīx**, *flattery, promoter of evils*

Yet **flūmen Rhēnus**, *the River Rhine*; and always in good prose **urbs Rōma**, *the city Rome*.

3. The **Vocative** usually follows one or more words; as,—

   audī, Caesar, *hear, Caesar!*

4. **Adjectives.** No general law can be laid down for the position of Adjectives. On the whole they precede the noun oftener than they follow it.

   a) Adjectives of *quantity* (including *numerals*) regularly precede their noun; as,—

      omnēs hominēs, *all men*
      septingentae nāvēs, *seven hundred vessels*

   b) Note the force of position in the following:—

      media urbs, *the middle of the city*
      urbs media, *the middle city*
      extrēmum bellum, *the end of the war*
      bellum extrēmum, *the last war*

   c) **Rōmānus** and **Latīnus** regularly follow; as,—

      senātus populusque Rōmānus, *the Roman Senate and People*
      lūdī Rōmānī, *the Roman games*
      fēriae Latīnae, *the Latin holidays*

   d) When a Noun is modified both by an Adjective and by a Genitive, a favorite order is: Adjective, Genitive, Noun; as,—

      summa omnium rērum abundantia, *the greatest abundance of all things*

5. **Pronouns**

   a) The Demonstrative, Relative, and Interrogative Pronouns regularly precede the Noun; as,—

      hīc homō, *this man*
      ille homō, *that man*
      erant duo itinera, quibus itineribus, *etc.*, *there were two routes, by which, etc.* (*B.G.* i.6.1)
      quī homō? *what sort of man?*

   b) But **ille** in the sense of '*that well known*,' '*that famous*,' usually stands after its Noun; as,—

      testula illa, *that well-known custom of ostracism*
      Mēdēa illa, *that famous Medea*

   c) Possessive and Indefinite Pronouns usually follow their Noun; as,—

pater meus, *my father*
homō quīdam, *a certain man*
mulier aliqua, *some woman*

But for purposes of contrast the Possessive often precedes its Noun; as,—

meus pater, MY *father (i.e.* as opposed to *yours, his, etc.)*

d) Where two or more Pronouns occur in the same sentence, the Latin is fond of putting them in close proximity; as,—

nisi forte ego vōbīs cessāre videor, *unless perchance I seem to you to be doing nothing (de Sen.* 18)

6. Adverbs and Adverbial phrases regularly precede the word they modify; as,—

valdē dīligēns, *extremely diligent*
saepe dīxī, *I have often said*
tē jam diū hortāmur, *we have long been urging you*
paulō post, *a little after*

7. **Prepositions** regularly precede the words they govern.

a) But limiting words often intervene between the Preposition and its case; as,—

dē commūnī hominum memoriā, *concerning the common memory of men*
ad beātē vīvendum, *for living happily*

b) When a noun is modified by an Adjective, the Adjective is often placed before the preposition; as,—

magnō in dolōre, *in great grief*
summā cum laude, *with the highest credit*
quā dē causā, *for which cause*
hanc ob rem, *on account of this thing*

c) For Anastrophe, by which a Preposition is put after its case, see § 144, 3.

8. **Conjunctions. Autem, enim**, and **igitur** regularly stand in the second place in the sentence, but when combined with **est** or **sunt** they often stand third; as,—

ita est enim, *for so it is*

9. Words or Phrases referring to the preceding sentence or to some part of it, regularly stand first; as,—

id ut audīvit, Corcyram dēmigrāvit, *when he heard that* (referring to the contents of the preceding sentence), *he moved to Corcyra* (Nep. *Them.* 8.3).

eō cum Caesar vēnisset, timentēs cōnfirmat, *when Caesar had come thither (i.e.* to the place just mentioned), *he encouraged the timid (B.G.* vii.7.4).

10. The Latin has a fondness for putting side by side words which are etymologically related; as,—

ut ad senem senex dē senectūte, sīc hōc librō ad amīcum amīcissimus dē amīcitiā scrīpsī, *as I, an old man, wrote to an old man, on old age, so in this book, as a fond friend, I have written to a friend, concerning friendship (Lael.* 5).

11. Special rhetorical devices for indicating emphasis are the following:—

a) **Hypérbaton,** which consists in the separation of words that regularly stand together; as,—

septimus mihi Orīginum liber est in manibus, *the seventh book of my 'Origines' is under way (de Sen.* 38).

receptō Caesar Ōricō proficīscitur, *having recovered Oricus, Caesar set out (B.C.* iii.12.1).

b) **Anáphora,** which consists in the repetition of the same word or the same word-order in successive phrases; as,—

sed plēnī omnēs sunt librī, plēnae sapientium vōcēs, plēna exemplōrum vetustās, *but all books are full of it, the voices of sages are full of it, antiquity is full of examples of it (Arch.* 14).

c) **Chiásmus,**[55] which consists in changing the relative order of words in two antithetical phrases; as,—

multōs dēfendī, laesī nēminem, *many have I defended, I have injured no one.*

horribilem illum diem aliīs, nōbīs faustum, *that day dreadful to others, for us fortunate (Tusc. Disp.* i.188).

d) **Sýnchysis,** or the interlocked arrangement. This is mostly confined to poetry, yet occurs in rhetorical prose, especially that of the Imperial Period; as,—

---

55 So named from a fancied analogy to the strokes of the Greek letter X (*chi*). Thus:—   multōs   laesī

                                 ✕

                    dēfendī   nēminem

> **simulātam Pompejānārum grātiam partium,**
> *pretended interest in the Pompeian party* (Tac. A. i.10)

12. **Metrical Close**. At the end of a sentence certain cadences were avoided; others were much employed. Thus:—

a) Cadences avoided.

$-\cup\cup-\cup$;   as, esse vidētur (close of hexameter)

$-\cup\cup\cup$;   as, **esse potest** (close of pentameter)

b) Cadences frequently employed.

$-\cup-$;   as, **auxerant**

$-\cup-\cup$;   as, **comprobāvit**

$-\cup\cup\cup-\cup$;   as, **esse videātur**

$\cup--\cup-$;   as, **rogātū tuō**

Sentence Structure

351

1. **Unity of Subject.**—In complex sentences the Latin regularly holds to unity of Subject in the different members; as,—

Caesar prīmum suō, deinde omnium ex cōnspectū remōtīs equīs, ut aequātō perīculō spem fugae tolleret, cohortātus suōs proelium commīsit, *Caesar having first removed his own horse from sight, then the horses of all, in order, by making the danger equal, to take away hope of flight, encouraged his men and joined battle (B.G. i.25.1).*

2. A word serving as the common Subject or Object of the main clause and a subordinate one, stands before both; as,—

Haeduī cum sē dēfendere nōn possent, lēgātōs ad Caesarem mittunt, *since the Haedui could not defend themselves, they sent envoys to Caesar (B.G. i.11.2).*

ille etsī flagrābat bellandī cupiditāte, tamen pācī serviendum putāvit, *although he was burning with a desire to fight, yet he thought he ought to aim at peace (Nep. Ham. 1).*

a) The same is true also

i) When the Subject of the main clause is Object (Direct or Indirect) of a subordinate clause; as,—

Caesar, cum hōc eī nūntiatum esset, mātūrat ab urbe proficīscī, *when this had been reported to Caesar he hastened to set out from the city (B.G. i.7.1).*

ii) When the Subject of a subordinate clause is at the same time the Object (Direct or Indirect) of the main clause; as,—

L. Mānliō, cum dictātor fuisset, M. Pompōnius tribūnus plēbis diem dīxit, *M. Pomponius, tribune of the people, instituted proceedings against Lucius Manlius, though he had been dictator.*

3. Of subordinate clauses, temporal, conditional, and adversative clauses more commonly precede the main clause; indirect questions and clauses of purpose or result more commonly follow; as,—

postquam haec dīxit, profectus est, *after he said this, he set out.*

sī quis ita agat, imprūdēns sit, *if any one should act so, he would be devoid of foresight.*

accidit ut ūnā nocte omnēs Hermae dēicerentur, *it happened that in a single night all the Hermae were thrown down* (Nep. *Alc.* 3.2).

4. Sometimes in Latin the main verb is placed within the subordinate clause; as,—

sī quid est in mē ingenī, quod sentiō quam sit exiguum, *if there is any talent in me, and I know how little it is (Arch. 1)*

5. **The Latin Period.** The term Period, when strictly used, designates a compound sentence in which the subordinate clauses are inserted within the main clause; as,—

Caesar etsī intellegēbat quā dē causā ea dīcerentur, tamen, nē aestātem in Trēverīs cōnsūmere cōgerētur, Indutiomārum ad sē venīre jussit, *though Caesar perceived why this was said, yet, lest he should be forced to spend the summer among the Treveri, he ordered Indutiomarus to come to him (B.G. v.4.1).*

In the Periodic structure the thought is suspended until the end of the sentence is reached. Many Roman writers were extremely fond of this sentence-structure, and it was well adapted to the inflectional character of their language; in English we generally avoid it.

6. When there are several subordinate clauses in one Period, the Latin so arranges them as to avoid a succession of verbs. Thus:—

> **At hostēs cum mīsissent, quī, quae in castrīs gererentur, cognōscerent, ubi sē dēceptōs intellēxērunt, omnibus cōpiīs subsecūtī ad flūmen contendunt,** *but the enemy when they had sent men to learn what was going on in camp, after discovering that they had been outwitted, followed with all their forces and hurried to the river.*

HINTS ON LATIN STYLE

352

In this chapter brief consideration is given to a few features of Latin diction which belong rather to style than to formal grammar.

Nouns

353

1. Where a distinct reference to several persons or things is involved, the Latin is frequently *much more exact in the use of the Plural* than is the English; as,—

> **domōs eunt,** *they go home (i.e. to their homes)*
>
> **Germānī corpora cūrant,** *the Germans care for the body*
>
> **animōs mīlitum recreat,** *he renews the courage of the soldiers*
>
> **diēs noctēsque timēre,** *to be in a state of fear day and night*

2. In case of Neuter Pronouns and Adjectives used substantively, the Latin often employs the Plural where the English uses the Singular; as,—

> **omnia sunt perdīta,** *everything is lost*
>
> **quae cum ita sint,** *since this is so*

haec omnibus pervulgāta sunt, *this is very well known to all*

3. The Latin is usually *more concrete* than the English, and especially *less bold in the personification* of abstract qualities. Thus:—

ā puerō, ā puerīs, *from boyhood*
Sullā dictātōre, *in Sulla's dictatorship*
mē duce, *under my leadership*
Rōmānī cum Carthāginiēnsibus pācem fēcērunt =
Rome made peace with Carthage
liber doctrīnae plēnus = *a learned book*
prūdentiā Themistoclīs Graecia servāta est =
Themistocles's foresight saved Greece

4. The Nouns of Agency in **-tor** and **-sor** (see § 147, 1) denote a permanent or characteristic activity; as,—

accūsātōrēs, *(professional) accusers*
ōrātōrēs, *pleaders*
cantōrēs, *singers*
Arminius, Germāniae līberātor, *Arminius, liberator of Germany*

a) To denote single instances of an action, other expressions are commonly employed; as,—

Numa, quī Rōmulō successit, *Numa, successor of Romulus*
quī mea legunt, *my readers*
quī mē audiunt, *my auditors*

5. The Latin avoids the use of prepositional phrases as modifiers of a Noun. In English we say: 'The war against Carthage'; 'a journey through Gaul'; 'cities on the sea'; 'the book in my hands'; 'the fight at Salamis'; etc. The Latin in such cases usually employs another mode of expression. Thus:—

a) A Genitive; as,—

dolor injūriārum, *resentment at injuries*

b) An Adjective; as,—

urbēs maritimae, *cities on the sea*
pugna Salamīnia, *the fight at Salamis*

c) A Participle; as,—

pugna ad Cannās facta, *the battle at Cannae*

d) A Relative clause; as,—

liber quī in meīs manibus est, *the book in my hands*

NOTE—Yet within certain limits the Latin does employ
Prepositional phrases as Noun modifiers. This is particularly
frequent when the governing noun is derived from a verb. The
following are typical examples:—

> **trānsitus in Britanniam**, *the passage to Britain*
> **excessus ē vītā**, *departure from life*
> **odium ergā Rōmānōs**, *hatred of the Romans*
> **liber dē senectūte**, *the book on old age*
> **amor in patriam**, *love for one's country.*

Adjectives

354

1. **Special Latin Equivalents for English Adjectives**
are—

a) A Genitive; as,—

> **virtūtēs animī** = *moral virtues*
> **dolōrēs corporis** = *bodily ills*

b) An Abstract Noun; as,—

> **novitās reī** = *the strange circumstance*
> **asperitās viārum** = *rough roads*

c) Hendiadys (see § 374, 4); as,—

> **ratiō et ōrdō** = *systematic order*
> **ārdor et impetus** = *eager onset*

d) Sometimes an Adverb; as,—

> **omnēs circā populī**, *all the surrounding tribes*
> **suōs semper hostēs**, *their perpetual foes*

2. Often a Latin Noun is equivalent to an English Noun
modified by an Adjective; as,—

> **doctrīna**, *theoretical knowledge*
> **prūdentia**, *practical knowledge*
> **oppidum**, *walled town*
> **libellus**, *little book*

3. Adjectives are not used in immediate agreement with
proper names; but an Adjective may limit **vir**, **homō**, **ille**,
or some other word used as an Appositive of a proper name;
as,—

> **Sōcratēs, homō sapiēns** = *the wise Socrates*
> **Scīpiō, vir fortissimus** = *the doughty Scipio*
> **Syrācūsae, urbs praeclārissima** = *famous Syracuse*

4. An Adjective *may be* equivalent to a Possessive or Subjective Genitive; as,—

pāstor rēgius, *the shepherd of the king*
tumultus servīlis, *the uprising of the slaves*

Pronouns

355

1. In Compound Sentences the Relative Pronoun has a fondness for connecting itself with the subordinate clause rather than the main one; as,—

ā quō cum quaererētur, quid maximē expedīret, respondit, *when it was asked of him what was best, he replied.* (Less commonly, **quī, cum ab eō quaererētur, respondit.**)

2. **Uterque, ambō. Uterque** means *each of two*; **ambō** means *both*; as,—

uterque frāter abiit, *each of the two brothers departed* (*i.e.* separately)

ambō frātrēs abiērunt, *i.e.* the two brothers departed together.

a) The Plural of **uterque** occurs—

   i) With Nouns used only in the Plural (see § 56); as,—

   in utrīsque castrīs, *in each camp.*

   ii) Where there is a distinct reference to two groups of persons or things; as,—

   utrīque ducēs clārī fuērunt, *the generals on each side* (several in number) *were famous.*

Verbs

356

1. In case of Defective and Deponent Verbs, a Passive is supplied:—

a) By the corresponding verbal Nouns in combination with **esse,** *etc.*; as,—

   in odiō sumus, *we are hated*
   in invidiā sum, *I am envied*
   admīrātiōnī est, *he is admired*
   oblīviōne obruitur, *he is forgotten* (lit. *is overwhelmed by oblivion*)
   in ūsū esse, *to be used*

b) By the Passive of Verbs of related meaning. Thus:—

    agitārī as Passive of **persequī**
    temptārī as Passive of **adorīrī**

2. The lack of the Perfect Active Participle in Latin is supplied—

a) Sometimes by the Perfect Passive Participle of the Deponent; as,—

    adhortātus, *having exhorted*
    veritus, *having feared.*

b) By the Ablative Absolute; as,—

    hostium agrīs vāstātīs Caesar exercitum redūxit, *having ravaged the country of the enemy, Caesar led back his army (B.G. iii.29.3).*

c) By subordinate clauses; as,—

    eō cum advēnisset, castra posuit, *having arrived there, he pitched a camp.*

    hostes quī in urbem irrūperant, *the enemy having burst into the city.*

3. The Latin agrees with English in the stylistic employment of the Second Person Singular in an indefinite sense (= 'one'). *Cf.* the English '*You can drive a horse to water, but you can't make him drink.*' But in Latin this use is mainly confined to certain varieties of the Subjunctive, especially the Potential (§ 280), Jussive (§ 275), Deliberative (§ 277), and the Subjunctive in conditional sentences of the sort included under § 302, 2, and 303. Examples:—

    vidērēs, *you could see*
    ūtāre vīribus, *use your strength*
    quid hōc homine faciās, *what are you to do with this man?*
    mēns quoque et animus, nisi tamquam lūminī oleum īnstīllēs, exstinguuntur senectūte, *the intellect and mind too are extinguished by old age, unless, so to speak, you keep pouring oil into the lamp (de Sen. 36).*
    tantō amōre possessiōnēs suās amplexī tenēbant, ut ab eīs membra dīvellī citius posse dīcerēs, *they clung to their possessions with such an affectionate embrace, that you would have said their limbs could sooner be torn from their bodies (Sull. 59).*

Special Uses of the Accusative

357

1. To denote '*so many years, etc., afterwards or before*' the Latin employs not merely the Ablative of Degree of Difference with **post** and **ante** (see § 223), but has other forms of expression. Thus:—

   post quīnque annōs, *five years afterward*
   paucōs ante diēs, *a few days before*
   ante quadriennium, *four years before*
   post diem quārtum quam ab urbe discesserāmus, *four days after we had left the city*
   ante tertium annum quam dēcesserat, *three years before he had died*

2. The Latin seldom combines both Subject and Object with the same Infinitive; as,—

   Rōmānōs Hannibalem vīcisse cōnstat.

   Such a sentence would be ambiguous, and might mean either that the Romans had conquered Hannibal, or that Hannibal had conquered the Romans. Perspicuity was gained by the use of the Passive Infinitive; as,—

   Rōmānōs ab Hannibale victōs esse cōnstat, *it is well established that the Romans were defeated by Hannibal.*

Special Uses of the Dative

358

1. The English *for* does not always correspond to a Dative notion in Latin, but is often the equivalent of **prō** with the Ablative, *viz.* in the senses—

   a) *In defense of*; as,—

      prō patriā morī, *to die for one's country*

   b) *Instead of, in behalf of*; as,—

      ūnus prō omnibus dīxit, *one spoke for all*
      haec prō lēge dicta sunt, *these things were said for the law.*

   c) *In proportion to*; as,—

      prō multitūdine hominum eōrum fīnēs erant angustī, *for the population, their territory was small (B.G. i.2.5).*

2. Similarly, English *to* when it indicates motion is rendered in Latin by **ad**.

a) Note, however, that the Latin may say either **scrībere ad aliquem**, or **scrībere alicui**, according as the idea of motion is or is not predominant. So in several similar expressions.

3. In the poets, verbs of *mingling with, contending with, joining, clinging to, etc.*, sometimes take the Dative. This construction is a Grecism. Thus:—

> **sē miscet virīs**, *he mingles with the men*
> **contendis Homērō**, *you contend with Homer*
> **dextrae dextram jungere**, *to clasp hand with hand*

Special Uses of the Genitive

359

1. The Possessive Genitive gives emphasis to the *possessor*, the Dative of Possessor emphasizes *the fact of possession*; as,—

> **hortus patris est**, *the garden is my father's.*
> **mihi hortus est**, *I possess a garden.*

2. The Latin can say either **stultī** or **stultum est dīcere**, *it is foolish to say*; but Adjectives of one ending permit only the Genitive; as,—

> **sapientis est haec sēcum reputāre**, *it is the part of a wise man to consider this.*

Part VI:
Prosody

360 Prosody treats of meters and versification.

361 **Latin Verse**. Latin Poetry was essentially different in character from English. In our own language, poetry is based upon *accent*, and poetical form consists essentially in a certain succession of *accented* and *unaccented* syllables. Latin poetry, on the other hand, was based not upon accent, but upon *quantity*, so that with the Romans poetical form consisted in a certain succession of *long and short syllables*, *i.e.* of long and short intervals of time.

This fundamental difference in the character of English and Latin poetry is a natural result of the difference in character of the two languages. English is a strongly accented language, in which quantity is relatively subordinate. Latin, on the other hand, was a quantitative language, in which accent was relatively subordinate.

Quantity of Vowels and Syllables

General Principles

362 The general principles for the quantity of vowels and syllables have been given above in § 5. The following peculiarities are to be noted here:—

1. A vowel is usually short when followed by another vowel (§ 5, A, 2), but the following exceptions occur:—

   a) In the Genitive termination -**īus** (except **alterĭus**); as, **illīus**, **tōtīus**. Yet the **i** may be short in poetry; as, **illĭus**, **tōtĭus**.

   b) In the Genitive and Dative Singular of the Fifth Declension; as, **diēī**, **aciēī**. But **fidĕī**, **rĕī**, **spĕī** (§ 52, 1).

   c) In **fīō**, excepting **fit** and forms where **i** is followed by **er**. Thus: **fīēbam**, **fīat**, **fīunt**; but **fĭerī**, **fĭerem**.

    d) In a few other words, especially words derived from the Greek; as, **dīus, Aenēās, Dārīus, hērōes,** *etc.*

2. A diphthong is usually long (§ 5, B, 2), but the preposition prae in composition is often shortened before a vowel; as, **prăĕacūtus.**

3. A syllable containing a short vowel followed by two consonants (§ 5, B, 2) is long, even when one of the consonants is in the following word; as, terret populum. Occasionally the syllable is long when both consonants are in the following word; as, prō segete spīcās.

4. Compounds of **jaciō,** though written **inicit, adicit,** *etc.*, have the first syllable long, as though written **inj-, adj-.**

5. Before **j, ă** and **ĕ** made a long syllable, e.g. in **major, pejor, ejus, ejusdem, Pompejus, rejēcit,** *etc.* These were pronounced, **mai-jor, pei-jor, ei-jus, Pompei-jus, rei-jēcit,** *etc.* So also sometimes before **i,** e.g. **Pompe-ī,** pronounced **Pompei-ī; re-iciō,** pronounced **rei-iciō.**

QUANTITY OF FINAL SYLLABLES

FINAL SYLLABLES ENDING IN A VOWEL

363

1. Final **a** is mostly short, but is long:—

    a) In the Ablative Singular of the First Declension; as, **portā.**

    b) In the Imperative; as, **laudā.**

    c) In indeclinable words (except **ită, quiă**); as, **trīgintā, contrā, posteā, intereā,** *etc.*

2. Final **e** is usually short, but is long:—

    a) In the Ablative Singular of the Fifth Declension; as, **diē, rē;** hence **hodiē, quārē.** Here belongs also **famē** (§ 59, 2, b).

    b) In the Imperative of the Second Conjugation; as, **monē, habē,** *etc.*; yet occasionally **cavĕ, valĕ.**

    c) In Adverbs derived from Adjectives of the Second Declension, along with **ferē** and **fermē. Benĕ, malĕ, temerĕ, saepĕ** have **ĕ.**

    d) In **ē, dē, mē, tē, sē, nē** (*not, lest*), **nē** (*verily*).

3. Final **i** is usually long, but is short in **nisĭ** and **quasĭ. Mihi, tibi, sibi, ibi, ubi,** have regularly **ĭ,** but sometimes **ī;** yet always **ibīdem, ibīque, ubīque.**

4. Final **o** is regularly long, but is short:—

   a) In **egŏ, duŏ, modŏ** (*only*), **citŏ**.

   b) Rarely in the First Person Singular of the Verb, and in Nominatives of the Third Declension; as, **amŏ, leŏ**.

   c) In a few compounds beginning with the Preposition **pro**, especially before **f**; as **prŏfundere, prŏficīscī, prŏfugere**.

5. Final **u** is always long.

FINAL SYLLABLES ENDING IN A CONSONANT.

364

1. Final syllables ending in any other consonant than **s** are short. The following words, however, have a long vowel: **sāl, sōl, Lār, pār, vēr, fūr, dīc, dūc, ēn, nōn, quīn, sīn, sīc, cūr**. Also the adverbs **hīc, illīc, istīc**.[56]

2. Final syllables in -**as** are long; as, **terrās, amās**.

3. Final syllables in -**es** are regularly long, but are short:—

   a) In the Nominative and Vocative Singular of dental stems (§ 33) of the Third Declension which have a short penult in the Genitive; as, segĕs (segetis), obsĕs (obsidis), mīlĕs, dīvĕs. But a few have -ēs; viz. pēs, ariēs, abiēs, pariēs.

   b) In **ēs** (*thou art*), **penēs**.

4. Final -**os** is usually long, but short in **ŏs** (**ossis**), **compŏs, impŏs**.

5. Final -**is** is usually short, but is long:—

   a) In Plurals; as, **portīs, hortīs, nōbīs, vōbīs, nūbīs** (Acc.).

   b) In the Second Person Singular Perfect Subjunctive Active; as, **amāverīs, monuerīs, audīverīs**, *etc.* Yet occasional exceptions occur.

   c) In the Second Person Singular Present Indicative Active of the Fourth Conjugation; as, **audīs**.

   d) In **vīs**, *force*; **īs**, *thou goest*; **fīs; sīs; velīs; nōlīs; vīs**, *thou wilt* (**māvīs, quamvīs, quīvīs**, *etc.*).

6. Final -**us** is usually short, but is long:—

   a) In the Genitive Singular and in the Nominative, Accusative, and Vocative Plural of the Fourth Declension; as, **frūctūs**.

   b) In the Nominative and Vocative Singular of those nouns of the Third Declension in which the **u** belongs to the stem; as, **palūs** (-**ūdis**), **servitūs** (-**ūtis**), **tellūs** (-**ūris**).

---

56 The pronouns **hic, hoc**, and the adverb **huc**, probably had a short vowel. The syllable was made long by pronouncing **hicc, hocc**, etc.

365 Greek Nouns retain in Latin their original quantity; as, Aenēā, epitomē, Dēlos, Pallas, Simoīs, Salamīs, Dīdūs, Paridī, āēr, aethēr, crātēr, hērōăs. Yet Greek nouns in -ωρ (-ōr) regularly shorten the vowel of the final syllable; as, rhētŏr, Hectŏr.

Verse Structure

General Principles

366 1. The metrical unit in versification is a short syllable, technically called a **mora** (◡). A long syllable (–) is equivalent to two morae.

2. A **verse** is a metrical structure, ending with a prosodic pause. A verse consists of one or more **cola** (singular **colon**); these are the building blocks of verses, typically eight to twelve syllables long. Each metrical family has its own characteristic cola. The point in a verse at which two cola are joined together is called the **principal caesura.** There is necessarily a word end at the principal caesura; any position in the verse where a word ends can also be called a caesura. The symbol ✕ represents an **anceps** syllable, a position that may contain either a long syllable or a short one.

3. Older texts analyze verse by **feet.** While this analysis is sensible for English verse, it is not historically accurate for Latin, and works only for a subset of Latin meters. The terminology is quite old—Roman poets referred to the "feet" of their verses—but it does not reflect the way the verses are actually constructed. In this kind of analysis, the long syllable of each foot is considered to have greater prominence. This prominence is called **ictus.** In analyses it is indicated with an accent mark, though this does not mean that this syllable is to be stressed or accented in reading. The syllable which receives the ictus is called the **thesis;** the rest of the foot is called the **arsis.** In more modern analysis, a position normally filled by a long syllable is called a **princeps** position.

4. The principal metrical families used by Roman poets are aeolic, iambic and trochaic, dactylic, anapestic, and ionic.

An **aeolic** colon consists of a variable part, called the "base," in which one or more syllables may be either long or short; a central "nucleus" normally in the form of a choriamb, $-\cup\cup-$; and a "tail" of one or more syllables to round out the verse. For example, the **glyconic** has the form × × $-\cup\cup-\cup-$. These meters are used in lyric poetry.

An **iambic** verse can be analyzed as a series of iambic **metra** (singular **metron**), each of the form ×$-\cup-$. The most common iambic verse is the trimeter, three metra in succession. A **trochaic verse is a series of trochaic metra,** $-\cup-$×. The long syllables in an iambic or trochaic metron can be **resolved**; that is, the poet may substitute two short syllables for a long one.[57] Note that the Latin iambic metron is not the same as the "iambic foot" of English verse. Iambics and trochaics are used in drama and in lyrics; see section 370.

A **dactylic** verse can be analyzed as a series of dactylic metra, each of the form $-\cup\cup$. The most common dactylic verse is the hexameter, a series of six metra. The two short syllables in a dactylic metron can be **contracted**; that is, the poet may use one long syllable in place of the two short ones.

The **hemiepes** is a dactylic colon that is not made up of dactylic metra; its form is $-\cup\cup-\cup\cup-$.

The dactylic family are used in lyric and epic poetry; see sections 368-369.

An **anapestic** verse is a series of anapestic metra, $\cup\cup-\cup\cup-$. In these verses **both** contraction **and** resolution are permitted. This form is used in drama.

An **ionic** verse may be a series of ionic metra, $\cup\cup--$, or it may be a related colon called the **anacreontic**, of the form $\cup\cup-\cup-\cup--$. This metrical family is used in lyric poetry.

Most of these verse forms are beyond the scope of this grammar; a good commentary on a poetic text will generally explain the meters used.

---

57 In reality the iambic trimeter is made of two cola, ×$\cup-$×|$-\cup-$×$\cup-$ or ×$\cup-$×$\cup-$|- ×$\cup-$, but by the time the Romans took over this metrical form from the Greeks, that fact had been forgotten.

5. **Elision**. Final syllables ending in a vowel, a diphthong, or -**m** are regularly elided before a word beginning with a vowel or **h**. In reading, we omit the elided syllable entirely. This may be indicated as follows: **corpor^e in ūnō; mult^{um} ill^e et; mōnstr^{um} horrendum; caus^{ae} īrārum.**

Omission of elision is called Hiátus. It occurs especially before and after monosyllabic interjections, as, **Ō et praesidium.**

6. Verses are distinguished as Catalectic or Acatalectic. A Catalectic verse is one in which the last metron or colon is not complete, but lacks one or more syllables; an Acatalectic verse has its last metron complete. Typically, though not always, a catalectic verse ends in two long syllabues.

7. At the end of a verse a slight pause occurred. Hence the final syllable may be either long or short (syllaba anceps), and may terminate in a vowel or m, even though the next verse begins with a vowel.

Special Peculiarities

367

1. **Synizésis** (**synaéresis**). Two successive vowels in the interior of a word are often united into a long syllable; as,—

   aureīs, deinde, anteīre, deesse.

2. **Diástole**. A syllable usually short is sometimes long; as,—
   vidēt, audīt

3. **Sýstole**. A syllable usually long is sometimes short; as,—
   stetĕrunt

   a) Diastole and Systole are not mere arbitrary processes. They usually represent an earlier pronunciation which had passed out of vogue in the ordinary speech.

4. After a consonant, **i** and **u** sometimes become **j** and **v**. The preceding syllable then becomes long; as,—
   abjete for **abiete; genva** for **genua**

5. Sometimes **v** becomes **u**; as,—
   silua for **silva; dissoluō** for **dissolvō**.

6. Sometimes a verse has an extra syllable. Such a verse is called **hypermetric**. The extra syllable ends in a vowel or -**m**, and is united with the initial vowel or **h** of the next verse by **Synaphéia**. Thus:—

. . . . ignārⁱ hominumque locōrum^{que}
errāmus.

7. **Tmesis** (*cutting*). Compound words are occasionally separated into their elements; as,—

   quō mē cumque rapit tempestās, for **quōcumque**, *etc.*

8. **Sýncope**. A short vowel is sometimes dropped between two consonants; as,—

   repostus for **repositus**

The Dactylic Hexameter

368

1. The Dactylic Hexameter, or Heroic Verse, consists of six dactylic metra. According to the rule for the dactylic family, the two short syllables in each metron can be contracted. By convention, the fifth metron usually is not contracted. Because the last syllable of a verse is always long, the last metron must be contracted. The resulting scheme is:

$$- \smile\smile - \smile\smile - \smile\smile - \smile\smile - \smile\smile - -$$

2. A contracted dactylic metron, two long syllables, is sometimes called a spondee. Although the fifth metron of a dactylic hexameter is generally not contracted, sometimes it is. Such verses are called Spondaic because of the so-called spondee in the fifth metron. In this case the fourth metron is generally not contracted, and the fifth and sixth metra are generally made up of a single four-syllable word; as,—

   armātum^{que} aurō circumspicit Ōrīōna. (*Aen.* 3.517)
   cāra deum subolēs, magnum Jovis incrēmentum.
   (*Ecl.* iv.49)

3. Caesura

   a) The principal caesura in the dactylic hexameter is generally after the princeps in the third metron, as:

   arma virumque canō ‖ Trōjae quī prīmus ab ōrĭs.
   (*Aen.* i.1)

   That is, this line is made up of two cola, the first a hemiepes (366.4). This is called a Masculine caesura.

   b) The Feminine caesura occurs between the two short syllables of the third metron, as:

   Ō passī graviōra ‖ dabit deus hīs quoque fīnem.
   (*Aen.* i.199)

The terms "masculine" and "feminine" in this sense refer to languages like French in which the ending of a feminine adjective is typically one syllable longer than that of a masculine adjective.[58]

c) The verse may also be divided into three cola, with two caesurae, one in the second metron and one in the fourth, as:

inde torō || pater Aenēās || sīc ōrsus ab altō est.
(*Aen.* ii.2)

d) A caesura sometimes occurs at the end of the fourth foot. This is called the Bucolic Diaeresis, as it was borrowed by the Romans from the Bucolic poetry of the Greeks.[59] Thus:—

sōlstitium pecorī dēfendite; || jam venit aestās.
(*Ecl.* vii.47)

The Elegiac Couplet

369

The Elegiac Couplet is a two-line stanza form. The first line is a dactylic hexameter. The second line contains two hemiepes cola, with a caesura between them (that is, there must be word-end at the end of the first colon). The pairs of short syllables in the first colon may be contracted, but *not those in the second*. Because a hemiepes looks like 2 ½ dactyls, and this line contains two of them, it is usually called the "dactylic pentameter," even though it does not actually contain *five* dactyls. The scheme is the following:—

$$- \smile\smile - \smile\smile - \smile\smile - \smile\smile - \smile\smile - -$$

$$- \smile\smile - \smile\smile - - \smile\smile - \smile\smile -$$

For example:—

Vergilium vīdī tantum, nec avāra Tibullō
tempus amīcitiae fāta dedēre meae. (Ov. *Tr.* 4.10.51-52)

---

58   Masculine and feminine rhymes in English verse, or masculine and feminine line-endings, are named by the same principle.

59   In analyses by feet, a "caesura" is a word end that comes within a foot, and a "diaeresis" is a word end that coincides with the end of a foot. In fact both are the same kind of phenomenon, a junction of cola. A verse with a bucolic diaeresis simply has two cola, which consist of four and two dactylic metra respectively.

Iambic Verse Forms

370

1. The most important Iambic verse is the **Iambic Trimeter**, called also **Senarius**. This is an acatalectic verse. It consists of three iambic metra. Its pure form is:—

$$ \times - \cup - \times - \cup - \times - \cup - $$

The principal caesura generally comes in the second metron, either after the anceps or after the short syllable. As always in iambic meter, the long syllables may be resolved (except the last one). For example:—

Phasellus ille, quem videtis, hospites,
ait fuisse navium celerrimus. (Catul. 4.1-2)

Quam bene parentis sceptra Polybi fugeram!
curis solutus exul, intrepidus uagans
(caelum deosque testor) in regnum incidi. (Sen. *Oed.*
12-14)

2. In the Latin comic writers, Plautus and Terence, great freedom is permitted. The anceps positions may be treated like long syllables and resolved into two shorts, and the short syllables may be treated like ancipitia and replaced by long syllables. It is in this form that the verse is called senarius, as if it were made of six iambic "feet"—

Ne mox erretis, iam nunc praedico prius:
idem est ambobus nomen geminis fratribus. (Pl. *Men.*
47-48)

3. Other iambic forms are used in lyric verse.

Part VII:
Supplements

Julian Calendar

371

1. The names of the Roman months are: **Jānuārius, Februārius, Mārtius, Aprīlis, Majus, Jūnius, Jūlius** (**Quīntīlis** prior to 46 B.C.), **Augustus** (**Sextīlis** before the Empire), **September, Octōber, November, December**. These words are properly Adjectives in agreement with **mēnsis** understood. Originally the Roman year began with March. This explains the names **Quīntīlis, Sextīlis, September**, etc., which mean fifth month, sixth month, etc.

2. Dates were reckoned from three points in the month:—

   a) The Calends, the first of the month.

   b) The Nones, usually the fifth of the month, but the seventh in March, May, July, and October.

   c) The Ides, usually the thirteenth of the month, but the fifteenth in March, May, July, and October.

3. From these points dates were reckoned backward; consequently all days after the Ides of any month were reckoned as so many days before the Calends of the month next following.

4. The day before the Calends, Nones, or Ides of any month is designated as **prīdiē Kalendās, Nōnās, Īdūs**. The second day before was designated as **diē tertiō ante Kalendās, Nōnās,** etc. Similarly the third day before was designated as **diē quārtō**, and so on. These designations appear arithmetically inaccurate, but the Romans reckoned both ends of the series. The Roman numeral indicating the date is therefore always larger by one than the number of days before Nones, Ides, or Calends: it is the number of days up to Nones, Ides, or Calends including the day in question.

5. In indicating dates, the name of the month is added in the form of an Adjective agreeing with Kalendās, Nōnās, Īdūs. Various forms of expression occur, of which that given under d) is most common:—

   a) **diē quīntō ante Īdūs Mārtiās**

   b) **quīntō ante Īdūs Mārtiās**

   c) **quīntō (V) Īdūs Mārtiās**

   d) **ante diem quīntum Īdūs Mārtiās**

6. These designations may be treated as nouns and combined with the prepositions in, ad, ex; as,—

> **ad ante diem IV Kalendās Octōbrēs**, *up to the 28th of September*

> **ex ante diem quīntum Īdūs Octōbrēs**, *from the 11th of October*

7. In leap-year the 25th was reckoned as the extra day in February. The 24th was designated as **ante diem VI Kalendās Mārtiās**, and the 25th as **ante diem bis VI Kal Mārt**.

372   Calendar

Days of the month	March, May, July, October	January, August, December	April, June, September, November	February *(parenthesized forms for leap years)*
1	Kalendīs	Kalendīs	Kalendīs	Kalendīs
2	VI. Nōnās	IV. Nōnās	IV. Nōnās	IV. Nōnās
3	V. "	III. "	III. "	III. "
4	IV. "	Prīdiē Nōnās	Prīdiē Nōnās	Prīdiē Nōnās
5	III. "	Nōnīs	Nōnīs	Nōnīs
6	Prīdiē Nōnās	VIII. Īdūs	VIII. Īdūs	VIII. Īdūs
7	Nōnīs	VII. "	VII. "	VII. "
8	VIII. Īdūs	VI. "	VI. "	VI. "
9	VII. "	V. "	V. "	V. "
10	VI. "	IV. "	IV. "	IV. "
11	V. "	III. "	III. "	III. "
12	IV. "	Prīdiē Īdūs	Prīdiē Īdūs	Prīdiē Īdūs
13	III. "	Īdibus	Īdibus	Īdibus
14	Prīdiē Īdūs	XIX. Kalend.	XVIII. Kalend.	XVI. Kalend
15	Īdibus	XVIII. "	XVII. "	XV. "

16	XVII. Kalend.	XVII. "	XVI. "	XIV. "
17	XVI. "	XVI. "	XV. "	XIII. "
18	XV. "	XV. "	XIV. "	XII. "
19	XIV. "	XIV. "	XIII. "	XI. "
20	XIII. "	XIII. "	XII. "	X. "
21	XII. "	XII. "	XI. "	IX. "
22	XI. "	XI. "	X. "	VIII. "
23	X. "	X. "	IX. "	VII. "
24	IX. "	IX. "	VIII. "	VI. "
25	VIII. "	VIII. "	VII. "	V. (bis VI.) "
26	VII. "	VII. "	VI. "	IV. (V.) "
27	VI. "	VI. "	V. "	III. (IV.) "
28	V. "	V. "	IV. "	Prīdiē Kalend. (III. Kal.)
29	IV. "	IV. "	III. "	(Prīd. Kal.)
30	III. "	III. "	Prīdiē Kalend.	
31	Prīdiē Kalend.	Prīdiē Kalend.		

Proper Names

373

1. The name of a Roman citizen regularly consisted of three parts: the **praenōmen** (or given name), the **nōmen** (name of the gens or clan), and the **cognōmen** (family name). Such a typical name is exemplied by **Mārcus Tullius Cicerō**, in which **Mārcus** is the **praenōmen**, **Tullius** the **nōmen**, and **Cicerō** the **cognōmen**. Sometimes a second **cognōmen** (in later Latin called an **agnōmen**) is added—expecially in honor of military achievements; as,—

Gāius Cornēlius Scīpiō Āfricānus

2. Abbreviations of Proper Names

A. = Aulus	Mam. = Māmercus
App. = Appius	N. = Numerius
C. = Gāius	P. = Pūblius
Cn. = Gnaeus	Q. = Quīntus
D. = Decimus	Sex. = Sextus
K. = Kaesō	Ser. = Servius
L. = Lūcius	Sp. = Spurius
M. = Mārcus	T. = Titus
M'. = Mānius	Ti. = Tiberius

Figures of Syntax and Rhetoric

Figures of Syntax

374

1. **Ellípsis** is the omission of one or more words; as,—

   quid multa, *why (should I say) much?*

2. **Brachýlogy** is a brief or condensed form of expression; as,—

   > **ut ager sine cultūrā frūctuōsus esse nōn potest,**
   > **sīc sine doctrīnā animus,** *as a field cannot be*
   > *productive without cultivation, so the mind (cannot*
   > *be productive) without learning (Tusc. Disp. ii.13).*

   Special varieties of Brachylogy are—

   a) **Zeugma,** in which one verb is made to stand for two; as,—

      > **minīs aut blandīmentīs corrupta** = (terrified) by
      > threats or corrupted by flattery (Tusc. Disp. v.87)

   b) **Compendiary Comparison,** by which a modifier of an object is mentioned instead of the object itself; as,—

      > **dissimilis erat Charēs eōrum et factīs et mōribus,**
      > lit. *Chares was different from their conduct and*
      > *character* i.e. *Chares's conduct and character were*
      > *different,* etc. (Nep. *Chab.* 3.4)

3. **Pléonasm** is an unnecessary fullness of expression; as,—

   prius praedīcam, lit. *I will first say in advance*

4. **Hendíadys** (ἓν διὰ δυοῖν, *one through two*) is the use of two nouns joined by a conjunction, in the sense of a noun modified by a Genitive or an Adjective; as,—

   febris et aestus, *the heat of fever* (Cat. 1.31)
   celeritāte cursūque, *by swift running*

5. **Prolépsis,** or **Anticipation,** is the introduction of an epithet in advance of the action which makes it appropriate; as,—

   submersās obrue puppēs, lit. *overwhelm their*
   submerged ships, i.e. *overwhelm and sink their ships*
   (Aen. i.69)

a) The name Prolepsis is also applied to the introduction of a noun or pronoun as object of the main clause where we should expect it to stand as subject of a subordinate clause. Thus:—

> **nōstī Mārcellum quam tardus sit,** *you know how slow Marcellus is* (lit. *you know Marcellus, how slow he is*) (Fam. viii.10.3).

Both varieties of Prolepsis are chiefly confined to poetry.

6. **Anacolúthon** is a lack of grammatical consistency in the construction of the sentence; as,—

> **tum Ancī fīliī ... impēnsius eīs indignitās crēscere,** *then the sons of Ancus ... their indignation increased all the more* (Liv. i.40.2).

7. **Hýsteron Próteron** consists in the inversion of the natural order of two words or phrases; as,—

> **moriāmur et in media arma ruāmus** = *let us rush into the midst of arms and die* (Aen. ii.353).

Figures of Rhetoric

375

1. **Lítotes** (literally *softening*) is the expression of an idea by the denial of its opposite; as,—

> **haud parum labōris,** *no little toil* (i.e. *much toil*)
> **nōn ignōrō,** *I am not ignorant* (i.e. *I am well aware*).

2. **Oxymóron** is the combination of contradictory conceptions; as,—

> **sapiēns īnsānia,** *wise folly*

3. **Alliteration** is the employment of a succession of words presenting frequent repetition of the same letter (mostly initial); as,—

> **sēnsim sine sēnsū aetās senēscit**

4. **Onomatopoéia** is the suiting of sound to sense; as,—

> **quadrupedante putrem sonitū quatit ungula campum,** '*And shake with horny hoofs the solid ground.*' (Aen. viii.596).

Abbreviations Used
in the Illustrative Examples

Ac., Cicero, Academica.
Acc., Accius.
ad Her., ad Herennium
Aen., Virgil, Aeneid.
Arch., Cicero, pro Archia.
Att., Cicero, Epistulae ad Atticus.
B.C., Caesar, de Bello Civili.
B.G., Caesar, de Bello Gallico.
Brut., Cicero, Brutus.
Caec., Cicero, pro Caecina.
Cat., Cicero, in Catilinam.
Catul., Catullus.
Cluent., Cicero, pro Cluentio.
Curt., Quintus Curtius
de Dom., Cicero, de Domo Sua.
de Or., Cicero, de Oratore.
de Sen., Cicero, de Senectute.
D., Cicero, de Divinatione.
Div. Caec., Cicero, Divinatio in Caecilium.
Ecl., Virgil, Eclogues.
Eut., Eutropius.
F., Cicero, de Finibus.
Fam., Cicero, Epistulae ad Familiares.
Flac., Cicero, pro Flacco.
Gell, Aulus Gellius.
Hor., Horace.
— Epp., Epistles.
— Od., Odes.
— Sat., Satires.
Inv., Cicero, de Inventione.
Juv., Juvenal.
Lael., Cicero, Laelius, de Amicitia.
Leg., Cicero, de Legibus.
Lig., Cicero, pro Ligario.
Liv., Livy.
Lucr., Lucretius.
Marc., Cicero, pro Marcello.
Mil., Cicero, pro Milone.
N.D., Cicero, de Natura Deorum.
Nep., Nepos.
— Alc., Alcibiades.
— Ar., Aristides.
— Att., Atticus.
— Cat., Cato.
— Chab. Chabrias.

— Cim., Cimon.
— Con., Conon.
— Dat., Datames.
— Ep., Epaminondas.
— Ham., Hamilcar.
— Milt., Miltiades.
— Paus., Pausanias.
— Them., Themistocles.
— Thras., Thrasybulus.
— Tim., Timoleon.
Off., Cicero, de Officiis.
Or., Cicero, Orator.
Ov., Ovid.
— Am., Amores,
— Met., Metamorphoses,
— Tr., Tristia.
Par., Cicero, Paradoxa.
Phil., Cicero, Philippics.
Pis., Cicero, in Pisonem.
Planc., Cicero, pro Plancio.
Pl., Plautus.
— Amph., Amphitruo.
— Aul., Aulularia.
— Bacch., Bacchides.
— Capt., Captivi.
— Curc., Curculio.
— Men., Menaechmi.
— Merc., Mercator.
— M.G., Miles Gloriosus.
— Pers., Persa.
— Poen., Poenulus.
— Rud., Rudens.
— Tr., Trinummus.
— Vid., Vidularia.
Plin. Epp., Pliny the Younger, Letters.
Pub. Syr., Publilius Syrus.
Q.F., Cicero, ad Quintum Fratrem.
Rep., Cicero, de Re Publica.
Rosc. Am., Cicero, pro Roscio Amerino.
Sall., Sallust.
— C., Catiline.
— Fr., Fragments.
— Jug., Jugurtha.
Sen., Seneca.
— Ep., Epistles.

—   N.Q., Naturales Quaestiones.
—   Oed., Oedipus.
Sest., Cicero, pro Sestio.
Sex. Rosc., Cicero, pro Sexto Roscio.
Sil., Silius Italicus.
Stat., Caecilius Statius.
Sull., Cicero, pro Sulla.
Tac., Tacitus.
—   A., Annals.
—   Agr., Agricola.
—   Dial., Dialogus de Oratoribus.
—   Ger., Germania.
—   H., Histories.

Ter., Terence.
—   Ad., Adelphoi.
—   And., Andria.
—   Eun., Eunuchus.
—   Hec., Hecyra.
—   H.T., Hautontimoroumenos.
—   Phor., Phormio.
Tusc. Disp., Cicero, Tusculan Disputations.
Twelve Tables, Laws of the Twelve Tables.
Vatin., Cicero, in Vatinium.
Verr., Cicero, in Verrem.
Verr. Act. Pr., Cicero, Actio Prima in C. Verrem.

Index of the Sources
of the Illustrative Examples
Cited in the Syntax

References are to sections.

Index to the Principal Parts of the Most Important Verbs

NOTE—Compounds are not given unless they present some special irregularity. The references are to sections.

A

abdō, 122, I, 4. abiciō, 122, III. abnuō, 122, II. aboleō, 121, I. abstergeō, 121, III absum, 125. accendō, 122, I, 4. accidit, 138, III. acciō, 121, I, N. accipiō, 122, III. acquīrō, 122, I, 6. acuō, 122, II. addō, 122, I, 2. adhaerēscō, 122, IV, 2. adipīscor, 122, V. adolēscō, 122, IV, 1. adsum, 125. adveniō, 123, IV. afferō, 129. afficiō, 122, III. afflīgō, 122, I, 1, a. agnōscō, 122, IV, 1. agō, 122, I, 3. algeō, 121, III. alō, 122, I, 5. amiciō, 123, III. amō, 120, I. amplector, 122, V. angō, 122, I, 7. aperiō, 123, II. appetō, 122, I, 6. arceō, 121, II, a. accessō, 122, I, 6. ārdeō, 121, III. ārēscō, 122, IV, 2. arguō, 122, II. ascendō, 122, I, 4. aspiciō, 122, III. assentior, 123, VII. assuēfaciō, 122, III. assuēfīō, 122, III. audiō, 123, I. auferō, 129. augeō, 121, III. aveō, 121, II, a, N. 2.

C

cadō, 122, I, 2. caedō, 122, I, 2. calefaciō, 122, III. calefīō, 122, III. caleō, 121, II, a. calēscō, 122, IV, 2. canō, 122, I, 2. capessō, 122, I, 6. capiō, 122, III. careō, 121, II, a. carpō, 121, I, 1, a. caveō, 121, V. cēdō, 122, I, 1, b. cēnseō, 121, II, b. cernō, 122, I, 6. cieō, 121, I. cingō, 122, I, 1, a. circumsistō, 122, I, 2. claudō, 122, I, 1, b. claudō, 122, I, 7. coëmō, 122, I, 3. coepī, 133. coërceō, 121, II, a. cognōscō, 122, IV, 1. cōgō, 122, I, 3. colligō, 122, I, 3. colō, 122, I, 5. comminīscor, 122, V. comperiō, 123, V. compleō, 121, I. concutiō, 122, III. condō, 122, I, 2. cōnferō, 129. cōnfiteor, 121, VII. congruō, 122,

II. cōnsenēscō, 122, IV, 2. cōnserō, 122, I, 5. cōnserō, 122, I, 6 (plant). cōnsīdō, 122, I, 4. cōnsistō, 122, I, 2. cōnspiciō, 122, III. cōnstat, 138, III. cōnstituō, 122, II. cōnsuēscō, 122, IV, 1. cōnsulō, 122, I, 5. contineō, 121, II, b. contingit, 138, III. coquō, 122, I, 1, a. crepō, 120, II. crēscō, 122, IV, 1. cubō, 120, II. cupiō, 122, III. currō, 122, I, 2.

D

dēbeō, 121, II, a. dēcernō, 122, I, 6. decet, 138, II. dēdecet, 138, II. dēdō, 122, I, 2. dēfendō, 122, I, 4. dēleō, 121, I dēligō, 122, I, 3. dēmō, 122, I, 3. dēsērō, 122, I, 5 dēsinō, 122, I, 6. dēsum, 125. dīcō, 122, I, 1, a. differō, 129. dīligō, 122, I, 3. dīmicō, 120, II. dirimō, 122, I, 3. dīripiō, 122, III. dīruō, 122, II. discernō, 122, I, 6. discō, 122, IV, 1. disserō, 122, I, 5. distinguō, 122, I, 1, a., footnote 44. dīvidō, 122, I, 1, b. dō, 127. doceō, 121, II, b. doleō, 121, II, a. domō, 120, II. dūcō, 122, I, 1, a.

E

ēdō, 122, I, 2. edō, 122, I, 3. efferō, 129. effugiō, 122, III. egeō, 121, II, a, N. 1. ēliciō, 122, III. ēmineō, 121, II, a, N. 1. emō, 122, I, 3. eō, 132. ēsuriō, 123, VI. ēvādō, 122, I, 1, b., footnote 45. ēvānēscō, 122, IV, 3. excolō, 122, I, 5. excūdō, 122, I, 4. exerceō, 121, II, a. experior, 123, VII. expleō, 121, I, N. explicō, 120, II. exstinguō, 122, I, 1, a., footnote 44. extimēscō, 122, IV, 2.

F

faciō, 122, III. fallō, 122, I, 2. fateor, 121, VII. faveō, 121, V. feriō, 123, VI. ferō, 129. ferveō, 121, VI fīgō, 122, I,

1, b. findō,122, I, 2, N. fingō, 122, I,
1, a. fiō, 131. flectō, 122, I, 1, b. fleō,
121, I. flōreō, 121, II, a, N. 1. flōrēscō,
122, IV, 2. fluō, 122, II. fodiō, 122, III.
foveō, 121, V. frangō, 122, I, 3. fremō,
122, I, 5. fricō, 120, II. frīgeō, 121, II,
a, N. 2. fruor, 122, V. fugiō, 122, III.
fulciō, 123, III. fulgeō, 121, III. fulget,
138, I. fundō, 122, I, 3. fungor, 122, V.
furō, 122, I, 7.

G

gemō, 122, I, 5. gerō, 122, I, 1, a.
gignō, 122, I, 5. gradior, 122, V.

H

habeō, 121, II, a. haereō, 121, III.
hauriō, 123, III. horreō, 121, II, a, N.
1.

I

ignōscō, 121, IV, 2. illiciō, 122, III.
imbuō, 122, II. immineō, 121, II, a,
N. 2. impleō, 121, I, N. implicō, 120 ,
II. incipiō, 122, III. incolō, 122, I, 5.
incumbō, 122, I, 5. indulgeō, 121, III.
induō, 122, II. īnferō, 129. ingemīscō,
122, IV, 2. īnsum, 125. intellegō, 122,
I, 3. interficiō, 122, III. intersum,
125. invādō, 122, I, 1, b., footnote 45.
inveniō, 123, IV. īrāscor, 122, V.

J

jaceō, 121, II, a. jaciō, 122, III. jubeō,
121, III. jungō, 122, I, 1, a. juvō, 120,
III.

L

lābor, 122, V. lacessō, 122, I, 6. laedō,
122, I, 1, b. lambō, 122, I, 7. largior,
123, VII. lateō, 121, II, a, N. 1. lavō,
120, III. legō, 122, I, 3. libet, 138, II.
liceor, 121, VII. licet, 138, II. loquor,
122, V. lūceo, 121, III. lūdō, 122, I, 1,
b. lūgeō, 121, III. luō, 122, II.

M

maereō, 121, II, a, N. 2. mālō, 130.
maneō, 121, III. mātūrēscō, 122, IV,
3. medeor, 121, VII. meminī, 133.
mereō, 121, II, a. mereor, 121, VII.
mergō, 122, I, 1, b. mētior, 123, VII.
metuō, 122, II. micō, 120, II. minuō,
122 , II. misceō, 121, II, b. miseret,
138, II. misereor, 121, VII. mittō, 122,
I, 1, b. molō, 122, I, 5. moneō, 121, II,
a. mordeō, 121, IV. morior, 122, V.
moveō, 121, V.

N

nancīscor, 122, V. nāscor, 122, V.
nectō, 122, I, 1, b. neglegō, 122, I, 3.
ningit, 138, . niteō, 121, II, a, N. 1.
nītor, 122, V. noceō, 121, II, a. nōlō,
130. nōscō, 122, IV, 1. nūbō, 122, I, 1,
a.

O

obdūrēscō, 122, IV, 3. oblinō, 122, I,
6. oblīvīscor, 122, V. obmūtēscō, 122,
IV, 3. obruō, 122, II. obsolēscō, 122,
IV, 1. obsum, 125. obtineō, 121, II, b.
ōdī, 133. offerō, 129. oleō, 121, II, a,
N. 1. operiō, 123, II. oportet, 138, II.
opperior, 123 , VII. ōrdior, 123, VII.
orior, 123, VII.

P

paenitet, 138, II. palleō, 121, II, a,
N. 1. pandō, 122, I, 4. parcō, 122, I,
2. pāreō, 121, II, a. pariō, 122, III.
pāscō, 122, IV, 1. pāscor, 122, IV, 1.
patefaciō, 122, III. patefīō, 122 , III.
pateō, 121, II, a, N. 1. patior, 122, V.
paveō, 121, V. pelliciō, 122, III. pellō,
122, I, 2. pendeō, 121, IV. pendō,
122, I, 2. peragō, 122, I, 3. percellō,
122, I, 2, N. percrēbrēscō, 122, IV,
3. perdō, 122, I, 2. perficiō, 122, III.
perfringō, 122, I, 3. perfruor, 122, V.
perlegō, 122, I, 3. permulceō, 121, III.
perpetior, 122, V. pervādō, 122, I, 1,
b., footnote 45. petō, 122, I, 6. piget,
138, II. pingō, 122, I, 1, a. placeō, 121,
II, a. plaudō, 122, I, 1, b. pluit, 138, I.
polleō, 121, II, a, N. 2. polliceor, 121,
VII. polluō, 122, II. pōnō, 122, I, 6.
poscō, 122, IV, 1. possīdō, 122, I, 4.
possum, 126. pōtō, 120, I. praebeō,
121, II, a. praestat, 138, III. praesum,
125. prandeō, 121, VI. prehendō, 122,
I, 4. premō, 122, I, 1, b. prōdō, 122,
I, 2. prōmō, 122, I, 3. prōsum, 125.
prōsternō, 122, I, 6. pudet, 138, II.
pungō, 122, I, 2.

Q

quaerō, 122, I, 6. quatiō, 122, III.
queror, 122, V. quiēscō, 122, IV, 1.

R

rādō, 122, I, 1, b. rapiō, 122, III.
reddō, 122, I, 2. redimō, 122, I, 3.
referciō, 123, III. referō, 129. rēfert,
138, II. regō, 122, I, 1, a. relinquō,
122 , I, 3. reminīscor, 122, V. reor,
121, VII. reperiō, 123, V. rēpō, 122,

General Index

The references are to sections and paragraphs.

ABBREVIATIONS—Abl., ablative; acc., accusative; adj., adjective; adv., adverb, adverbial, or adverbially; cf., compare; comp., comparison or comparative; conj., conjunction or conjugation; const., constr., construction; dat., dative; decl., declension; gen., genitive; ind., indicative; indir. disc., indirect discourse; loc., locative; N., note; nom., nominative; plu., plural; prep., preposition; pron., pronoun or pronunciation; sing., singular; subj., subject; subjv., subjunctive; voc., vocative; w., with.

A

ă, vowel, 2, 1; pronunciation, 3, 1; development of ă, before a single consonant, 7, 1, a; before two consonants, 7, 1, b; ă as ending of nom. sing. of 1st decl., 20; in voc. sing. of Greek nouns in -ēs of 1st decl., 22; in nom. sing. of Greek nouns in -ē of 1st decl., 22, 3; termination of nom. and acc. plu. of neuters, 23; 35; 48; termination of nom. sing. of nouns of 3d decl., 28; gender of nouns in -ă of 3d decl., 43, 3; ending of acc. sing. of Greek nouns of 3d decl., 47, 1; regular quantity of final a, 363, 1; exceptions to quantity of final a, 363, 1, a-c.

ā, pronunciation, 3, 1; arising by contraction, 7, 2; as ending of stem in 1st decl., 18; ā-stems inflected, 20; in voc. sing. of Greek nouns of 1st decl., 22; in voc. sing. of Greek nouns in -ās of 3d decl., 47, 4; distinguishing vowel of 1st conjugation, 98; ending of imperative act. of 1st conj., 101; final a long by exception, 363, 1, a-c.

ā, ab, abs, use, 142, 1; with town names, 229, 2.

ā to denote agency, 216. to denote separation, 214. place from which, 229.

— with town names, 229, 2.

— with abl. of gerund, 338, 4, b.

ā-stems, 20; 98; 101.

Abbreviations of proper names, 373.

Ablative case, 17; 213 f.

— in -ābus, 21, 2, e.

— in -d in prons., 84, 3; 85, 3.

— formation of sing. of adjs. of 3d decl., 67, a; 70, 1-5.

— of ī-stems, 37; 38.

— genuine abl. uses, 214 f.

— absolute, 227.

— of agent, 216.

— of accompaniment, 222.

— of accordance, 220, 3.

— of association, 222A.

— of attendant circumstance, 221; 227, 2, e).

— of cause, 219.

— of comparison, 217.

— of degree of difference, 223.

— of fine or penalty, 208, 2, b.

— of manner, 220.

— of material, 224, 3.

— of means, 218.

— of penalty, 208, 2, b.

— of place where, 228.

— of place whence, 229.

— of price, 225.

— of quality, 224.

— of separation, 214;

— — with compounds of *dis-* and *sē-*, 214, 3.

— of source, 215.

— of specification, 226.

frēnum, plu. of, 60, 2.
Frequentatives, 155, 2.
frētus w. abl., 218, 3.
Fricatives, 2, 7.
Friendly, dat. w. adjs. signifying, 192, 1.
frūctus, decl., 48.
frūgi, compared, 72; 70, 6.
frūgis, 57, 6.
fruor, with abl., 218, 1;
—   in gerundive constr., 339, 4.
fugiō, conj., 109, 2, a).
fuī, fuistī, etc., for *sum, es*, etc., in
        compound tenses, 102, footnotes.
Fullness, adjs. of, w. abl., 218, 8;
—   w. gen., 204, 1.
fungor, w. abl., 218, 1;
—   in gerundive constr., 339, 4.
fūr, decl., 40, 1, d.
fūrtō, abl. of manner, 220, 2.
Future tense, 161;
—   w. imperative force, 261, 3.
—   time in the subjv., 269.
—   perfect, 264;
—   —   with future meaning, 133, 2;
—   —   inf., 270, 4.
—   imperative, 281, 1.
—   infinitive, 270;
—   —   periphrastic fut. inf., 270, 3, and
        a.
—   participle, 337, 4.
futūrum esse ut, with subjv., 270, 3.

G

gaudeō, semi-deponent, 114, 1.
gemō, w. acc., 175, 2, b.
Gender 13-15;
—   in 1st decl., 20; 21;
—   in 2d decl., 23;
—   exceptions, 26;
—   in 3d decl., 43 f.;
—   in 4th decl., 50;
—   in 5th decl., 53;
—   determined by endings, 14;
—   —   by signification, 15, A;
—   heterogeneous nouns, 60.
gener, decl, 23, 2.
General relatives, 312, 1;
—   general truths, 259, 1; 262, B, 1;
—   'general' conditions, 302, 2; 3.
Genitive, 17;
—   in *-ī* for *-iī*, 25, 1 and 2;
—   of 4th decl., in *-ī*, 49, 1;
—   of 5th decl. in *-ī*, 52, 2;
—   of 5th decl. in *-ēī*, 52, 1;
—   —   in *-ē*, 52, 3;
—   of 1st decl. in *-āī*, 21, 2, b;

—   of 1st decl. in *-ās*, 21, 2, a;
—   gen. plu. *-um* for *-ārum*, 21, 2 d);
—   —   *-um* for *ōrum*, 25, 6; 63, 2;
—   —   *-um* for *-ium*, 70, 7;
—   gen. plu. lacking, 57, 7;
—   syntax of, 194 f.
—   of characteristic, 203, 1.
—   of charge with judicial verbs, 208.
—   of indefinite price, 203, 4.
—   of indefinite value, 203, 3.
—   of material, 197.
—   of measure, 203, 2.
—   of origin, 196.
—   of possession, 198.
—   of quality, 203.
—   of the whole, 201.
—   appositional, 202.
—   objective, 200.
—   of separation, 212, 3.
—   subjective, 199.
—   with adjs., 204;
—   —   with participles, 204, 1, a.
—   with *causā, grātiā*, 198, 1.
—   with verbs, 205 f.;
—   —   of plenty and want, 212;
—   —   with impers. verbs, 209.
—   position of gen., 350, 1.
genus, decl. 36;
—   *id genus*, 185, 1.
-ger, decl. of nouns in, 23, 2;
—   adjs., 65, 1.
Gerund, 95, 1;
—   1st conj., 101;
—   2d conj., 103;
—   3d conj., 105;
—   4th conj., 107;
—   syntax, 338;
—   with object, 338, 5.
Gerundive, 95, 1;
—   1st conj., 102;
—   2d conj., 104;
—   3d conj., 106;
—   4th conj., 108;
—   in periphrastic conj., 115; 337, 8.
Gerundive, const., 339, 1-6;
—   in passive periphrastic conj., 337, 8 f.;
—   gen. denoting purpose, 339, 6;
—   with dat. of purpose, 191, 3; 339, 7.
gnārus, not compared, 75, 2.
Gnomic present, 259, 1;
—   perfect, 262, 1.
gradior, conj., 109, 2, c.
Grammatical gender, 15.
grātiā, with gen., 198, 1;
—   *grātia, grātiae*, 61.